YOUR CHINESE
HOROSCOPE 1998

ABOUT THE AUTHOR

Neil Somerville is one of the leading writers in the West on Chinese horoscopes. He has been interested in Eastern forms of divination for many years and believes that much can be learned from the ancient wisdom of the East. His annual book on Chinese horoscopes has built up an international following and he is also the author of *Chinese Love Signs* (Thorsons, 1995).

Neil Somerville was born in the year of the Water Snake. His wife was born under the sign of the Monkey, his son is an Ox and daughter a Horse.

YOUR CHINESE
HOROSCOPE 1998

NEIL SOMERVILLE

What the Year of the Tiger holds in store for you

Thorsons
An Imprint of HarperCollinsPublishers

TO ROS, RICHARD AND EMILY

Thorsons
An Imprint of HarperCollins*Publishers*
77–85 Fulham Palace Road
Hammersmith, London W6 8JB
1160 Battery Street
San Francisco, California 94111–1213

Published by Thorsons 1997

10 9 8 7 6 5 4 3 2 1

© Neil Somerville 1997

Neil Somerville asserts the moral right to
be identified as the author of this work

A catalogue record for this book
is available from the British Library

ISBN 0 7225 3440 X

Printed in Great Britain by
Caledonian International Book Manufacturing Ltd,
Glasgow, G64

CONTENTS

———◆◆◆———

ACKNOWLEDGEMENTS

In writing *Your Chinese Horoscope 1998* I am grateful for the assistance and support that those around me have given. I wish to acknowledge Theodora Lau's *The Handbook of Chinese Horoscopes* (Harper & Row, 1979; Arrow, 1981), which was particularly useful to me in my research.

In addition to Ms Lau's work, I commend the following books to those who wish to find out more about Chinese horoscopes: Kristyna Arcarti, *Chinese Horoscopes for Beginners* (Headway, 1995); Catherine Aubier, *Chinese Zodiac Signs* (Arrow, 1984), series of 12 books; Paula Delsol, *Chinese Horoscopes* (Pan, 1973); E. A. Crawford and Teresa Kennedy, *Chinese Elemental Astrology* (Piatkus, 1992); Barry Fantoni, *Barry Fantoni's Chinese Horoscopes* (Warner, 1994); Bridget Giles and the Diagram Group, *Chinese Astrology* (Collins Gem, HarperCollins*Publishers*, 1996); Jean-Michel Huon de Kermadec, *The Way to Chinese Astrology* (Unwin, 1983); Kwok Man-Ho, *Authentic Chinese Horoscopes* (Arrow, 1987), series of 12 books; Paul Rigby and Harvey Bean, *Chinese Astrologics* (Publications Division, South China Morning Post Ltd, 1981); Derek Walters, *Ming Shu* (Pagoda Books, 1987) and *The Chinese Astrology Workbook* (The Aquarian Press, 1988); Suzanne White,

ACKNOWLEDGEMENTS

Suzanne White Book of Chinese Chance (Fontana/Collins, 1978) and *The New Astrology* (Pan, 1987) and *The New Chinese Astrology* (Pan, 1994).

INTRODUCTION

The origins of Chinese horoscopes have been lost in the mists of time. It is known that Oriental astrologers practised their art many thousands of years ago and, even today, Chinese astrology continues to fascinate and intrigue.

In Chinese astrology there are 12 signs named after 12 different animals. No one quite knows how the signs acquired their names, but there is one legend that offers an explanation.

According to this legend, one Chinese New Year the Buddha invited all the animals in his kingdom to come before him. Unfortunately – for reasons best known to the animals – only 12 turned up. The first to arrive was the Rat, followed by the Ox, Tiger, Rabbit, Dragon, Snake, Horse, Goat, Monkey, Rooster, Dog and finally Pig.

In gratitude, the Buddha decided to name a year after each of the animals and those born during that year would inherit some of the personality of that animal. Therefore those born in the year of the Ox would be hard-working, resolute and stubborn – just like the Ox – while those born in the year of the Dog would be loyal and faithful – just like the Dog.

While not everyone can possibly share all the characteristics of a sign, it is incredible what similarities do occur and this is partly where the fascination of Chinese horoscopes lies.

In addition to the 12 signs of the Chinese zodiac there are also five elements and these have a strengthening or moderating influence upon the sign. Details about the effects of the elements are given in each of the chapters on the 12 signs.

To find out which sign you were born under, refer to the tables on pages x–xiii. As the Chinese year is based on the lunar year and does not start until late January or early February, it is particularly important for anyone born in those two months to check carefully the dates of the Chinese year in which they were born.

Also included, in the Appendix, are two charts showing the compatibility between the signs for both personal and business relationships, and details about the signs ruling the different hours of the day. From this it is possible to locate your ascendant and, as in Western astrology, this has a significant influence on your personality.

In writing this book, I have taken the unusual step of combining the intriguing nature of Chinese horoscopes with the Western desire to know what the future holds and have based my interpretations upon various factors relating to each of the signs. This is the eleventh year in which *Your Chinese Horoscope* has been published and I am pleased that so many have found the sections on the forthcoming year of benefit and hope that the horoscope has been constructive and of help. Remember, though, that at all times you are the master of your own destiny. I sincerely hope that *Your Chinese Horoscope 1998* will prove interesting and helpful for the year ahead.

THE CHINESE YEARS

Rat	31 January	1900	to	18 February	1901
Ox	19 February	1901	to	7 February	1902
Tiger	8 February	1902	to	28 January	1903
Rabbit	29 January	1903	to	15 February	1904
Dragon	16 February	1904	to	3 February	1905
Snake	4 February	1905	to	24 January	1906
Horse	25 January	1906	to	12 February	1907
Goat	13 February	1907	to	1 February	1908
Monkey	2 February	1908	to	21 January	1909
Rooster	22 January	1909	to	9 February	1910
Dog	10 February	1910	to	29 January	1911
Pig	30 January	1911	to	17 February	1912
Rat	18 February	1912	to	5 February	1913
Ox	6 February	1913	to	25 January	1914
Tiger	26 January	1914	to	13 February	1915
Rabbit	14 February	1915	to	2 February	1916
Dragon	3 February	1916	to	22 January	1917
Snake	23 January	1917	to	10 February	1918
Horse	11 February	1918	to	31 January	1919
Goat	1 February	1919	to	19 February	1920
Monkey	20 February	1920	to	7 February	1921
Rooster	8 February	1921	to	27 January	1922
Dog	28 January	1922	to	15 February	1923
Pig	16 February	1923	to	4 February	1924

Rat	5 February	1924	to	23 January	1925
Ox	24 January	1925	to	12 February	1926
Tiger	13 February	1926	to	1 February	1927
Rabbit	2 February	1927	to	22 January	1928
Dragon	23 January	1928	to	9 February	1929
Snake	10 February	1929	to	29 January	1930
Horse	30 January	1930	to	16 February	1931
Goat	17 February	1931	to	5 February	1932
Monkey	6 February	1932	to	25 January	1933
Rooster	26 January	1933	to	13 February	1934
Dog	14 February	1934	to	3 February	1935
Pig	4 February	1935	to	23 January	1936
Rat	24 January	1936	to	10 February	1937
Ox	11 February	1937	to	30 January	1938
Tiger	31 January	1938	to	18 February	1939
Rabbit	19 February	1939	to	7 February	1940
Dragon	8 February	1940	to	26 January	1941
Snake	27 January	1941	to	14 February	1942
Horse	15 February	1942	to	4 February	1943
Goat	5 February	1943	to	24 January	1944
Monkey	25 January	1944	to	12 February	1945
Rooster	13 February	1945	to	1 February	1946
Dog	2 February	1946	to	21 January	1947
Pig	22 January	1947	to	9 February	1948
Rat	10 February	1948	to	28 January	1949
Ox	29 January	1949	to	16 February	1950
Tiger	17 February	1950	to	5 February	1951
Rabbit	6 February	1951	to	26 January	1952
Dragon	27 January	1952	to	13 February	1953
Snake	14 February	1953	to	2 February	1954
Horse	3 February	1954	to	23 January	1955

Goat	24 January	1955	to	11 February	1956
Monkey	12 February	1956	to	30 January	1957
Rooster	31 January	1957	to	17 February	1958
Dog	18 February	1958	to	7 February	1959
Pig	8 February	1959	to	27 January	1960
Rat	28 January	1960	to	14 February	1961
Ox	15 February	1961	to	4 February	1962
Tiger	5 February	1962	to	24 January	1963
Rabbit	25 January	1963	to	12 February	1964
Dragon	13 February	1964	to	1 February	1965
Snake	2 February	1965	to	20 January	1966
Horse	21 January	1966	to	8 February	1967
Goat	9 February	1967	to	29 January	1968
Monkey	30 January	1968	to	16 February	1969
Rooster	17 February	1969	to	5 February	1970
Dog	6 February	1970	to	26 January	1971
Pig	27 January	1971	to	14 February	1972
Rat	15 February	1972	to	2 February	1973
Ox	3 February	1973	to	22 January	1974
Tiger	23 January	1974	to	10 February	1975
Rabbit	11 February	1975	to	30 January	1976
Dragon	31 January	1976	to	17 February	1977
Snake	18 February	1977	to	6 February	1978
Horse	7 February	1978	to	27 January	1979
Goat	28 January	1979	to	15 February	1980
Monkey	16 February	1980	to	4 February	1981
Rooster	5 February	1981	to	24 January	1982
Dog	25 January	1982	to	12 February	1983
Pig	13 February	1983	to	1 February	1984
Rat	2 February	1984	to	19 February	1985
Ox	20 February	1985	to	8 February	1986

Tiger	9 February	1986	to	28 January	1987
Rabbit	29 January	1987	to	16 February	1988
Dragon	17 February	1988	to	5 February	1989
Snake	6 February	1989	to	26 January	1990
Horse	27 January	1990	to	14 February	1991
Goat	15 February	1991	to	3 February	1992
Monkey	4 February	1992	to	22 January	1993
Rooster	23 January	1993	to	9 February	1994
Dog	10 February	1994	to	30 January	1995
Pig	31 January	1995	to	18 February	1996
Rat	19 February	1996	to	6 February	1997
Ox	7 February	1997	to	27 January	1998
Tiger	28 January	1998	to	15 February	1999

Note: The names of the signs in the Chinese zodiac occasionally differ in the various books on Chinese astrology, although the characteristics of the signs remain the same. In some books the Ox is referred to as the Buffalo or Bull, the Rabbit as the Hare or Cat, the Goat as the Sheep and the Pig as the Boar.

For the sake of convenience, the male gender is used throughout this book. Unless otherwise stated, the characteristics of the signs apply to both sexes.

Once the mind is set on something,
no distance can be a barrier.
Chinese proverb

WELCOME TO
THE YEAR OF THE TIGER

Alone ... watchful ... and fierce. When the Tiger hunts, other animals cower, hide or flee. Such is the power, the strength and sheer ferocity of this beast. The Tiger commands respect. No one can ignore – dare ignore – its presence. Everything changes in its wake. Everyone takes notice.

And so it is with the Year of the Tiger – a year of often dramatic change, a year of opportunity but also one that can bring disaster and tragedy. Indeed, few will remain unmoved by the events of 1998.

So far the Tiger year has produced some of the major news stories of this century and 1998 will be no exception. This will be a time of intense activity, considerable change and, regrettably, armed conflict and disaster.

It was in a previous Tiger year that the First World War began and in another, 1938, that events brought the Second World War inextricably closer. It was also in a Tiger year that the Cuban missile crisis occurred, Chinese troops occupied Tibet, North Korean troops invaded South Korea and Turkish troops invaded Cyprus. In 1998 further conflicts and acts of aggression will take place and several areas of the world, particularly the Middle East, will see military action. In addition, some of the developing nations of the world will experience times of political instability, and a spate of military coups, sometimes with significant repercussions, could occur. However, unlike previous Tiger years, international pressure and condemnation will be so strong that many of the conflicts will be brought to a speedy and effective resolution.

As well as some tense international situations, many world leaders will face considerable domestic pressure, with factions calling for change and more rights. Some leaders will also be facing investigations into their past actions. It was in a previous Tiger year that some of President Nixon's top aides were indicted and Nixon resigned. Other Tiger years have also seen the resignation of prominent politicians for past actions or disagreements over policy and again, 1998 will be no different. Politically, this promises to be an active year.

Industrial relations will also figure prominently, with several countries facing disruption, and it is likely that certain sectors of the workforce will be vigorous in campaigning for wage increases, legislative changes or other causes. In Britain the General Strike and 1974 miners' strike both occurred in Tiger years and other countries too have experienced industrial problems in these years. Again, this pattern could be repeated. Also, certain proposals within the EEC could give rise to much dissension among some member states, with several polices being rigorously challenged.

Another disquieting aspect of the year will be the disasters, both natural and man-made, that are likely to occur. The last Tiger year saw the radiation leak at the Chernobyl nuclear power plant and the worst mining disaster in South African history, while the weather and natural phenomena also have a tendency to wreak havoc in these years. Late in 1962 much of Europe was plunged into the coldest and severest winter for many years, while earthquakes, cyclones and volcanoes have caused much destruction in Tiger years. This again could be the case in 1998.

However, although the year will bring its tragedies, there are also some highly positive aspects and many interesting developments will take place. In particular this will be year of considerable technological advance. This could include the setting up of more 'techno-villages' and, with the growth and ease of communication, a greater number of people will be tempted to work from home. Cable services will continue to expand and the growth of the home entertainment market will continue with the introduction of new and more sophisticated products. The year will also see major growth in the number of services available over the Internet and a game that can be played on-line could well develop into a world-wide craze. With the exciting developments that will take place in 1998, it seems a long way from a previous Tiger year (1962) when millions watched in awe as the first television pictures were relayed live from America to Europe via Telstar.

The Tiger year is also a year which favours innovation and enterprise and during 1998 several interesting products are likely to be introduced and find widespread appeal. The ballpoint pen is just one of the many Tiger year inventions. In addition, new and striking fashions will find their way into the shops, with bright colours and zany designs proving popular. The Tiger year favours the bold, the bright and razzmatazz, and 1998 could see some interesting and exciting trends. Similarly there could also be some lavish productions on both stage and screen. Appropriately, *Ben Hur*, complete with a real chariot race, was just one of the many spectacular productions to have first been performed in a Tiger year. Also, with the approach of the millennium, further projects will be announced which, in true Tiger style, will be great and spectacular and destined to become a legacy of our time.

The year will also see the launch and completion of several major building projects. These could include the redevelopment of inner city areas and industrial wasteland as well as the completion of several major buildings and complexes. Indeed, previous Tiger years have seen the opening of many famous structures and sites, including the Forth bridge, the Panama canal, the Aswan dam and the Trans-Canada highway. The coming year will see this pattern of development continue.

As far as economic activity is concerned, the Tiger year will be a time of considerable fluctuation. Money can be made and lost over the year and investors will need to keep their wits about them. The year will see some significant rises in stock markets around the world but also some dramatic falls. However, the general improvement in the economies of many countries will continue and this will be reflected in a positive and buoyant job market. In many countries unemployment levels will stabilize or fall.

For many, the Year of the Tiger will be a time of change and activity; some of the Chinese signs will relish this while others will feel uneasy about the many developments taking place. However, unsettling though some aspects of the year may be, out of the changes that occur new opportunities will arise – opportunities just waiting to be grasped. And it is those who are prepared to make the effort, to be enterprising and adventurous in their outlook, who stand to make the greatest gains during the year. The Tiger year is one that holds much potential and I sincerely hope that you will fare well and will be able to make the most of the considerable opportunities that the year will bring.

31 JANUARY 1900 〜 18 FEBRUARY 1901	*Metal Rat*
18 FEBRUARY 1912 〜 5 FEBRUARY 1913	*Water Rat*
5 FEBRUARY 1924 〜 23 JANUARY 1925	*Wood Rat*
24 JANUARY 1936 〜 10 FEBRUARY 1937	*Fire Rat*
10 FEBRUARY 1948 〜 28 JANUARY 1949	*Earth Rat*
28 JANUARY 1960 〜 14 FEBRUARY 1961	*Metal Rat*
15 FEBRUARY 1972 〜 2 FEBRUARY 1973	*Water Rat*
2 FEBRUARY 1984 〜 19 FEBRUARY 1985	*Wood Rat*
19 FEBRUARY 1996 〜 6 FEBRUARY 1997	*Fire Rat*

THE
RAT

THE PERSONALITY OF THE RAT

> The secret of success in life is for a man to be ready for his opportunity when it comes.
>
> *– Benjamin Disraeli: a Rat*

The Rat is born under the sign of charm. He is intelligent, popular and loves attending parties and large social gatherings. He is able to establish friendships with remarkable ease and people generally feel relaxed in his company. He is a very social creature and is genuinely interested in the welfare and activities of others. He has a good understanding of human nature and his advice and opinions are often sought.

The Rat is a hard and diligent worker. He is also very imaginative and is never short of ideas. However, he does sometimes lack the confidence to promote his ideas as much as he should and this can often prevent him from securing the recognition and credit he so often deserves.

The Rat is very observant and many Rats have made excellent writers and journalists. The Rat also excels at personnel and PR work and any job which brings him into contact with people and the media. His skills are particularly appreciated in times of crisis, for the Rat has an incredibly strong sense of self-preservation. When it comes to finding a way out of an awkward situation, he is certain to be the one who comes up with a solution.

The Rat loves to be where there is a lot of action, but should he ever find himself in a very bureaucratic or restrictive environment he can become a stickler for discipline and routine.

He is also something of an opportunist and is constantly on the look-out for ways in which he can improve his wealth and lifestyle. He rarely lets an opportunity go by and can become involved in so many plans and schemes that he sometimes squanders his energies and achieves very little as a result. He is also rather gullible and can be taken in by those less scrupulous than himself.

Another characteristic of the Rat is his attitude to money. He is very thrifty and to some he may appear a little mean. The reason for this is purely that he likes to keep his money within his family. He can be most generous to his partner, his children and close friends and relatives. He can also be generous to himself, for he often finds it impossible to deprive himself of any luxury or object he fancies. The Rat is also very acquisitive and can be a notorious hoarder. He hates waste and is rarely prepared to throw anything away. He can also be rather greedy and will rarely refuse an invitation for a free meal or a complimentary ticket to some lavish function.

The Rat is a good conversationalist, although he can occasionally be a little indiscreet. He can be highly critical of others – for an honest and unbiased opinion, the Rat is a superb critic – and sometimes will use confidential information to his own advantage. However, as the Rat has such a bright and irresistible nature, most are prepared to forgive him for his slight indiscretions.

Throughout his long and eventful life, the Rat will make many friends and will find that he is especially well suited to those born under his own sign and those of the Ox, Dragon and Monkey. He can also get on well with those born under the signs of the Tiger, Snake, Rooster, Dog and

Pig, but the rather sensitive Rabbit and Goat will find the Rat a little too critical and blunt for their liking. The Horse and Rat will also find it difficult to get on with each other – the Rat craves security and will find the Horse's changeable moods and rather independent nature a little unsettling.

The Rat is very family orientated and will do anything to please his nearest and dearest. He is exceptionally loyal to his parents and can himself be a very caring and loving parent. He will take an interest in all his children's activities and will see that they want for nothing. The Rat usually has a large family.

The female Rat has a kindly, outgoing nature and involves herself in a multitude of different activities. She has a wide circle of friends, enjoys entertaining and is an attentive hostess. She is also conscientious about the upkeep of her home and has superb taste in home furnishings. She is most supportive to the other members of her family and, due to her resourceful, friendly and persevering nature, can do well in practically any career she enters.

Although the Rat is essentially outgoing and something of an extrovert, he is also a very private individual. He tends to keep his feelings to himself and, while he is not averse to learning what other people are doing, he resents anyone prying too closely into his own affairs. He also does not like solitude and if he is alone for any length of time he can easily get depressed.

The Rat is undoubtedly very talented, but more often than not he fails to capitalize on his many abilities. He has a tendency to become involved in too many schemes and chase after too many opportunities all at one time. If he were to slow down and concentrate on one thing at a time he could become very successful. If not, success and wealth could elude him. But the Rat, with his tremendous ability to charm, will rarely, if ever, be without friends.

THE FIVE DIFFERENT TYPES OF RAT

In addition to the 12 signs of the Chinese zodiac, there are five elements and these have a strengthening or moderating influence on the sign. The effects of the five elements on the Rat are described below, together with the years in which the elements were exercising their influence. Therefore all Rats born in 1900 and 1960 are Metal Rats, those born in 1912 and 1972 are Water Rats, and so on.

Metal Rat: 1900, 1960

This Rat has excellent taste and certainly knows how to appreciate the finer things in life. His home is comfortable and nicely decorated and he is forever entertaining or mixing in fashionable circles. He has considerable financial acumen and invests his money well. On the surface the Metal Rat appears cheerful and confident, but deep down he can be troubled by worries that are quite often of his own making. He is exceptionally loyal to his family and friends.

Water Rat: 1912, 1972

The Water Rat is intelligent and very astute. He is a deep thinker and can express his thoughts clearly and persuasively. He is always eager to learn and is talented in many different areas. The Water Rat is usually very popular, but his fear of loneliness can sometimes lead him into mixing with the wrong sort of company. He is a particularly skilful writer, but he can get side-tracked very easily and should try to concentrate on just one thing at a time.

Wood Rat: 1924, 1984

The Wood Rat has a friendly, outgoing personality and is most popular with his colleagues and friends. He has a quick, agile brain and likes to turn his hand to anything he thinks may be useful. His one fear is insecurity, but given his intelligence and capabilities, this fear is usually unfounded. He has a good sense of humour, enjoys travel and, due to his highly imaginative nature, can be a gifted writer or artist.

Fire Rat: 1936, 1996

The Fire Rat is rarely still and seems to have a never-ending supply of energy and enthusiasm. He loves being involved in the action – be it travel, following up new ideas or campaigning for a cause in which he fervently believes. He is an original thinker and hates being bound by petty restrictions or the dictates of others. He can be forthright in his views, but can sometimes get carried away in the excitement of the moment and commit himself to various undertakings without checking what all the implications might be. He has a resilient nature and, with the right support, can often go far in life.

Earth Rat: 1948

This Rat is astute and very level-headed. He rarely takes unnecessary chances and, while he is constantly trying to improve his financial status, he is prepared to proceed slowly and leave nothing to chance. The Earth Rat is probably not as adventurous as the other types of Rat and prefers to remain in familiar areas rather than rush headlong into something he knows little about. He is talented, conscientious and caring towards his loved ones, but at the same time can be self-conscious and worry a little too much about the image he is trying to project.

PROSPECTS FOR THE RAT IN 1998

The Chinese New Year starts on 28 January 1998. Until then, the old year, the Year of the Ox, is still making its presence felt.

The Year of the Ox (7 February 1997 to 27 January 1998) will have been an interesting year for the Rat, with the latter part being a pleasant and productive time. Throughout the year the Rat will have found that concentrated effort will have brought good results and in what remains of the Ox year he must resist the all too strong temptation of engaging in too many activities at the same time. He needs to decide upon his priorities and concentrate on these, especially as far as his work and career are concerned. Determined action on his part could bring pleasing results.

The closing stages of the Ox year could, however, be an expensive time and the Rat needs to keep a watchful eye over his level of spending. While usually thrifty, he should think twice before engaging in too many expensive whims and, if he is planning any costly purchase, he could save himself considerable outlay by comparing prices in several different outlets rather than taking the first he sees.

Domestically and socially the Ox year will have gone reasonably well for the Rat. His family and friends will have provided him with much useful support and he would do well to listen closely to any advice he is given as well as be forthcoming over any matter that might be causing him concern. However, should any difference of opinion have arisen with either colleagues or those close to him, the Rat would do well to use the remaining months of the year to sort the situation out rather than have it lingering in the background. If he is not careful, a contretemps could take the edge off what will have been a generally pleasant year.

If he bears these points in mind, the Rat will enjoy the closing months of the Ox year and will have every reason to feel satisfied with his accomplishments over the last 12 months.

The Year of the Tiger starts on 28 January and will be a variable year for the Rat. Although there will be parts he will enjoy, 1998 will not be without its difficulties.

Overall the Tiger year is one of change and the Rat, who so much likes to be in control of events, will feel ill at ease with some of what happens. Not all his existing plans will work out in the manner he had hoped and there could be a few disappointments in store. However, while the Tiger year will bring its challenges, it can also bring its rewards.

Throughout the year the Rat will undoubtedly be helped by his resourceful nature. The Rat is tenacious and always strives to make the best out of any situation in which he finds himself. In many cases over the year he will find that new situations will lead to new opportunities and that by being adaptable he can profit from many of the changes that take place. Also, some events that occur will cause him to reassess his current situation and lead him to make newer and sometimes better plans. For any Rat who might have felt staid or been in a rut in recent years, this can be the year which will bring the change and opportunity he has been seeking.

In his work the Rat needs to set about his activities in his usual determined way but remain aware of any new developments taking place and the views of those around him. This is not a year in which he can be too independent in his actions or ignore the opinions of others. Many Rats will also see changes in their duties and, while some of these may not be of the Rat's choosing, he should continue to give of his best and remain committed to the tasks before him. He will also find that some of the changes that occur will open up new possibilities for him and by showing himself adaptable, he will be well placed to take advantage of these. Work-wise, there will be parts of the year which will be demanding and sometimes difficult but, with care, the Rat can emerge from the year in a considerably enhanced position.

Similarly, those Rats seeking work or wanting to change their present position should remain alert for openings to pursue. They could also consider approaching those who may be in a position to help or advise. By taking the initiative they could be given some useful assistance and throughout the year will find much truth in the saying 'nothing ventured, nothing gained'. The Tiger year is, after all, a year which favours enterprise and the determined Rat will indeed find himself rewarded for his efforts and tenacity.

The Rat will generally find the second half of the year better for work matters than the first but if, during the year, he gets the opportunity to extend his skills or go on courses he should do so. Any knowledge and experience he can gain will certainly enhance his prospects for the latter part of the Tiger year as well as for the future.

As far as financial matters are concerned, care and vigilance is needed. Although the Rat is always striving to improve his financial position, he must not let his desires lead him into taking undue risks or speculating with money he cannot afford to lose. He should be particularly wary of any 'get rich quick schemes' he may hear about; all may not be as straightforward as it may at first appear. Also, if he intends to make a major purchase or investment, he should check the matter thoroughly and make sure he is conversant with any obligations he may be placed under. Provided the Rat exercises caution in his financial dealings he should be able to avert problems, but this is certainly not a year for complacency, for taking risks or spending without regard to his current situation.

As always, the Rat's family will prove most important to him and he will have good reason to value the support and encouragement of those around him. Domestically this could be quite an active year and at busy times the Rat should not hesitate to ask for additional assistance or seek advice on any matter that may be troubling him. He may also have to assist a more senior relation over the year and the time and support he is able to give will be much appreciated. The love that the Rat has for those close to him and they for him will certainly be amply demonstrated over the year. Also, despite the pressures and demands he may face, there will be many family occasions the Rat will enjoy and savour. At busy times, to ease some of the pressure, he could also find it helpful to suggest activities all can enjoy – perhaps a meal out, visit to the cinema or some other pleasurable activity. Such occasions could turn out to be happy and meaningful events.

With the active nature of the year, the Rat may sometimes feel he is not able to devote as much time to his interests and hobbies as he would like. However it is important he does not neglect these, as they do provide him with a valuable source of relaxation. He could also find it beneficial to take up any activities that would give him some additional exercise, especially if he is sedentary for much of the day. Also, despite the many demands on his time, he should not neglect his social life. His friends will be most important to him over the year, providing company, support and some truly pleasurable occasions. Any Rats seeking additional friends or romance should make every effort to go out more and get in contact with others, perhaps by joining a club or interest group. They will find, as with most areas of their life, that positive action will be well rewarded.

Travel is another area which will figure prominently and for any Rat who has been wanting to visit a certain place for some time, gain work experience abroad or visit relations living some distance away, this could be a good year to do so. Many Rats will find themselves travelling considerable distances over the year and generally the journeys they take will go well. However, before visiting any destination new to him, the Rat would find it helpful to read up about the area before he leaves. This way his visit will be made all the more meaningful.

Generally, 1998 will prove an interesting year for the Rat. Admittedly there will be challenges and not all will go as smoothly as he would like, but he will learn much from what happens. Some of the changes that occur will bring forth new opportunities and, with his resourceful nature, the Rat is sure to make the most of them. This may not be the easiest of years, but for the determined and enterprising Rat, it still holds much potential.

As far as the different types of Rat are concerned, this will be an eventful year for the *Metal Rat*. Although some of what happens in 1998 may not be of his own choosing, he will still be able to profit from the year as well as gain much useful experience. Throughout the year it is important he remains alert to all that is taking place around him and is prepared to adapt to any changes that occur. In some cases he may have to revise existing ideas, but better this than remain inflexible and lose out on new opportunities. Fortunately though, the Metal Rat is resourceful and good at assessing the situations in which he finds himself, and both these abilities will serve him well. In 1998 progress is possible, but may not always be in the manner he originally envisaged. Although the Metal Rat does need to be cautious in his actions this should not prevent him from following up any opportunities he sees, especially as far as his work is concerned. If he feels uncomfortable with his present position, wishes to move to new duties or is seeking work, he should keep alert for openings to pursue. He would also do well to investigate positions which he may not have fully considered before and ways in which he can draw on past experience. The Metal Rat does, after all, possess many fine talents and some imaginative thinking could open up some interesting possibilities for him. As far as financial matters are concerned, 1998 calls for a certain watchfulness. This is not a year for taking financial risks or for spending without regard to his current situation. He should also be wary about entering into risky ventures and should he be involved in any large transaction, it would be in his interests to check the terms and any obligations he may be placed under. The Metal Rat's domestic life will prove quite busy over the year, with many calls upon his time. However, while there will be moments of pressure, the help and support that he is able to offer to family members will be much appreciated. Similarly, when he feels in need of assistance or advice, he should not hesitate to ask. Those around him will be only too keen to help and throughout the year this spirit of co-operation and mutual support will be a great value both to the Metal Rat and to his family. There will also be several opportunities for the Metal Rat to travel over the year and he should try to ensure that he goes away for a proper holiday or break; a rest and change of scene will prove most beneficial. Also, if he does not get much exercise during the day, the Metal Rat could find additional walking or activities such as swimming or cycling will do much to help his overall level of fitness. Although the Tiger year may bring its uncertainties, there are still some very positive elements. Out of the changes that occur will arise new and interesting opportunities and, in his true resourceful style, the Metal Rat will do much to turn these to his advantage.

Although 1998 will be a demanding year for the *Water Rat* it will also be a satisfying one. In recent years the Water Rat will have learned much and the Tiger year will give him the chance to put his knowledge and experience to good use. By acting determinedly and giving of his best the Water Rat can accomplish much as well as sow the seeds for future advancement. In his work he is likely to see considerable change. Some Water Rats will take on new responsibilities while others will change to a different type of work. In either case, what is asked of the Water Rat could appear daunting, but by rising up to the challenges he will acquit himself well and impress those around him. Also, further opportunities arise in the later part of the year and in 1999 he will be well placed to take advantage of them. Many of those Water Rats seeking work will also find their perseverance rewarded, sometimes in a most unexpected manner. Throughout the year these Water Rats should pursue any openings that interest them and if they are eligible for any training courses, they should take advantage of them. Anything the Water Rat can do to further his skills or improve his prospects will be very much to his advantage. The Water Rat's domestic life will be busy over the year; some Water Rats will see an addition to their family or spend much time assisting those around them. Although there may be occasions when he will despair of all he has to do, the Water Rat will still derive much pride and pleasure from his home life. He should also not hesitate to ask for help or advice if he feels under too much pressure or is anxious over any matter. Those around him will be glad to assist as well as give him much constructive support. He will also obtain considerable satisfaction from his social life and for any Water Rat who may have had some recent difficulty to bear or may be feeling lonely, there will be some excellent opportunities to meet others and build up a new and meaningful friendship. The summer months are especially favourable for social and personal matters, and at this time the lonely and unattached Water Rat should make every effort to go out more. The Water Rat should not incur any financial problems over the year, although he does need to keep watch over his level of spending, and if he has any large item of expenditure, he needs to budget accordingly. This is not a year for taking undue risks or over-stretching his resources. There will also be several opportunities for travel and for those Water Rats who wish to gain experience by working in another country or who have a destination they would like to visit, this would be a good year to do so. Generally, 1998 will be an active year for the Water Rat, but despite the pressures and changes that arise, he will be given ample opportunity to show his true worth and indeed will do well. Added to this, on a personal level this will be a pleasant and rewarding year.

This will be a mixed year for the *Wood Rat*; sometimes everything will be going splendidly for him while at other times he will feel under pressure or have matters giving him concern. His family and home life will, as always, prove most important to him and throughout the year he will greatly appreciate the support and encouragement that those around him give. When he does have any anxieties, no matter what area of his life they might concern, he will be greatly helped by discussing them openly rather than keeping them to himself. In some cases he could find he is worrying unnecessarily and that his concerns are not as bad as he first envisaged. One of the more awkward elements of the year could involve bureaucratic matters and if the Wood Rat has any important forms to complete or is entering into a complicated transaction, he should make sure he reads the small print carefully. If there is anything he does not understand, he should check rather than take risks or jump to conclusions. Those Wood Rats in education will make good progress over the year, although there will be times when they are daunted by what is being asked of them. At these times, they should not hesitate to seek assistance and will find that those around them will be glad to guide them and put their mind at ease. However, for others to be able to do this, the Wood Rat does need to be forthcoming and open about his concerns. While there are some challenging aspects to the year, 1998 will still contain some enjoyable occasions for the Wood Rat. In particular, he will delight in the achievements of those close to him and both domestically and socially there will be times of much happiness, especially over the summer and the second half of the year. Any holidays will go well and with travel favourably aspected, many Wood Rats will journey considerable distances over the year, some visiting friends and relations they have not seen for some time.

The Wood Rat will also obtain much satisfaction from his hobbies, especially from those that allow him to use his creative skills or take him out of doors. For Wood Rats who are artistically inclined, it could be worth furthering their skills and bringing their work to the attention of others this year, even perhaps entering an appropriate competition. As far as personal interests are concerned, the year could hold several major surprises! Although 1998 may not be an entirely problem-free year, it can still prove a satisfying and constructive one. However, the main thing for the Wood Rat to remember is not to keep any worries or concerns he has to himself. He is, after all, in the fortunate position of having many he can turn to for advice and assistance and in 1998 he should avail himself of this support.

This will be an important year for the *Fire Rat*, with some of its events having far-reaching implications. Several times the Fire Rat will have to make key decisions or adapt to new situations and so the year will contain some interesting possibilities. Some of the Fire Rats in work will choose to retire while others will opt to change their duties. In many cases the decisions they will need to take will not be easy, but the Fire Rat will be well supported by others and would be helped if he were to discuss his feelings and options with those around him. In time, he will be content with the decisions that he does take, but they are not something he can rush or enter into lightly. In addition to the work changes indicated, some Fire Rats will consider moving. Those that do could find the actual process protracted, but once settled, they will be well pleased with their new accommodation and location. These Fire Rats should also make an active effort to involve themselves in their new community. With their amiable nature and broad interests they will experience little difficulty in settling down. Also, should any Fire Rat have suffered some sadness in recent times, it would be in his interests to focus his attention more on the present and future, rather than dwell too much on the past, and decide on what he would now like to do. For many Fire Rats, 1998 will mark the start of a new phase in their life, with the latter part of the year ushering in better and more stable times. As far as the Fire Rat's domestic life is concerned, this will be quite an active year with many matters requiring his attention. This is particularly so for those who move or have alterations or renovations carried out on their home. However, at busy times, the Fire Rat should not hesitate to ask those around him for additional assistance and again, if he has any problem or difficulty, he should raise it with others. However, despite some of the testing aspects of the year, there will also be much to enjoy. Over the year there will be good cause for a personal celebration – perhaps the birth of a grandchild or a wedding of someone in the family – and the Fire Rat will also take much delight in following the activities of those close to him. Socially, too, the year will go well and the aspects are particularly favourable for making new friends and adding to acquaintances. Travel is also well aspected and the holidays and outings that the Fire Rat takes will prove both pleasurable and beneficial. In addition, outdoor pursuits are favoured and for those Fire Rats who are keen gardeners, follow sport, enjoy walking or exploring the countryside, the year will contain some truly satisfying moments. Generally, this will be an active and sometimes demanding year, but what the Fire Rat accomplishes in it will have a positive impact over the next few years.

Although the *Earth Rat* is always keen to make the most of himself and his abilities he is nevertheless cautious and careful in his approach and such an attitude will help him considerably over the Tiger year. Throughout 1998 the Earth Rat should continue to set about his work and responsibilities in his usual thorough and conscientious way. However, should situations and circumstances change, he should show some willingness to adjust and see how he can make the most of the new situation. As a Rat he is blessed with a most inventive mind and over the year there will be several times when he can turn events to his advantage or see opportunities that perhaps others have missed. Admittedly, not all the year will be easy and the Earth Rat will feel unsettled by some of what happens, but he can still profit from it. In his work he needs to remain alert to all that is happening and act in conjunction with others rather than maintain too independent an attitude. Also, should any difficulties emerge, he should remain his usual discreet and diplomatic self. This is not a year to rock the boat! Any Earth Rat seeking work or wanting to change his present duties should continue to follow up any openings but also investigate other ways in which he can use his talents. Some innovative thinking on his part could pay off and, in work matters, the Tiger year could bring the Earth Rat several surprises and unexpected rewards. As far as finance is concerned, the Earth Rat will need to remain watchful. This is not a year in which to take undue risks and if he enters into any involved transaction, particularly concerning his accommodation, he needs to check the terms and implications of the agreement carefully. If not, problems could ensue. Domestically, this will be a pleasant although busy year. Several family matters will require the Earth Rat's attention and if a close relation has a dilemma or is facing some difficulty, any advice and assistance he feels able to give will do much to help. Others do think highly of the Earth Rat's judgement and this will be especially so in the Tiger year. With travel being well aspected, the Earth Rat should aim to go away at least once over the year. Such a break will be of considerable benefit to him and if there is a particular destination he has been longing to visit, this could be the year to make the journey. He should also make sure he does not neglect his own interests, particularly those that give him additional exercise and provide a break from his usual daily concerns. Indeed, he could obtain much satisfaction by extending one of his existing interests in some way, perhaps by learning about another aspect or getting in contact with fellow enthusiasts. By doing so, he could make the interest even more meaningful for him. Although the year will bring moments of uncertainty and pressure, it will also bring its opportunities and with his careful and yet enterprising manner, the Earth Rat is well placed to make much of it. Added to which, his family, friends, travel and interests will all bring him considerable pleasure.

FAMOUS RATS

Alan Alda, Dave Allen, Ursula Andress, Louis Armstrong, Charles Aznavour, Lauren Bacall, Shirley Bassey, Jeremy Beadle, Irving Berlin, Virginia Bottomley, Kenneth Branagh, Marlon Brando, Charlotte Brontë, Chris de Burgh, George Bush, Lord Callaghan, Glen Campbell, Jimmy Carter, Dick Cavett, Maurice Chevalier, Linford Christie, Lloyd Cole, Barbara Dickson, Benjamin Disraeli, David Duchovny, Noël Edmonds, T. S. Eliot, Albert Finney, Clark Gable, Liam Gallagher, Al Gore, Hugh Grant, Thomas Hardy, Vaclav Havel, Haydn, Charlton Heston, Damon Hill, Ian Hislop, Buddy Holly, Mick Hucknall, Jeremy Irons, Glenda Jackson, Jean-Michel Jarre, Gene Kelly, F. W. de Klerk, Kris Kristofferson, Lawrence of Arabia, Gary Lineker, Sir Andrew Lloyd Webber, Claude Monet, Robert Mugabe, Richard Nixon, Robert Palmer, Sean Penn, Terry Pratchett, the Queen Mother, Vanessa Redgrave, Burt Reynolds, Jonathan Ross, Rossini, William Shakespeare, Yves St Laurent, Tommy Steele, Donna Summer, James Taylor, Leo Tolstoy, Spencer Tracey, Anthea Turner, Tim Vincent, the Prince of Wales, George Washington, Dennis Waterman, Dennis Weaver, Roger Whittaker, Richard Wilson, Bill Wyman, the Duke of York, Emile Zola.

19 FEBRUARY 1901 ～ 7 FEBRUARY 1902	*Metal Ox*
6 FEBRUARY 1913 ～ 25 JANUARY 1914	*Water Ox*
24 JANUARY 1925 ～ 12 FEBRUARY 1926	*Wood Ox*
11 FEBRUARY 1937 ～ 30 JANUARY 1938	*Fire Ox*
29 JANUARY 1949 ～ 16 FEBRUARY 1950	*Earth Ox*
15 FEBRUARY 1961 ～ 4 FEBRUARY 1962	*Metal Ox*
3 FEBRUARY 1973 ～ 22 JANUARY 1974	*Water Ox*
20 FEBRUARY 1985 ～ 8 FEBRUARY 1986	*Wood Ox*
7 FEBRUARY 1997 ～ 27 JANUARY 1998	*Fire Ox*

THE
OX

THE PERSONALITY OF THE OX

> The great thing in this world is not so much where we
> stand, as in what direction we are moving.
>
> — *Oliver Wendell Holmes: an Ox*

The Ox is born under the signs of equilibrium and tenacity.
He is a hard and conscientious worker and sets about
everything he does in a resolute, methodical and determined manner. He has considerable leadership qualities
and is often admired for his tough and uncompromising
nature. He knows what he wants to achieve in life and, as
far as possible, will not be deflected from his ultimate
objective.

The Ox takes his responsibilities and duties very
seriously. He is decisive and quick to take advantage of any
opportunity that comes his way. He is also sincere and
places a great deal of trust in his friends and colleagues. He
is, nevertheless, something of a loner. He is a quiet and
private individual and often keeps his thoughts to himself.
He also cherishes his independence and prefers to set about
things in his own way rather than be bound by the dictates
of others or be influenced by outside pressures.

The Ox tends to have a calm and tranquil nature, but if
something angers him or he feels that someone has let
him down, he can have a fearsome temper. He can also be
stubborn and obstinate and this can lead him into conflict
with others. Usually the Ox will succeed in getting his own
way, but should things go against him, he is a poor loser
and will take any defeat or setback extremely badly.

The Ox is often a deep thinker and rather studious. He is not particularly renowned for his sense of humour and does not take kindly to new gimmicks or anything too innovative. The Ox is too solid and traditional for that and he prefers to stick to the more conventional norm.

His home is very important to him and in some respects he treats it as a private sanctuary. His family tends to be closely knit and the Ox will make sure that each member does their fair share around the house. The Ox tends to be a hoarder, but he is always well organized and neat. He also places great importance on punctuality and there is nothing that infuriates him more than to be kept waiting – particularly if it is due to someone's inefficiency. The Ox can be a hard taskmaster!

Once settled in a job or house the Ox will quite happily remain there for many years. He does not like change and he is also not particularly keen on travel. He does, however, enjoy gardening and other outdoor pursuits and he will often spend much of his spare time out of doors. The Ox is usually an excellent gardener and whenever possible he will always make sure he has a large area of ground to maintain. He usually prefers to live in the country than the town.

Due to his dedicated and dependable nature, the Ox will usually do well in his chosen career, providing he is given enough freedom to act on his own initiative. He invariably does well in politics, agriculture and in careers which need specialized training. The Ox is also very gifted in the arts and many Oxen have enjoyed considerable success as musicians or composers.

The Ox is not as outgoing as some and it often takes him a long time to establish friendships and feel relaxed in another person's company. His courtships are likely to be long, but once he is settled he will remain devoted and loyal to his partner. The Ox is particularly well suited to those born under the signs of the Rat, Rabbit, Snake and Rooster. He can also establish a good relationship with the Monkey, Dog, Pig and another Ox, but he will find that he has little in common with the whimsical and sensitive Goat. He will also find it difficult to get on with the Horse, Dragon and Tiger – the Ox prefers a quiet and peaceful existence and those born under these three signs tend to be a little too lively and impulsive for his liking.

The female Ox has a kind and caring nature, and her home and family are very much her pride and joy. She always tries to do her best for her partner and can be a most conscientious and loving parent. She is an excellent organizer and also a very determined person who will often succeed in getting what she wants in life. She usually has a deep interest in the arts and is often a talented artist or musician.

The Ox is a very down-to-earth character. He is sincere, loyal and unpretentious. He can, however, be rather reserved and to some he may appear distant and aloof. He has a quiet nature, but underneath he is very strong-willed and ambitious. He has the courage of his convictions and is often prepared to stand up for what he believes is right, regardless of the consequences. He inspires confidence and trust and throughout his life he will rarely be short of people who are ready to support him or who admire his strong and resolute manner.

THE FIVE DIFFERENT TYPES OF OX

In addition to the 12 signs of the Chinese zodiac, there are five elements and these have a strengthening or moderating influence on the sign. The effects of the five elements on the Ox are described below, together with the years in which the elements were exercising their influence. Therefore all Oxen born in 1901 and 1961 are Metal Oxen, those born in 1913 and 1973 are Water Oxen, and so on.

Metal Ox: 1901, 1961
This Ox is confident and very strong-willed. He can be blunt and forthright in his views and is not afraid of speaking his mind. He sets about his objectives with a dogged determination, but he can become so wrapped up in his various activities that he is oblivious to the thoughts and feelings of those around him, and this can sometimes be to his detriment. He is honest and dependable and will never promise more than he can deliver. He has a good appreciation of the arts and usually has a small circle of very good and loyal friends.

Water Ox: 1913, 1973
This Ox has a sharp and penetrating mind. He is a good organizer and sets about his work in a methodical manner. He is not as narrow-minded as some of the other types of Oxen and is more willing to involve others in his plans and aspirations. He usually has very high moral standards and is often attracted to careers in public service. He is a

good judge of character and has such a friendly and persuasive manner that he usually experiences little difficulty in securing his objectives. He is popular and has an excellent way with children.

Wood Ox: 1925, 1985

The Wood Ox conducts himself with an air of dignity and authority and will often take a leading role in any enterprise in which he gets involved. He is very self-confident and is direct in his dealings with others. He does, however, have a quick temper and has no hesitation in speaking his mind. He has tremendous drive and will-power and has an extremely good memory. The Wood Ox is particularly loyal and devoted to the members of his family and has a most caring nature.

Fire Ox: 1937, 1997

The Fire Ox has a powerful and assertive personality and is a hard and conscientious worker. He holds strong views and has very little patience when things do not go his own way. He can also get carried away in the excitement of the moment and does not always take into account the views of those around him. He nevertheless has many leadership qualities and will often reach positions of power, eminence and wealth. He usually has a small group of loyal and close friends and is very devoted to his family.

Earth Ox: 1949

This Ox sets about everything he does in a sensible and level-headed manner. He is ambitious, but also realistic in his aims and is often prepared to work long hours in order to secure his objectives. He is shrewd in financial and business matters and is a very good judge of character. He has a quiet nature and is greatly admired for his sincerity and integrity. He is also very loyal to his family and friends and his views and opinions are often sought by others.

PROSPECTS FOR THE OX IN 1998

The Chinese New Year starts on 28 January 1998. Until then, the old year, the Year of the Ox, is still making its presence felt.

The Year of the Ox (7 February 1997 to 27 January 1998) will have been a pleasing and constructive year for the Ox and the aspects remain encouraging right to the end.

By nature, the Ox is a prodigious planner and sets about his activities in a determined and conscientious manner. In the Ox year, such an attitude will have helped his progress as well as won favour with those around him. In the closing stages of the year the Ox will continue to make progress and will find his recent efforts rewarded. Some Oxen will be given new and more varied responsibilities in their work, while others will go a long way towards realizing an ambition or receiving some sort of financial bonus. These are promising times and the Ox should make every effort to promote himself and his talents.

On a personal level, too, the Ox year will have gone well. The Ox will have had many enjoyable times with his family and friends and many Oxen will have had good reason for a personal celebration over the year. These gratifying trends will continue and the Ox can look forward to some enjoyable family and social gatherings at the end of the year. He would also do well to heed the advice someone senior gives him over the Christmas holidays; there will be much wisdom in their words. For the lonely or unattached Ox there will be occasions to meet others towards the end of the Ox year and the aspects for building new friendships are good, especially in the period from late October to mid January.

One area which could, however, prove problematical for the Ox is paperwork and matters of a bureaucratic nature. The Ox needs to deal with important forms and items of correspondence he receives promptly and with care. If not, he could find himself involved in some protracted correspondence. It would also be in his interests to check any invoices and statements he receives and the terms of any transactions he enters into. By doing so he could spot a mistake and save himself some unnecessary outlay.

These warnings apart, the closing months of the year will go well for the Ox and he should aim to make the most of the auspicious trends that prevail.

The Year of the Tiger begins on 28 January 1998 and will be a variable year for the Ox. The Tiger year is generally characterized by activity and change and such an atmosphere will not always be to the cautious and steadfast Ox's liking. However, despite any misgivings he might have, the Ox can, with care, emerge from the year with some useful gains to his credit.

As far as his work is concerned, the Ox should aim to build on the progress of recent years and consolidate any gains he has made. If he is in a new position or has taken on different duties, he should concentrate on learning these and establishing himself. Over the year he will greatly impress others with his meticulous approach as well as usefully extend his experience. However, the Tiger year will bring additional changes for him and when these occur he should show some willingness to adapt. Admittedly, change does not always come easily to the Ox, but this is not a year in which he can risk undermining his position by appearing too inflexible. At times of transition it would sometimes be in his interests to watch and assess developments rather than speak out too hastily. He could ultimately find that some of what happens is to his advantage and presents new opportunities for him.

The Ox will, however, greatly benefit from any training courses he is able to go on and all Oxen should try to add to their skills and qualifications. The Ox will find learning a new skill a satisfying challenge for him as well as being a constructive use of his time. Similarly, for Oxen seeking work, any training or study they can undertake will certainly do much to help their prospects. These Oxen should also remain active in following up any openings that they see. Although their quest for work may be not be easy, their persistence will in time be rewarded. It could also be to their advantage to look at different ways in which they can use their skills and past experience. Some enterprising thinking on their part could open up additional opportunities.

The Ox is generally careful when dealing with financial matters and over the Tiger year he does need to keep a watchful eye over his level of spending. When he does incur any large expenses, particularly connected with his accommodation or transport, he should make sure he budgets accordingly and is aware of any obligations he may be placed under. His vigilance and prudent nature should help avert problems, but this is a year for careful financial management.

Domestically, this will be a generally pleasing year and the Ox will draw much comfort from the support and encouragement of those around him. While he has a tendency to keep his thoughts to himself, he would certainly be helped if he were prepared to be more forthcoming over the year and to discuss his ideas and any concerns he might have with those around him. In 1998 he will benefit much from the input of others. In addition, he can also look forward to some pleasing family occasions and one, concerning the achievements of a younger relation, will be a source of considerable joy and pride.

Many Oxen will also carry out large-scale projects on their home over the year, either in redecorating or making some alterations. However, while he will be satisfied with the end result, carrying out some of these projects could prove challenging for the Ox. If, at any time, he feels he is undertaking too much or is not overly confident with what he is doing, he should seek assistance and advice. In 1998 practical and DIY activities must not be rushed and the Ox must not take risks or compromise his safety.

With projects around his home and the many other demands upon his time the Ox may sometimes feel that he is not able to devote too much attention to his hobbies and personal interests. However, it is important he does not neglect these. His interests do provide an important break from his usual daytime concerns and help him unwind. The Ox could even find it helpful to consider taking up a new hobby over the year, perhaps something unrelated to anything he has done before. This could turn into an absorbing challenge for him and allow him to discover talents he did not realize he possessed. In addition, many Oxen have a fine ear for music and the Ox could find pursuing his musical interests most satisfying.

The Ox will lead a quiet but pleasant social life over the year. Admittedly, he may not be as keen a socializer as some, but he selects his friends well and in 1998 will spend many enjoyable times in their company. He will also attend several interesting social events over the year and these will give him the chance to meet others as well as build up some useful contacts. For the young and unattached Ox, a friendship made last year or early in 1998 could develop and become significant during the course of the year.

However, while there are aspects that will go well for the Ox in the Tiger year, there are some areas which could prove more troublesome. Over the year he could face several irritating problems which, while not serious, could take up valuable time and prove an unwelcome distraction. These problems could range from bureaucratic muddles, delays in the delivery of items or equipment he has ordered or a difference of opinion with someone. As far as possible, the Ox should aim to sort out the problem as quickly and amicably as he can rather than let it escalate and get out of proportion. Also, if he finds himself in any fraught situation, he should try to remain his usual diplomatic self. Although he does not often lose his temper, when he does it can be an awesome experience and, if he is not careful, harsh words could undermine some of the goodwill he has recently built up.

Although the Tiger year may not be the smoothest of years for the Ox, by setting about his activities in his usual measured way and taking into account the situations that prevail, he will be able to make reasonable progress. In addition, he will usefully add to his experience and this, together with any new skills he is able to develop, will help him in future years. However, despite the pressures that the Tiger year will bring, there will be many enjoyable times for the Ox, especially those spent with his family and friends and in carrying out his hobbies. The Year of the Tiger may be a year which calls for care but it need not be an unduly adverse one.

As far as the different types of Ox are concerned, this will prove a challenging year for the *Metal Ox*. The Metal Ox is shrewd, decisive and knows exactly what he wants to achieve and accomplish. And while such traits are commendable, when changes and new situations arise the Metal Ox needs to show a certain flexibility in his attitude and this is not always easy for one so resolute. In his work several new developments will take place over the year and if he is to make any sort of headway he needs to be adaptable and prepared to make the most of new situations. If not, he could find himself losing out on opportunities and not making the progress he desires. Also, despite some of his early misgivings, the changes that take place will sometimes give him the chance to investigate other aspects of his work and present him with new challenges and incentives, all of which can be to his future advantage. It would also be in his interests to consider what he would like to do over the next few years and if he feels this requires further skills or training, then the Tiger year would be an excellent time to obtain this. In many respects, what the Metal Ox learns and accomplishes in 1998 will be laying the foundations for the more progressive times that lie ahead. He will, however, need to remain his usual cautious self when dealing with monetary matters and should not commit himself to any large transaction without checking the terms and obligations he may be placed under. If in doubt, he should seek further clarification rather than take risks. There will also be several opportunities for the Metal Ox to travel over the year and a holiday he takes in the late summer will prove especially pleasurable, particularly if it is a destination new to him and one that he has been keen to visit for some time. Visits to local attractions and places of interest will also bring him much satisfaction, and if ever the Metal Ox, or those around him, should feel tired or under pressure, he would do well to suggest an activity or outing all can enjoy rather than driving on without any respite. Domestically, this will be an active year, and while there will be several family matters and household projects that will take up much of the Metal Ox's time, the progress and successes of those around him will be a source of much pride. Any further assistance he feels able to give, particularly to younger relations, will be especially valued. The Metal Ox will also obtain much satisfaction from his hobbies over the year and if he is able to extend them in some way, perhaps by learning about a new aspect or contacting fellow enthusiasts, then he will find this will make the interest all the more fulfilling. Although the Tiger year will bring its pressures and some niggling irritations, the Metal Ox will still reap much value from what occurs. The changes will not only allow him to broaden his experience but also the challenges he faces and surmounts will teach him much about himself and where his abilities lie. In 1999 and beyond he will be able to put what he has learned to positive use. In the meantime, he should view the Tiger year as one for preparing for the future advances he will make as well as for enjoying the time spent with his family and friends and on his interests.

The last few years will have been quite active for the *Water Ox* and he will have accomplished much as well as gained useful experience. In 1998 he would do well to take stock of his position, consolidate any gains he has recently made and think about what he hopes to achieve over the next few years. In this he would do well to talk to those around him, especially to those who have relevant experience or are in a position to offer practical assistance. The ideas and plans that the Water Ox formulates in 1998 will have a major bearing on the next few years as well as give him an idea of where best he should now concentrate his energies. During the Tiger year, though, he should continue to set about his work and activities in his usual conscientious manner and while he should remain alert for opportunities, he does need to be realistic in his expectations. This is more a year for planning and gaining further skills than for making major advances. Those Water Oxen seeking work or wanting to change their current position could, however, enjoy some good fortune in the early months of the year, with April and May being active months for employment matters. As far as financial affairs are concerned, this could prove an expensive year, especially as many Water Oxen will decide to buy some major items of equipment for their accommodation. Before making any sizeable purchase though, it would certainly be in the Water Ox's interests to check the range of prices on offer rather than accepting the first he sees. He should also make allowances for any major outlay in his budget; if not, he could find himself having to make economies later. On a personal level this will be a busy year, with many calls upon his time. However, despite the sometimes hectic nature of his domestic life, the Water Ox will take much satisfaction in following and encouraging the activities of those around him and, as always, his help will be highly valued. He should also not hesitate to ask for assistance at particularly demanding times, especially when he has many household tasks to deal with in addition to all his other commitments. Assistance will be forthcoming, but sometimes he may have to prompt others into action! It is important, too, that the Water Ox does not neglect his own interests, particularly those that allow him to meet others, take him out of doors or enable him to get some additional exercise. For those Water Oxen who enjoy gardening, exploring the countryside, travelling or following sport, the year will contain some truly satisfying moments. Generally, this will be a reasonable year for the Water Ox and the experience he gains and plans he makes will prove of considerable importance to him in the future. Added to which, the Tiger year, for all its pressures, will still contain many pleasurable and satisfying times for him.

This will be a mixed year for the *Wood Ox*, containing some highly positive aspects as well as some negative ones. To deal with the negative first, the Wood Ox may find it difficult to achieve as much as he would like over the year. Some of his plans could be affected by problems and delays and he could find it takes him longer to accomplish tasks than he originally anticipated. In 1998, before starting any new undertaking, he should allow plenty of time and avoid committing himself to too many tasks all at the same time. Over the Tiger year he will find he will achieve more by concentrating on a small range of activities than by spreading his energies too widely. However, despite any problems that occur, the Wood Ox will be well supported by those around him and he should not hesitate to seek their opinions and advice on any matter that might be troubling him. He could find that some of the problems that do arise are not as bad as he envisaged and talking to others will do much to put his mind at ease. It is also important he seeks assistance when engaging in any hazardous or strenuous activity; without care there is a risk he could hurt or strain himself. Wood Oxen, be warned! Care too is needed when dealing with important forms, correspondence or financial matters; if the Wood Ox has any doubts about what is being asked or uncertainties over any obligations he might be placed under, he should seek further advice. More positively, however, the Wood Ox's domestic and social life will bring him much satisfaction. He will delight in following the progress of those around him and can look forward to attending several pleasant social occasions during the course of the year. Any Wood Ox who may be feeling lonely should also make the effort to go out more and get in contact with others. The prospects for building new friendships are good, but it does require the Wood Ox to make the initial effort. His hobbies, too, will bring him much pleasure and any Wood Ox who has an interest of a creative nature would do well to bring his work to the notice of others; by doing so he could receive some positive encouragement and well-deserved praise. Travel will go well and many Wood Oxen will particularly enjoy a holiday they take during the summer months. Trips and outings arranged at short notice could also prove most memorable. Generally, there will be much in the Tiger year that the Wood Ox will enjoy, but he needs to be realistic in his undertakings and be prepared for some delays as well as a few niggling problems. But overall, these should not mar what will prove a varied and interesting year for him. And throughout, the Wood Ox should remember he has many around him he can call on for assistance and advice and that those around him will support him well.

The *Fire Ox* possesses a resolute and determined nature and often has set ideas about what he wishes to undertake and achieve. While such clear-sightedness has served him well in the past, in 1998 he will need to exercise caution and show a certain amount of flexibility. Despite his good intentions, not all his activities will work out in the manner he intended. He could find his plans are delayed or have to be changed because of new situations that arise. However, although the year will contain its irritations and frustrations, the Fire Ox can still make some worthwhile

41

accomplishments. Projects that he carries out on his home and garden will bring him much satisfaction and any Fire Ox who moves over the year will take considerable pleasure in setting up his new home and settling into a new area. Admittedly, the moving process may at times be stressful but the Fire Ox will, in the end, feel that the effort has been worthwhile. He does, however, need to take care when dealing with important items of paperwork. He should check any forms or agreements he has to complete and if he has any queries, he should seek clarification rather than take risks. There may be times in 1998 when the Fire Ox will be irritated by matters of a bureaucratic nature but failure to attend to these properly could result in more aggravation in the long run. More favourably aspected, though, is his domestic life. He can look forward to some most agreeable times with those around him and will not only take much pleasure in following the activities of those close to him but will also himself receive much useful support and advice. Socially, too, this will be a generally pleasant year and the Fire Ox would also do well to consider contacting those who share similar hobbies and interests to his own. By doing so he will be able to add to his circle of acquaintances and extend his interests in a most constructive way. Travel, too, is well aspected and the Fire Ox will enjoy and get much benefit from any holidays and breaks he is able to take over the year. This may not be the easiest of years for the Fire Ox and will require a fair amount of patience and flexibility on his part. However, despite its irritations (most of which will be over by midsummer), there will be many enjoyable and fulfilling times for him.

Although the aspects for the Ox are variable in the Tiger year, the *Earth Ox* can still make much of the year. The Earth Ox is both perceptive and realistic in his outlook and has a good sense of timing. He knows when conditions are right to advance his ideas and similarly shows restraint when a more cautious attitude is needed. This ability will serve him well throughout the year. In his work the Earth Ox should continue to set about his duties in his usual conscientious way but all the time remain alert to all that is happening around him. Although he may not be able to promote his plans and ideas as much as he would like, there will still be opportunities to pursue and the Earth Ox will be sure to make the most of these, limited though they may be. He would also do well to take advantage of any training courses that he might be eligible for or opportunities to extend his skills; by doing this he will not only be enhancing his future prospects but will also find this a satisfying and constructive use of his time. Those Earth Oxen seeking work should remain active in their quest for a position. Although opportunities may not be plentiful, many of them will hear of an opening by chance which could prove ideally suitable. The Tiger year, while not an easy one, will be a time when enterprise, persistence – and also sometimes the unexpected – will pay off! The Earth Ox does, however, need to handle financial matters with care. Several times during the year he could face large outlays, especially involving his accommodation and travel and, to avoid problems, he does need to keep a watchful eye over his financial situation. This is a year for vigilance and a certain restraint, not for taking risks! The Earth Ox's domestic life will be generally busy over the year and there will be some family matters that will take him much time to sort out. As always, his calm, level-headed manner will be appreciated and his advice and opinions often sought. However, to compensate for any aggravations that do arise, there will be many pleasurable family and social occasions for the Earth Ox to look forward to and at one he could find he is taking centre stage. He should also ensure he takes a proper break or holiday over the year as well as set a regular time aside for his hobbies and interests. The Earth Ox may usually possess much stamina, but with the demanding nature of the year, he does need to make sure he takes time to regularly relax and unwind. If not, he could find himself becoming tired, tense and not making as much of himself as he otherwise could. Generally, if the Earth Ox remains his usual vigilant self and makes the most of any opportunities that he sees, he can emerge from the year with some gains to his credit. And what he achieves and learns in 1998 will do much to prepare him for the growth and success he is soon to enjoy in the Year of the Rabbit.

FAMOUS OXEN

Madeleine Albright, Martin Amis, Hans Christian Andersen, Johann Sebastian Bach, Warren Beatty, Tony Benn, Jon Bon Jovi, Napoleon Bonaparte, Rory Bremner, Jeff Bridges, Benjamin Britten, Frank Bruno, Richard Burton, Barbara Cartland, Charlie Chaplin, Martin Clunes, George Cole, Natalie Cole, Bill Cosby, Tom Courtenay, Tony Curtis, Donald Dewar, Walt Disney, Patrick Duffy,

Dick van Dyke, Harry Enfield, Jane Fonda, Gerald Ford, Edward Fox, Michael J. Fox, Peter Gabriel, Richard Gere, Ryan Giggs, Whoopi Goldberg, William Hague, Handel, Robert Hardy, King Harold V of Norway, Nigel Havers, Adolf Hitler, Dustin Hoffman, Anthony Hopkins, Saddam Hussein, Billy Joel, Don Johnson, King Juan Carlos of Spain, B. B. King, Mark Knopfler, Burt Lancaster, k. d. Lang, Jessica Lange, Angela Lansbury, Jack Lemmon, Nick Lowe, Nicholas Lyndhurst, Kate Moss, Alison Moyet, Eddie Murphy, Benjamin Netanyahu, Paul Newman, Jack Nicholson, Leslie Nielsen, Billy Ocean, Oscar Peterson, Colin Powell, Robert Redford, Rubens, Meg Ryan, Arthur Scargill, Monica Seles, Sibelius, Sissy Spacek, Bruce Springsteen, Rod Steiger, Meryl Streep, Elaine Stritch, Loretta Swit, Lady Thatcher, Mel Torme, Scott F. Turow, Twiggy, Mary Tyler Moore, the Princess of Wales, Zoë Wanamaker, Tom Watson, the Duke of Wellington, Alan Whicker, Barbara Windsor, Ernie Wise, W. B. Yeats.

8 FEBRUARY 1902 ～ 28 JANUARY 1903   *Water Tiger*

26 JANUARY 1914 ～ 13 FEBRUARY 1915   *Wood Tiger*

13 FEBRUARY 1926 ～ 1 FEBRUARY 1927   *Fire Tiger*

31 JANUARY 1938 ～ 18 FEBRUARY 1939   *Earth Tiger*

17 FEBRUARY 1950 ～ 5 FEBRUARY 1951   *Metal Tiger*

5 FEBRUARY 1962 ～ 24 JANUARY 1963   *Water Tiger*

23 JANUARY 1974 ～ 10 FEBRUARY 1975   *Wood Tiger*

9 FEBRUARY 1986 ～ 28 JANUARY 1987   *Fire Tiger*

28 JANUARY 1998 ～ 15 FEBRUARY 1999   *Earth Tiger*

THE
TIGER

THE PERSONALITY OF THE TIGER

The true perfection of man lies not in what man has, but in what man is.

— Oscar Wilde: a Tiger

The Tiger is born under the sign of courage. He is a charismatic figure and usually holds very firm views and beliefs. He is strong-willed and determined, and sets about most of the things he does with a tremendous energy and enthusiasm. He is very alert and quick-witted and his mind is forever active. He is a highly original thinker and is nearly always brimming with new ideas or full of enthusiasm for some new project or scheme.

The Tiger adores challenges and loves to get involved in anything which he thinks has an exciting future or which catches his imagination. He is prepared to take risks and does not like to be bound either by convention or the dictates of others. The Tiger likes to be free to act as he chooses and at least once during his life he will throw caution to the wind and go off and do the things he wants to do.

The Tiger does, however, have a somewhat restless nature. Even though he is often prepared to throw himself wholeheartedly into a project, his initial enthusiasm can soon wane if he sees something more appealing. He can also be rather impulsive and there will be occasions in his life when he acts in a manner which he later regrets. If the Tiger were to think things out or to persevere in his various activities, he would almost certainly enjoy a greater degree of success.

Fortunately, the Tiger is lucky in most of his enterprises, but should things not work out as he had hoped, he is liable to suffer from severe bouts of depression and it will often take him a long time to recover. His life often consists of a series of ups and downs.

The Tiger is, however, very adaptable. He has an adventurous spirit and rarely stays in the same place for long. In the early stages of his life he is likely to try his hand at several different jobs and he will also change his residence fairly frequently.

The Tiger is very honest and open in his dealings with others. He hates any sort of hypocrisy or falsehood. He is also well known for being blunt and forthright and has no hesitation in speaking his mind. He can also be most rebellious at times, particularly against any form of petty authority, and while this can lead the Tiger into conflict with others, he is never one to shrink from an argument or avoid standing up for what he believes is right.

The Tiger is a natural leader and can invariably rise to the top of his chosen profession. He does not, however, care for anything too bureaucratic or detailed and he also does not like to obey orders. He can be stubborn and obstinate, and throughout his life he likes to retain a certain amount of independence in his actions and be responsible to no one but himself. He likes to consider that all his achievements are due to his own efforts and unless he cannot avoid it, he will rarely ask for support from others.

Ironically, despite his self-confidence and leadership qualities, the Tiger can be indecisive and will often delay making a major decision until the very last moment. He can also be sensitive to criticism.

Although the Tiger is capable of earning large sums of money, he is rather a spendthrift and does not always put his money to its best use. He can also be most generous and will often shower lavish gifts on friends and relations.

The Tiger cares very much for his reputation and the image that he tries to project. He carries himself with an air of dignity and authority and enjoys being the centre of attention. He is very adept at attracting publicity, both for himself and for the causes he supports.

The Tiger often marries young and he will find himself best suited to those born under the signs of the Pig, Dog, Horse and Goat. He can also get on well with the Rat, Rabbit and Rooster, but will find the Ox and Snake a bit too quiet and too serious for his liking, and he will also be highly irritated by the Monkey's rather mischievous and inquisitive ways. The Tiger will also find it difficult to get on with another Tiger or a Dragon – both partners will want to dominate the relationship and could find it difficult to compromise on even the smallest of matters.

The Tigress is lively, witty and a marvellous hostess at parties. She is usually most attractive and takes great care over her appearance. She can also be a very doting mother and while she believes in letting her children have their freedom, she makes an excellent teacher and will ensure that her children are brought up well and want for nothing. Like her male counterpart, she has numerous interests and likes to have sufficient independence and freedom to go off and do the things that she wants to do. She also has a most caring and generous nature.

The Tiger has many commendable qualities. He is honest, courageous and often a source of inspiration for others. Providing he can curb the wilder excesses of his restless nature, he is almost certain to lead a most fulfilling and satisfying life.

THE FIVE DIFFERENT TYPES OF TIGER

In addition to the 12 signs of the Chinese zodiac, there are five elements and these have a strengthening or moderating influence on the sign. The effects of the five elements on the Tiger are described below, together with the years in which the elements were exercising their influence. Therefore all Tigers born in 1950 are Metal Tigers, those born in 1902 and 1962 are Water Tigers, and so on.

Metal Tiger: 1950

The Metal Tiger has an assertive and outgoing personality. He is very ambitious and, while his aims may change from time to time, he will work relentlessly until he has obtained what he wants. He can, however, be impatient for results and also get highly strung if things do not work out as he would like. He is distinctive in his appearance and is admired and respected by many.

Water Tiger: 1902, 1962

This Tiger has a wide variety of interests and is always eager to experiment with new ideas or go off and explore distant lands. He is versatile, shrewd and has a kindly nature. The Water Tiger tends to remain calm in a crisis, although he can be annoyingly indecisive at times. He communicates well with others and through his many capabilities and persuasive nature he usually achieves what he wants in life. He is also highly imaginative and is often a gifted orator or writer.

Wood Tiger: 1914, 1974

The Wood Tiger has a very friendly and pleasant personality. He is less independent than some of the other types of Tiger and is more prepared to work with others to secure a desired objective. However, he does have a tendency to jump from one thing to another and can get easily distracted. He is usually very popular, has a large circle of friends and invariably leads a busy and enjoyable social life. He also has a good sense of humour.

Fire Tiger: 1926, 1986

The Fire Tiger sets about everything he does with great verve and enthusiasm. He loves action and is always ready to throw himself wholeheartedly into anything which catches his imagination. He has many leadership qualities and is capable of communicating his ideas and enthusiasm to others. He is very much an optimist and can be most generous. He has a likeable nature and can be a witty and persuasive speaker.

Earth Tiger: 1938, 1998

This Tiger is responsible and level-headed. He studies everything objectively and tries to be scrupulously fair in all his dealings. Unlike other Tigers, he is prepared to specialize in certain areas rather than get distracted by other matters, but he can become so involved with what he is doing that he does not always take into account the views and opinions of those around him. He has good business sense and is usually very successful in later life. He has a large circle of friends and pays great attention to both his appearance and his reputation.

PROSPECTS FOR THE TIGER IN 1998

The Chinese New Year starts on 28 January 1998. Until then, the old year, the Year of the Ox, is still making its presence felt.

The Year of the Ox (7 February 1997 to 27 January 1998) will not have been the easiest of years for the Tiger. Progress will have been slow and many Tigers will have encountered problems and delays with their various activities. Also there will have been times over the year when the Tiger will have felt he has not been making as much of himself or his abilities as he would have liked. Generally, the Ox year will have been a challenging one for him, but there is good reason for the Tiger now to take heart.

By October 1997 the more adverse aspects of the Ox year will have passed and a new and more positive trend will start to emerge; this will gather pace as the Tiger's own year approaches. With this upturn, all Tigers should give serious thought to what they would like to achieve over the next 12 months. They should discuss their ideas with those around them and particularly seek out those with relevant experience who are in a position to give expert advice. Also, if the Tiger feels he needs additional training or experience to accomplish what he has in mind, he should take steps to obtain this. Anything positive he can do now will certainly be to his advantage.

The Tiger would also do well to complete any outstanding matters that he might have, including unanswered correspondence, at this time. With a concerted effort, he will be able to accomplish much and this will leave him freer to enjoy the end of the year and to start the new year reasonably up to date. Also, if he has experienced strain in his relations with anyone, this would be an ideal time to rectify this. A positive and understanding approach will do much to improve any differences and all Tigers will, in any case, find that their relations with others will go much better in the closing stages of the year. In particular, the Tiger can look forward to having some most agreeable times with family and friends at this time as well as to attending some highly enjoyable parties and functions. The Christmas and New Year holidays will go especially well and will give him a much needed break after the pressures of the previous 12 months. Rested and revitalized, the Tiger can look forward to the exciting prospects that await him in his own year.

The Year of the Tiger begins on 28 January 1998 and will herald an upturn in the Tiger's fortunes. This will be a much more positive year for him and he will now be able to make the progress that has been eluding him of late. Throughout the year he should aim to promote himself and his abilities as much as he can. The Tiger year favours enterprise and indeed few are as enterprising or as innovative as the Tiger. His own year, therefore, offers him considerable potential.

In his work the Tiger should remain alert for any openings to pursue. The period from late January to May could prove especially active for work matters and the Tiger should make every effort to follow up any opportunities that he sees at this time. He should also promote his ideas; as a Tiger he has a most inventive mind and some of his suggestions and thoughts will be well received by those around him and will help both his position and progress. Many times during 1998 the Tiger will find that positive and enterprising action on his part will be recognized and rewarded.

Although the Tiger possesses an independent streak in his nature, he would, however, find it in his interests to work closely and in co-operation with others rather than retain too independent an approach. Indeed, several times during the year he will gain much from the input of others and throughout he does need to be mindful of what those around him advise.

The Tiger is also likely to see changes in the nature of his duties over the year and while sometimes these may be different from what he had envisaged, often they will represent new and exciting opportunities for him and will enable him to extend his experience. In 1998 events may sometimes be unexpected and arise in a surprising manner, but almost always the Tiger will be able to turn them to his advantage, such are the powerful and auspicious aspects that prevail.

Those Tigers who may have felt in a rut lately, who are feeling staid in their present position or who are seeking work will also enjoy some positive developments over the year. Again, they should follow up any opportunities they see but also actively promote their skills. They could even find it helpful to make a direct approach to organizations or employers they would like to work for, setting out ideas and their past experience or seeking advice over possible employment. Bold and enterprising action on the Tiger's part could lead to some favourable results, but to do well he does need to take the initiative.

Tigers in education are also likely to make good progress and will find the time and attention they give to their studies will be well rewarded. And for any Tiger who is keen to extend his skills and qualifications, this is an excellent year to do so.

Financial matters are also favourably aspected and most Tigers will enjoy a noticeable improvement in their situation over the year. However, while the Tiger will enjoy this upturn, if he does find himself with surplus funds, he would do well to consider saving part of them rather than spending too freely or engaging in too many expensive whims. He could find savings made in the Tiger year will build into a useful asset and will be something he will be grateful for in future years. However, while the Tiger should aim to make some savings in 1998, he could also spot some excellent bargains over the year, especially in the home furnishing line. At sale times it would certainly be in his interest to keep alert!

The favourable aspects also extend to the Tiger's personal life and in both his domestic and social life he can look forward to some pleasing times. Domestically, those around the Tiger will be most encouraging and will give him much useful support. The Tiger himself will also take delight in following the activities of those close to him and will have every reason to be proud of the achievements of a loved one.

He will also spend considerable time on household matters – in redecorating, carrying out alterations or, for some Tigers, moving. Generally, the Tiger will feel well satisfied with what he is able to accomplish and will find that projects of a practical nature go well. Those Tigers who do move will, in particular, enjoy settling into, and finding out about, their new area and establishing a new social life. Any Tiger who may have had some sadness or adversity to bear in recent years should try now to turn his attention to the present and the future. For many, 1998 will represent the start of a new chapter in their life and it rests with them to make the most of positive aspects that prevail and the chances that the year will bring.

Socially, too, the year will go well and all Tigers will get much pleasure from going out and meeting others. There will also be several enjoyable occasions and functions for the Tiger to attend during the year which will give him the opportunity to add to his circle of friends. For the unattached Tiger, the prospects for romance and marriage are excellent, with spring and summer being a well aspected time.

Overall, this is a year of opportunity for the Tiger. In his work, there will be chances to progress, while personally, domestically and socially the year holds much promise. However, while the trends are so auspicious, there are several points the Tiger will need to bear in mind.

To get the best from the year he should have some idea about what he wishes to accomplish. By giving himself some objectives he will find he is making more effective use of his time and will also have a better idea of where to concentrate his efforts. Without this, he could easily drift and miss out on some marvellous opportunities.

He should also keep his sometimes restless nature in check. To make progress will require some discipline on his part and in 1998 he must resist the temptation of getting too easily distracted or of jumping from one activity to another. These are really great times for him and he must not squander them.

With these points in mind, this can be an excellent and enjoyable year. Tigers are both resourceful and enterprising and by using their skills and talents well they will enjoy considerable success. And, in much of what the Tiger does in 1998, luck and good fortune will accompany him.

As far as the different types of Tiger are concerned, this will be a significant year for the *Metal Tiger*. He will be given the chance to draw on his past experience and put some of his ideas and plans into practice. This is a year which holds much potential for him and, given the Metal Tiger's drive and ambition, he will certainly make much of it. In his work he will make considerable headway. Many Metal Tigers will be given greater responsibilities, be promoted or transfer to new and more varied duties. They will delight in the challenges they are given as well as greatly impress those around them. Also, any Metal Tiger who may have been disappointed with his recent progress or felt he has not been making as much of his abilities as he would have liked will find that this will certainly change now. This is a year of significant advance and one in which the Metal Tiger will receive recognition for his past work and his skills. There will also be openings for those Metal Tigers seeking work and many will find their persistence and quest for a position rewarded in quite a surprising way. Financial matters too are well aspected and if the Metal Tiger finds himself in a position to make some savings he could find these will develop into a useful asset in the future. With luck on his side he could also enjoy good fortune in a competition and would do well to enter any that particularly catch his eye. On a personal level, too, the year holds much promise. The Metal Tiger can look forward to some pleasing times with both family and friends, and those around him will give him much valuable support in his activities. Many Metal Tigers will also have good cause for a personal celebration over the year, either fulfilling an ambition or having some other piece of favourable news. In addition, the Metal Tiger is likely to attend several parties and functions during the spring and summer, some of which could turn out to be highly pleasant and memorable occasions. As far as his interests are concerned, he will particularly delight in outdoor activities and there will also be several opportunities for him to indulge in his love of travel. Generally, this will be a most favourable year for the Metal Tiger and by using his talents and giving of his best he will be able to make excellent progress as well as enjoy himself. It has been some time since the aspects have been so auspicious for him and he really should aim to make the most of them.

In recent years the *Water Tiger* will have learned much and in 1998 he will be able to draw on his past experience and his skills and put them to good use. In his work he will make good progress and almost all Water Tigers will take on new and more varied responsibilities as the year progresses. The Water Tiger will delight in the challenges given him and these will help give him an added incentive to do well. Those around him will look favourably on his undertakings and be impressed by his diligent and enterprising manner. He should also advance any ideas he has; he could find these will develop in quite a pleasing and unexpected way. For Water Tigers seeking work or feeling that the time has come for a change, the year will again hold some interesting possibilities and they should actively follow up any openings they see. The Water Tiger should also explore other ways in which he can use his skills; by doing so he will discover further opportunities that could be suitable for him. Some innovative thinking could pay off handsomely! There will also be a marked improvement in his financial position and any problems he may have been experiencing will be considerably eased. However, if he finds he has any spare funds at his disposal he should aim to put these towards a specific purpose, such as his accommodation or travel, as well as making provision for his longer-term future. Without a certain care, he could find he is spending money that could be put to more purposeful use. The Water Tiger's domestic and social life will, however, be most agreeable and he can look forward to some splendid times with those around him. In the interests of domestic harmony, he could find it helpful to encourage activities all can take part in, such as joint projects in the home or garden or an occasional treat or trip out. Such activities will give all concerned much satisfaction and the year could be marked by some distinguished occasions. The Water Tiger can also look forward to some pleasant times with his friends and for those who are unattached, lonely or seeking new friends, the year will bring some ideal opportunities to meet others. In particular, the Water Tiger could find joining a local interest group will lead to new friendships as well as some pleasurable social occasions. Generally, 1998 is a year of considerable potential for the Water Tiger and by taking advantage of the positive aspects that prevail, he will do much to improve his position. Added to which, the year will also contain some most enjoyable and personally satisfying times.

With his outgoing and agreeable manner, the *Wood Tiger* is highly regarded by others and in 1998 he will find himself much in demand. This will be a busy and fulfilling year for him and one in which he will make good progress. However, to maximize the favourable aspects that prevail, the Wood Tiger should set himself some priorities and have some idea about what he hopes to achieve over the next 12 months. Without any such plan, he could easily drift and not make as much of himself, his skills or the opportunities that occur as he otherwise could. In his work the Wood Tiger will make considerable progress. There will be several excellent opportunities for him to further his position and put his skills to good use. He should also actively promote any ideas he has; these are likely to impress others and this again can do much to advance his position. Indeed, enterprising and determined action on his part will be well received, and throughout the year he will find much truth in the old saying 'nothing ventured, nothing gained'. The Wood Tiger will also enjoy an improvement in his financial situation over the year, although he still needs to keep a watchful eye over his level of spending. During the year he could find he has to meet several large expenses, especially as far as his accommodation is concerned, and he needs to budget carefully and avoid succumbing to too many expensive indulgences! With care, and a certain restraint, he will end the year in a much improved financial position. Personally, this will also be a splendid year for the Wood Tiger and he can look forward to having some memorable times with those around him. In addition, there will be good cause for some personal celebration; many Wood Tigers who are unattached will either get engaged or married, while others could see an addition to their family. In so many respects, this will prove a positive and memorable year and it rests with the Wood Tiger to make the maximum use of his many fine talents and skills. In 1998 he really does have much going in his favour.

This will be a year that the *Fire Tiger* will enjoy. During 1998 he will be able to devote time to his various interests and hobbies and these will provide him with considerable satisfaction. Indeed, he would do well to consider extending his interests in some way or perhaps even taking up a new one. Both out-of-door and creative activities are favoured and for any Fire Tiger involved in the creative arts, whether in writing, photography, the theatre, music or in some other aspect, it would be worthwhile bringing his work to the attention of others and perhaps entering an appropriate competition. His skills and talents will be favourably received and he could obtain much constructive and encouraging comment as a result. It would also be worth contacting fellow enthusiasts; this will allow the Fire Tiger to extend his interest even further as well as lead to some pleasurable social occasions. His personal life too will go well. Those close to him will provide him with much support for his activities and should he feel in need of any assistance or have any matter concerning him, he should not hesitate to seek their views. This is particularly so for those Fire Tigers in education. While they will make pleasing progress with their studies, some of what is asked of them will be challenging and at these times they should seek guidance rather than struggling on unaided. Those close to the Fire Tiger are keen to see him do well and will readily help if asked. Similarly, those Fire Tigers born in 1926 should seek assistance when tackling any complex matter, especially of a bureaucratic nature, or when undertaking any strenuous or hazardous activity. Again, help and practical assistance will be readily forthcoming. Socially, the Fire Tiger can look forward to some pleasant times with his friends and at a gathering held in the spring he could make some new and what will become significant acquaintances. Travel, too, is well aspected and any journeys and holidays that the Fire Tiger takes will go well and prove beneficial for him. In addition to visiting places new to him, he will also take much delight in finding out about places of local interest and one local outing he takes could turn out to be highly fortuitous and memorable. Generally, 1998 will be a fulfilling year for the Fire Tiger and by using his time wisely he will accomplish much as well as greatly enjoy the year.

The last few years will not have been the easiest for the *Earth Tiger*. He could have faced challenging decisions and may not have been able to accomplish as much as he would have liked. However, in 1998 he will be able to put many of his former troubles behind him and should regard this, his own year, as marking an upturn in his fortunes. This is a time when he can turn his attention to new plans, new projects and some ideas he has long been nurturing. With a positive and determined attitude he can accomplish much and achieve successes that may not have been possible before. This will be a year of many interesting possibilities for him and one in which he will also make some far-reaching decisions. Some Earth Tigers will consider retiring, some moving, some going on a lengthy journey and some pursuing a personal goal, but whatever the Earth Tiger has in mind, he will receive much valuable support from those around him and will find that his plans generally work out well. However, although the aspects are so much in his favour, he does need to exercise care with bureaucratic matters, especially with any important correspondence and forms he receives. If he has any uncertainties he should seek clarification rather than take risks. If not, he could find himself involved in some protracted correspondence and wasting time he could be spending on more pleasurable activities. More positively, however, financial matters are well aspected and many Earth Tigers can look forward to receiving an extra sum of money over the year, either in recognition for some work they have done or as a gift. And with luck so much on his side, it would also be worth the Earth Tiger entering any competitions that interest him. His domestic life will prove particularly pleasurable and he will take much delight in following and encouraging the activities of those around him. The year will also mark an upturn in his social life and he could be invited to several interesting and enjoyable functions. For the lonely or unattached Earth Tiger, the aspects for building new and meaningful friendships are good, particularly in the spring, and also during a holiday. Overall, this will be a fulfilling year for the Earth Tiger and one in which he can look forward to many agreeable times with his family and friends and in carrying out his wide and varied interests.

FAMOUS TIGERS

Sir David Attenborough, Queen Beatrix of the Netherlands, Beethoven, Tony Bennett, Tom Berenger, Chuck Berry, Richard Branson, Garth Brooks, Mel Brooks, Isambard Kingdom Brunel, Agatha Christie, David Coleman, Phil Collins, Robbie Coltrane, Alan Coren, Gemma Craven, Tom Cruise, Paul Daniels, Emily Dickinson, David Dimbleby, Isadora Duncan, Dwight Eisenhower, Queen Elizabeth II, Enya, Roberta Flack, E. M. Forster, Frederick Forsyth, Jodie Foster, Connie Francis, Charles de Gaulle, Crystal Gayle, Elliott Gould, Buddy Greco, Sir Alec Guinness, Naseem Hamed, Harriet Harman, Ed Harris, Tim Henman, William Hurt, Derek Jacobi, Bianca Jagger, Matthew Kelly, Stan Laurel, Ian

McCaskill, Karl Marx, Marilyn Monroe, Demi Moore, Eric Morecambe, Neil Morrissey, Lord Owen, Marco Polo, Jonathan Porritt, Beatrix Potter, John Prescott, the Princess Royal, Oliver Reed, Renoir, Lionel Ritchie, Kenny Rogers, Sir Jimmy Savile, Phillip Schofield, Dick Spring, Sir David Steel, Dame Joan Sutherland, Dylan Thomas, Terence Trent-D'Arby, Liv Ullman, Jon Voight, Julie Walters, Oscar Wilde, Tennessee Williams, Terry Wogan, Stevie Wonder, Natalie Wood.

29 JANUARY 1903 〜 15 FEBRUARY 1904   *Water Rabbit*

14 FEBRUARY 1915 〜 2 FEBRUARY 1916   *Wood Rabbit*

2 FEBRUARY 1927 〜 22 JANUARY 1928   *Fire Rabbit*

19 FEBRUARY 1939 〜 7 FEBRUARY 1940   *Earth Rabbit*

6 FEBRUARY 1951 〜 26 JANUARY 1952   *Metal Rabbit*

25 JANUARY 1963 〜 12 FEBRUARY 1964   *Water Rabbit*

11 FEBRUARY 1975 〜 30 JANUARY 1976   *Wood Rabbit*

29 JANUARY 1987 〜 16 FEBRUARY 1988   *Fire Rabbit*

THE
RABBIT

THE PERSONALITY OF THE RABBIT

> The talent of success is nothing more than doing what
> you can do well, and doing well whatever you do.
> — *Henry Wadsworth Longfellow: a Rabbit*

The Rabbit is born under the signs of virtue and prudence. He is intelligent, well-mannered and prefers a quiet and peaceful existence. He dislikes any sort of unpleasantness and will try to steer clear of arguments and disputes. He is very much a pacifist and tends to have a calming influence on those around him.

He has wide interests and usually has a good appreciation of the arts and the finer things in life. He also knows how to enjoy himself and will often gravitate to the best restaurants and night spots in town.

The Rabbit is a witty and intelligent speaker and loves being involved in a good discussion. His views and advice are often sought by others and he can be relied upon to be discreet and diplomatic. He will rarely raise his voice in anger and will even turn a blind eye to matters which displease him just to preserve the peace. The Rabbit likes to remain on good terms with everyone, but he can be rather sensitive and takes any form of criticism very badly. He will also be the first to get out of the way if he sees any form of trouble brewing.

The Rabbit is a quiet and efficient worker and has an extremely good memory. He is very astute in business and financial matters, but his degree of success often depends on the conditions that prevail. He hates being in a situation which is fraught with tension or where he has to make quick and sudden decisions. Wherever possible he will plan his various activities with the utmost care and a good deal of caution. He does not like to take risks and does not take kindly to changes. Basically, he seeks a secure, calm and stable environment, and when conditions are right he is more than happy to leave things as they are.

The Rabbit is conscientious in most of the things he does and, because of his methodical and ever-watchful nature, can often do well in his chosen profession. He makes a good diplomat, lawyer, shopkeeper, administrator or priest and he excels in any job where he can use his superb skills as a communicator. He tends to be loyal to his employers and is respected for his integrity and honesty, but if he ever finds himself in a position of great power he can become rather intransigent and authoritarian.

The Rabbit attaches great importance to his home and will often spend much time and money to maintain and furnish it and to fit it with all the latest comforts – the Rabbit is very much a creature of comfort! He is also something of a collector and there are many Rabbits who derive much pleasure from collecting antiques, stamps, coins, *objets d'art* or anything else which catches their eye or particularly interests them.

The female Rabbit has a friendly, caring and considerate nature, and will do all in her power to give her home a happy and loving atmosphere. She is also very sociable and enjoys holding parties and entertaining. She has a great ability to make the maximum use of her time and, although she involves herself in numerous activities, she always manages to find time to sit back and enjoy a good read or a chat. She has a great sense of humour, is very artistic and is often a talented gardener.

The Rabbit takes considerable care over his appearance and is usually smart and very well turned out. He also attaches great importance to his relations with others and matters of the heart are particularly important to him. He will rarely be short of admirers and will often have several serious romances before he settles down. The Rabbit is not the most faithful of signs, but he will find that he is especially well suited to those born under the signs of the Goat, Snake, Pig and Ox. Due to his sociable and easy-going manner he can also get on well with the Tiger, Dragon, Horse, Monkey, Dog and another Rabbit, but will feel ill at ease with the Rat and Rooster as both these signs tend to speak their mind and be critical in their comments, and the Rabbit just loathes any form of criticism or unpleasantness.

The Rabbit is usually lucky in life and often has the happy knack of being in the right place at the right time. He is talented and quick-witted, but he does sometimes put pleasure before work, and wherever possible will tend to opt for the easy life. He can at times be a little reserved and suspicious of the motives of others, but generally will lead a long and contented life and one which – as far as possible – will be free of strife and discord.

THE FIVE DIFFERENT TYPES OF RABBIT

In addition to the 12 signs of the Chinese zodiac, there are five elements and these have a strengthening or moderating influence on the sign. The effects of the five elements on the Rabbit are described below, together with the years in which the elements were exercising their influence. Therefore all Rabbits born in 1951 are Metal Rabbits, those born in 1903 and 1963 are Water Rabbits, and so on.

Metal Rabbit: 1951
This Rabbit is capable, ambitious and has very definite views on what he wants to achieve in life. He can occasionally appear reserved and aloof, but this is mainly because he likes to keep his thoughts and ideas to himself. He has a very quick and alert mind and is particularly shrewd in business matters. He can also be very cunning in his actions. The Metal Rabbit has a good appreciation of the arts and likes to mix in the best circles. He usually has a small but very loyal group of friends.

Water Rabbit: 1903, 1963
The Water Rabbit is popular, intuitive and keenly aware of the feelings of those around him. He can, however, be rather sensitive and tends to take things too much to heart. He is very precise and thorough in everything he does and

has an exceedingly good memory. He tends to be quiet and at times rather withdrawn, but he expresses his ideas well and is highly regarded by his family, friends and colleagues.

Wood Rabbit: 1915, 1975

The Wood Rabbit is likeable, easy going and very adaptable. He prefers to work in groups rather than on his own and likes to have the support and encouragement of others. He can, however, be rather reticent in expressing his views and it would be in his own interests to become a little more open and forthright and let others know how he feels on certain matters. He usually has many friends and enjoys an active social life. He is noted for his generosity.

Fire Rabbit: 1927, 1987

The Fire Rabbit has a friendly, outgoing personality. He likes socializing and being on good terms with everyone. He is discreet and diplomatic and has a very good understanding of human nature. He is also strong-willed and provided he has the necessary backing and support he can go far in life. He does not, however, suffer adversity well and can become moody and depressed when things are not working out as he would like. The Fire Rabbit is very intuitive and there are some who are even noted for their psychic ability. The Fire Rabbit has a particularly good manner with children.

Earth Rabbit: 1939

The Earth Rabbit is a quiet individual, but he is nevertheless very shrewd and astute. He is realistic in his aims and is prepared to work long and hard in order to achieve his objectives. He has good business sense and is invariably lucky in financial matters. He also has a most persuasive manner and usually experiences little difficulty in getting others to fall in with his plans. He is held in very high esteem by his friends and colleagues and his views and opinions are often sought and highly valued.

PROSPECTS FOR THE RABBIT IN 1998

The Chinese New Year starts on 28 January 1998. Until then, the old year, the Year of the Ox, is still making its presence felt.

The Year of the Ox (7 February 1997 to 27 January 1998) will not have been the easiest of years for the Rabbit. His progress will not have been all that he would have liked and he could also have faced several niggling problems. However, although the Ox year does contain some negative aspects, the Rabbit can still obtain much of value from it and this certainly applies to the closing months of the year.

In the Ox year the Rabbit should try to build on his experience and skills. This can be through taking on new and different duties in his work, personal study or following up subjects that have been intriguing him. Anything positive that the Rabbit can do at this time will certainly help his future prospects. He should also remain alert to all that is going on around him, particularly concerning work matters, as he could learn of something that could be to his advantage and worth following up.

As far as financial matters are concerned the Rabbit needs to remain his careful and prudent self. The closing stages of the year could prove expensive for him and he would do well to watch his level of spending and avoid taking unnecessary financial risks. If he has doubts over any monetary matter it would be in his interests to check and, if need be, seek further advice.

Although the Rabbit is renowned for his discreet and tactful manner, he could have found that some of his relations with others have become strained over the Ox year. In what remains of it he should make every effort to resolve any differences or ill feeling that might remain. Indeed, some social occasions during December and January would be an ideal time to do this, and by making the effort the Rabbit will do much to remove existing tensions. The latter part of the year will, in any case, be a more favourable time for personal relations and over the Christmas and New Year holidays the Rabbit will find himself much in demand, with many occasions he will thoroughly enjoy. Added to which, the holiday period will generally give him a good chance to relax and unwind after the pressures of the year.

The Year of the Tiger starts on 28 January 1998 and will be an important and eventful year for the Rabbit. What he undertakes and achieves will have a significant bearing on the progress that he will make in his own year, 1999, the Year of the Rabbit. The Year of the Tiger is very much a prelude and preparatory stage for the truly excellent times that await him.

However, before any period of success there is often a time of upheaval, a time when plans and ideas need to be reviewed, when certain changes take place and further knowledge is gained. And while the Rabbit may feel uneasy about some of the events and changes that do take place in the Tiger year, he must view much of what happens as opportunities in the making. Admittedly, the Rabbit is one who seeks a stable lifestyle and dislikes uncertainty, but change is an inevitable process and, as he will find, can often work to his advantage. Also, viewed positively, the changes that occur will add to his experience, prevent him from becoming staid in his present situation and give him new challenges – challenges that will revitalize him, absorb him and renew his incentive to do well. The Tiger year will mark an important stage in the Rabbit's development and the beginning of a major upturn in his fortunes, an upturn that will gather momentum as his own year approaches.

In the meantime, the Rabbit will need to remain alert to all that is happening around him and show himself willing to adapt to any changes that may be introduced, particularly in the workplace. By being flexible and accommodating in his attitude he will do much to impress others and accordingly enhance his reputation. The Rabbit should also take advantage of any opportunity to expand on his experience and if there are any courses he is eligible for or skills he can learn, he should follow these up. This particularly applies to those Rabbits seeking work or wanting to change their present position. Positive and persistent action on the Rabbit's part will ultimately be rewarded, with both the early and especially the later parts of the year being active times for work matters.

The Tiger year is also one which favours enterprise and if the Rabbit has some project he wishes to start, this would be an excellent year to prepare the groundwork and set his plans in motion. Indeed, what the Rabbit commences in 1998 could truly flourish over the next few years.

The Rabbit will, however, need to be careful when dealing with financial matters. Again, this is not a year for taking undue risks and neither should the Rabbit commit himself to any large transaction until he has checked all the clauses and obligations involved. Fortunately, his thorough nature will usually prevent him from making mistakes, but this is not a year in which he can let his vigilance slip. Also, should the Rabbit make any sizeable purchases over the year, especially equipment and furnishings for his home, he would do well to compare the prices in several outlets rather than take the first that he sees. By doing so he could save himself considerable outlay.

Domestically, this will be a busy year for the Rabbit with many calls upon his time. At particularly active times he would find it helpful to set himself priorities and concentrate on these rather than try to do too much all at once. Also, if he finds household chores and other matters are mounting up, he should not hesitate to ask for assistance. He will find it readily forthcoming. However, despite the demands of the year, there will also be times of much domestic happiness and the Rabbit will delight in following and encouraging the activities of those close to him. Some joint family activities, such as trips out or holidays, will prove especially pleasurable as well as help relieve some of the pressures of normal everyday routine.

The Rabbit is a keen socializer and can look forward to attending some interesting parties and functions over the year. In addition, there will be many chances for him to extend his circle of friends and acquaintances and, for the unattached Rabbit, a chance meeting in the second half of the year could truly blossom late in 1998 and particularly in 1999.

However, while he will get much pleasure from his domestic and social life, the Rabbit's relations with others will need careful handling. There will be occasions over the year when he will feel under pressure or ill at ease and at such times he does need to exercise care and thoughtfulness in his relations with others – a word said out of place or a snappy response could cause a certain ill feeling with others. The Rabbit should watch this. He will also undoubtedly find it helpful to discuss his feelings and concerns with those around him rather than bottle them up inside. Usually the Rabbit is masterful at handling his relations with others and, both for his own sake and for the sake of the good relations he so much values, he should strive to remain his usual tactful and diplomatic self over the year.

In view of the active nature of the year it is also important that the Rabbit regularly devotes time to his hobbies and interests and allows himself time to relax, unwind and just enjoy himself. It could also be worth considering taking up a new interest over the year, perhaps something unrelated to anything he has done before. By doing so the Rabbit could find a most fulfilling challenge that will provide him with many hours of pleasure. Also, if he does not get much exercise during the day, he could find additional walking or some activity such as cycling or swimming would be beneficial for him.

Generally, the Rabbit will achieve and learn much over the Tiger year. Though there will be pressures and uncertainties, they will often herald new opportunities and chances for him to develop and show his true worth. As such, the Tiger year will prove an important one for the Rabbit and will serve as a prelude to the exciting prospects that await him in 1999.

As far as the different types of Rabbit are concerned, this will be an important and active year for the *Metal Rabbit*. The Metal Rabbit possesses many fine abilities and high amongst these is his good sense of judgement. He is adept at reading the conditions that prevail as well as seeing how he can turn new situations to his advantage. And in 1998, he will indeed be involved in several changing situations. In his work he could be given new duties, new projects or see changes in the personnel around him. While some of this may be unsettling and daunting, by rising up to the challenges given him and opportunities that arise, he will do well. Furthermore, by extending his experience he will be placing himself in an excellent position to make progress in the future. However, throughout the Tiger year the Metal Rabbit does need to keep alert to all that is happening around him and, as always, remain his diligent and committed self. He should also promote any ideas that he has and if there has been some goal he has long been seeking, now is the time to take the initial steps. Plans started now could well come to fruition later in the year and particularly in 1999. Many of those Metal Rabbits looking for work could also enjoy some success in obtaining a new position. Although this may not always be in the capacity they were initially seeking, they could find that one position will, in time, lead to another, better one. As far as financial matters are concerned, the Metal Rabbit will need to keep a watchful eye over his level of spending and avoid taking unnecessary risks or entering into anything of a too speculative nature. While he is usually adept at dealing with finance, this is a year for care and prudence. The Metal Rabbit's domestic and social life will, however, be a source of much pleasure. Joint family activities, such as household or garden projects, will prove especially satisfying, as will family treats, such as trips or meals out. The Metal Rabbit will also take much pleasure in following and assisting with the activities of those close to him and, as always, his sound judgement will be most appreciated. However, although he may not like to trouble others with his own concerns, it really would be in his interests to be forthcoming about any anxieties that he may have, particularly in view of some of the pressures he will face over the year. Those around him will be only too pleased to assist and advise, should he ask. The Metal Rabbit should also make sure that he devotes sufficient time to recreational activities over the year and does not neglect his hobbies and interests. These do help him to unwind and also help to take his mind off some of the pressures he may feel under. Similarly, he will find that the holidays and breaks he is able to take will be most beneficial for him. Although this will be a busy year for the Metal Rabbit and care and watchfulness is needed with many of his activities, there will be much that he will find satisfying. Added to which, what he accomplishes in 1998 will do much to assist his progress in the even more positive times that await him in 1999.

Although the *Water Rabbit* will have accomplished much in recent years, many Water Rabbits will have felt they have not yet reached their full potential or been making as much use of their talents as they might. This is about to change and so the Tiger year will prove of considerable importance to them. Over the year the Water Rabbit should look closely at his aims and aspirations and ideally talk these over with those with experience who are in a position to offer expert advice. Then, having reflected over his plans and the best course of action for him to take, the Water Rabbit should put his schemes in motion. This will be the year when he will take the initial steps on the road to much greater things, and he will begin to see the results of his newfound determination towards the end of the Tiger year and during the Year of the Rabbit. In all he does, however, the Water Rabbit should take a keen interest in the changes and developments that take place around him. By doing so, he will not only learn of information that will be helpful to him but will also identify opportunities that might soon become available. Again, attentiveness, together with some enterprise on his part, will lead to him furthering his position. Similarly, those Water Rabbits seeking employment or wanting to move on from their present duties could also identify opportunities and openings that they can turn to their advantage. Again, it could be in their interests to think about their wide range of skills and how they can put them to most effective use. Some innovative thinking could pay off quite handsomely! Domestically, this will be an active year for the Water Rabbit, with many matters requiring his attention. However, at busy times he should try to give himself priorities and would find it helpful to tackle one task at a time rather than spread his energies too widely. Also, if the Water Rabbit intends to carry out any practical projects on his home he should allow plenty of time for them. To set himself tight deadlines or rush jobs will not only put him under greater pressure but will also lead to less satisfactory results. However, in spite of the demanding nature of the year, there will be many domestic and social occasions for the Water Rabbit to enjoy. In particular, trips out with his family or friends will prove most pleasurable, especially if arranged at short notice and as something of a surprise. The Water Rabbit should also ensure that he takes a proper break or holiday over the year; he will find it most beneficial for him as well as highly enjoyable, especially if he is able to visit an area he has long been wanting to see. Generally, the Tiger year is one which will offer the Water Rabbit considerable scope. He should decide what he wants to achieve over the next few years and start working towards his goals. He has the gifts and the abilities and it rests with him to use them wisely. His prospects over the next year are truly glittering.

The last few years will have been active for the *Wood Rabbit* and much will have happened, both in his personal life and work situation. At the start of the Tiger year he would do well to take stock of his present position and consider how he would like to see his life developing over the next few years. In contemplating future activities he should take into account his strengths, where his natural interests lie and how best he can draw on his past experience. He would also be helped by discussing his thoughts with those who have relevant experience behind them and are in a position to offer constructive advice. Once he has formed some idea of what he would like to do and has some goals to aim for, the Wood Rabbit should earnestly set about achieving them. He has many fine talents and by channelling his energies wisely and towards a specific purpose, he will make good progress. Throughout the Tiger year, however, he should actively follow up any openings he sees and use any opportunity he gets to extend his experience as well as promote his ideas. What the Wood Rabbit accomplishes in the Tiger year will stand him in good stead for the excellent aspects that prevail in 1999. As far as financial matters are concerned, he will, however, need to exercise caution and restraint. Many Wood Rabbits will face large expenses over the year, especially involving their accommodation, and they will need to make full allowance for this in their budget. The Wood Rabbit should also be wary of any speculative ventures that he may hear about and if he has any reservations or doubts over any commitment he is about to enter into, he should check. On a personal level, the Tiger year will be busy and memorable. The Wood Rabbit will take considerable delight in following the activities of those around him and can look forward to some rewarding times with both family and friends. In particular, the successes of a younger relation will be a source of considerable joy to him and the

Wood Rabbit will take much pleasure in encouraging and assisting the progress of those around him. However, there will be times over the year when he will feel under pressure or, because of the demands placed upon him, tired and dispirited. On such occasions, he should not hesitate to ask for assistance rather than struggle on unaided. Also, while usually considerate of others, he should try not to take out his tensions on others; to do so could undermine some of the goodwill he has built up with those around him. This warning apart, the Wood Rabbit will do much over the Tiger year and what he achieves will certainly help him towards greater things in the future.

Although there will be much to the year that the *Fire Rabbit* will enjoy, there will also be some aspects which could cause him concern. Looking at the more positive areas first, the Fire Rabbit's domestic and social life will provide him with considerable pleasure and satisfaction. He can look forward to some most enjoyable occasions with those close to him and throughout the year would do well to involve them in his interests and activities. He will not only be grateful for the encouragement and input others are able to give but also, by encouraging joint, rather than solitary pursuits, he will help maintain a good rapport with those around him. Also, if he intends to carry out projects to his home or garden, he should encourage others to join in rather than undertake the activity on his own. It will not only make the project more satisfying for all involved but will also make it quicker and easier to complete! The Fire Rabbit will obtain much pleasure from outdoor activities over the year and for those who enjoy gardening, exploring the countryside, travel or just visiting places of local interest, there will be many pleasurable moments. Any Fire Rabbit who may have had some recent adversity, is feeling lonely or hoping to make additional friends really should make the effort to go out more and perhaps consider joining a local club or society. As all Rabbits will find in the Tiger year, positive action will lead to constructive results. As far as financial matters are concerned, the Fire Rabbit will need to be vigilant. He should be wary of risky undertakings and any 'get rich schemes' he may hear about and if entering into any large transaction, should check the details carefully. Similarly, if he has any important forms or documents to complete, he needs to deal with these with care. If he has any doubts, he should check rather than jump to conclusions. Important forms and items of a bureaucratic nature could, if not dealt with properly, cause problems and waste valuable time over the year. Those Fire Rabbits in education will, however, make good progress and accomplish much. If, though, there is any aspect of their studies or schooling which is concerning them or which they do not quite understand, they should ask rather than struggle on single-handed. As they will find, those around them are keen to assist and will do much to help. Overall, the Fire Rabbit will be content with how much of the year works out for him and by using his time wisely, he will be well satisfied with his accomplishments.

The Tiger year will mark the emergence of a new and positive phase in the *Earth Rabbit*'s life. Accordingly, the actions that he takes in 1998, together with the events that occur, will have a significant bearing over the next few years. In the Tiger year the Earth Rabbit should give thought to his current position, to any changes and improvements he would like to take place and to what he would like to undertake over the next few years. The plans and ideas he formulates will prove of considerable value to him and will help him to direct his energies in a purposeful way. He would also find it helpful to talk over his ideas with others, but at no time should he feel pressurized into taking immediate decisions or irrevocable action. Time is on his side and he should only take action when he feels comfortable with the plans he proposes to carry out. As far as his work is concerned, some Earth Rabbits will consider retiring while others may feel they will benefit from a change and will transfer to other duties or channel their energies towards something new. Alternatively, there will be some Earth Rabbits who decide to move and during the Tiger year they could look more closely at the areas they might like to move to and take the initial steps in the process. In the Tiger year there are indeed many options for the Earth Rabbit to consider and by making plans he will be sowing the seeds for the better times to come. More immediately, most of the activities that the Earth Rabbit engages in over the year will go well, although they may sometimes take him longer to complete than he originally envisaged. This particularly applies to any jobs around the home or garden. The Earth Rabbit will also need to deal with important paperwork he receives with care. Similarly, with financial matters, he should check any agreement he enters into. Any problems that do arise in the Tiger year are more likely to be of a niggling than serious nature, but bureaucratic matters could, without this extra vigilance, prove troublesome. The Earth Rabbit will, however, derive much pleasure from his domestic and social life and there will be many occasions he will greatly enjoy. However, during the year someone close to him may have an awkward problem to deal with and, while he may not like to appear too interfering, the Earth Rabbit should not hold back from offering any advice or assistance he feels appropriate. As always, his judgement and sound reasoning will be much valued and appreciated. The Earth Rabbit should also take advantage of any opportunity that he gets to travel over the year and a holiday he takes in the second half of 1998 is likely to go especially well, particularly if it is to a destination new to him. Also, should he find himself with some spare time at his disposal, it would be beneficial for him to consider taking up a new interest, perhaps one he has been meaning to look into for some time. He could find it will lead to many absorbing and fulfilling hours as well as revealing talents he did not realize he possessed! Generally, 1998 will prove a satisfying year for the Earth Rabbit, with the period from August onwards becoming more positive. This upturn will gather pace as the Year of the Rabbit, 1999, approaches. In the meantime, what the Earth Rabbit undertakes in the Tiger year will, in time, prove of considerable significance.

FAMOUS RABBITS

Paula Abdul, Rob Andrew, Drew Barrymore, Cecil Beaton, Harry Belafonte, Ingrid Bergman, Melvyn Bragg, Gordon Brown, James Caan, Nicolas Cage, Lewis Carroll, Fidel Castro, John Cleese, Confucius, Christopher Cross, Dr Jack Cunningham, Marie Curie, Kenny Dalglish, Peter Davison, Johnny Depp, Albert Einstein, George Eliot, Peter Falk, W. C. Fields, Bridget Fonda, Peter Fonda, James Fox, Sir David Frost, James Galway, Cary Grant, Edvard Grieg, John Gummer, Oliver Hardy, Seamus Heaney, Paul Hogan, Bob Hope, Whitney Houston, John Howard, John Hurt, Chrissie Hynde, Clive James, Henry James, David Jason, Gary Kasparov, John Keats, Danny La Rue, Cheryl Ladd, Julian Lennon, Patrick Lichfield, Gina Lollobrigida, Robert Ludlum, Ali MacGraw, Trevor McDonald, George Michael, Arthur Miller, Colin Montgomerie, Roger Moore, James Naughtie, Nanette Newman, Brigitte Nielsen, Tatum O'Neal, Christina Onassis, George Orwell, John Peel, Eva Peron, William Perry, Edith Piaf, Chris Rea, John Redwood, Ken Russell, Mort Sahl, Elisabeth Schwarzkopf, Selina Scott, Neil Sedaka, Jane Seymour, Gillian Shephard, Neil Simon, Frank Sinatra, Dusty Springfield, Sting, Jimmy Tarbuck, Sir Denis Thatcher, J. R. R. Tolkien, Arturo Toscanini, Tina Turner, Luther Vandross, Queen Victoria, Terry Waite, Andy Warhol, Orson Welles, Walt Whitman.

16 FEBRUARY 1904 ~ 3 FEBRUARY 1905	*Wood Dragon*
3 FEBRUARY 1916 ~ 22 JANUARY 1917	*Fire Dragon*
23 JANUARY 1928 ~ 9 FEBRUARY 1929	*Earth Dragon*
8 FEBRUARY 1940 ~ 26 JANUARY 1941	*Metal Dragon*
27 JANUARY 1952 ~ 13 FEBRUARY 1953	*Water Dragon*
13 FEBRUARY 1964 ~ 1 FEBRUARY 1965	*Wood Dragon*
31 JANUARY 1976 ~ 17 FEBRUARY 1977	*Fire Dragon*
17 FEBRUARY 1988 ~ 5 FEBRUARY 1989	*Earth Dragon*

THE
DRAGON

THE PERSONALITY OF THE DRAGON

I will prepare and some day my chance will come.
> *— Abraham Lincoln: a Dragon*

The Dragon is born under the sign of luck. He is a proud and lively character and has a tremendous amount of self-confidence. He is also highly intelligent and very quick to take advantage of any opportunities that occur. He is ambitious and determined and will do well in practically anything he attempts. He is also something of a perfectionist and will always try and maintain the high standards he sets himself.

The Dragon does not suffer fools gladly and will be quick to criticize anyone or anything that displeases him. He can be blunt and forthright in his views and is certainly not renowned for being either tactful or diplomatic. He does, however, often take people at their word and can occasionally be rather gullible. If he ever feels that his trust has been abused or his dignity wounded he can sometimes become very bitter and it will take him a long time to forgive and forget.

The Dragon is usually very outgoing and is particularly adept at attracting attention and publicity. He enjoys being in the limelight and is often at his best when he is confronted by a difficult problem or tense situation. In some respects he is a showman and he rarely lacks an audience. His views and opinions are very highly valued and he invariably has something interesting – and sometimes controversial – to say.

He has considerable energy and is often prepared to work long and unsocial hours in order to achieve what he wants. He can, however, be rather impulsive and does not always consider the consequences of his actions. He also has a tendency to live for the moment and there is nothing that riles him more than to be kept waiting. The Dragon hates delay and can get extremely impatient and irritable over even the smallest of hold-ups.

The Dragon has an enormous faith in his abilities, but he does run the risk of becoming over-confident and unless he is careful he can sometimes make grave errors of judgement. While this may prove disastrous at the time, he does have the tenacity and ability to bounce back and pick up the pieces again.

The Dragon has such an assertive personality, so much will-power and such a desire to succeed that he will often reach the top of his chosen profession. He has considerable leadership qualities and will do well in positions where he can put his own ideas and policies into practice. He is usually successful in politics, show business, as the manager of his own department or business, and in any job which brings him into contact with the media.

The Dragon relies a tremendous amount on his own judgement and can be scornful of other people's advice. He likes to feel self-sufficient and there are many Dragons who cherish their independence to such a degree that they prefer to remain single throughout their lives. However, the Dragon will often have numerous admirers and there are many who are attracted by his flamboyant personality and striking looks. If he does marry, he will usually marry young and will find himself particularly well suited to those born under the signs of the Snake, Rat, Monkey and Rooster. He will also find that the Rabbit, Pig, Horse and Goat make ideal companions and will readily join in with many of his escapades. Two Dragons will also get on well together, as they understand each other, but the Dragon may not find things so easy with the Ox and Dog, as both will be critical of his impulsive and somewhat extrovert manner. He will also find it difficult to form an alliance with the Tiger, for the Tiger, like the Dragon, tends to speak his mind, is very strong-willed and likes to take the lead.

The female Dragon knows what she wants in life and sets about everything she does in a very determined and positive manner. No job is too small for her and she is often prepared to work extremely hard until she has secured her objective. She is immensely practical and some-what liberated. She hates being bound by routine and petty restrictions and likes to have sufficient freedom to be able to go off and do what she wants to do. She will keep her house tidy but is not one for spending hours on house-work – there are far too many other things that she feels are more important and that she prefers to do. Like her male counterpart, she has a tendency to speak her mind.

The Dragon usually has many interests and enjoys sport and other outdoor activities. He also likes to travel and often prefers to visit places that are off the beaten track rather than head for popular tourist attractions. He has a very adventurous streak in him and providing his financial circumstances permit – and the Dragon is usually sensible with his money – he will travel considerable distances during his lifetime.

The Dragon is a very flamboyant character and while he can be demanding of others and in his early years rather precocious, he will have many friends and will nearly always be the centre of attention. He has charisma and so much confidence in himself that he can often become a source of inspiration for others. In China he is the leader of the carnival and he is also blessed with an inordinate share of luck.

THE FIVE DIFFERENT TYPES OF DRAGON

In addition to the 12 signs of the Chinese zodiac, there are five elements and these have a strengthening or moderating influence on the sign. The effects of the five elements on the Dragon are described below, together with the years in which the elements were exercising their influence. Therefore all Dragons born in 1940 are Metal Dragons, those born in 1952 are Water Dragons, and so on.

Metal Dragon: 1940
This Dragon is very strong-willed and has a particularly forceful personality. He is energetic, ambitious and tries to be scrupulous in his dealings with others. He can also be blunt and to the point and usually has no hesitation in speaking his mind. If people disagree with him, or are not

prepared to co-operate, he is more than happy to go his own way. The Metal Dragon usually has very high moral values and is held in great esteem by his friends and colleagues.

Water Dragon: 1952

This Dragon is friendly, easy-going and intelligent. He is quick-witted and rarely lets an opportunity slip by. However, he is not as impatient as some of the other types of Dragon and is more prepared to wait for results rather than expect everything to happen that moment. He has an understanding nature and is prepared to share his ideas and co-operate with others. His main failing, though, is a tendency to jump from one thing to another rather than concentrate on the job in hand. He has a good sense of humour and is an effective speaker.

Wood Dragon: 1904, 1964

The Wood Dragon is practical, imaginative and inquisitive. He loves delving into all manner of subjects and can quite often come up with some highly original ideas. He is a thinker and a doer and has sufficient drive and commitment to put many of his ideas into practice. He is more diplomatic than some of the other types of Dragon and has a good sense of humour. He is very astute in business matters and can also be most generous.

Fire Dragon: 1916, 1976

This Dragon is ambitious, articulate and has a tremendous desire to succeed. He is a hard and conscientious worker and is often admired for his integrity and forthright nature. He is very strong-willed and has considerable leadership qualities. He can, however, rely a bit too much on his own judgement and fail to take into account the views and feelings of others. He can also be rather aloof and it would certainly be in his own interests to let others join in more with his various activities. The Fire Dragon usually gets much enjoyment from music, literature and the arts.

Earth Dragon: 1928, 1988

The Earth Dragon tends to be quieter and more reflective than some of the other types of Dragon. He has a wide variety of interests and is keenly aware of what is going on around him. He also has clear objectives and usually has no problems in obtaining support and backing for any of his ventures. He is very astute in financial matters and is often able to accumulate considerable wealth. He is a good organizer, although he can at times be rather bureaucratic and fussy. He mixes well with others and has a large circle of friends.

PROSPECTS FOR THE DRAGON
IN 1998

The Chinese New Year starts on 28 January 1998. Until then, the old year, the Year of the Ox, is still making its presence felt.

The Year of the Ox (7 February 1997 to 27 January 1998) will have been a variable year for the Dragon and, for one so active, will also have held its frustrations. His progress will not have been as swift or as easy as he would have liked and some Dragons could have experienced strains in their relations with others. In what remains of the Ox year, the Dragon will need to exercise care, restraint and also a certain amount of tact.

However, despite the inhibiting nature of the Ox year, the Dragon can do much to negate the more difficult aspects that prevail. In all his activities, he needs to remain alert to everything that is going on around him and particularly take into account the views and feelings of others. Although he might hold very definite views himself and likes to retain a certain independence in his actions, this is not a time when the Dragon can be too single-minded. To do so could undermine his position and it is something he should strive to avoid.

In his work the Dragon should continue to set about his activities in his usual enterprising way but avoid committing himself to risky or ill-prepared ventures. However, if he is seeking work or looking for a change of duties, he should remain alert for opportunities, with September and October 1997 being two key months for employment matters. The Dragon would also do well to give some thought to his future aspirations, particularly to what he would like to accomplish over the next 12 months. This will help to give him a better idea of where he should now concentrate his energies.

The Dragon will, however, need to be careful when dealing with financial matters and should keep a close watch on his level of spending. Savings that he has to dip into may not always be so easy to replenish as he first thought.

Domestically and socially, the closing months of the Ox year will generally go well and the Dragon can look forward to some happy and interesting occasions with those around him. The Christmas and New Year holidays will, on a personal level, be a particularly special and gratifying time. Also, if any strains have occurred in his relations with others over the year, the Dragon should make every effort to resolve any differences that might still remain. With a conciliatory and understanding manner, he can do much to rectify the situation.

Generally, through care and good sense, the Dragon can overcome many of the difficulties that the Ox year sometimes presents and with the approach of the Tiger year, he can look forward to a noticeable upturn in his fortunes.

The Year of the Tiger begins on 28 January 1998 and will be a considerably improved year for the Dragon. Tiger years are often times of change, when determination and enterprise are encouraged and rewarded, so the Dragon is well suited to the conditions that prevail.

In 1998 the Dragon will find progress much easier and most aspects of his life will go well. This is a year when he should aim to put past setbacks and misfortunes behind him and concentrate on the present and the future. For the active and enterprising Dragon – of which there are so many – this will be a good year indeed.

Particularly well aspected is the Dragon's work and over the year he will see several significant changes. These could concern the initiation of new projects, being given different responsibilities or a change in personnel. Out of these changes, there will be opportunities for the Dragon to pursue and throughout the year he should look at ways in which he can most effectively use his talents as well as promote his ideas. While some signs may feel unnerved by some of what will happen over the year, the Dragon is generally strong-willed and resourceful enough to tackle any challenges given him and demonstrate his true worth. Indeed, it is often at these times that he truly shines, and by being his bold and enterprising self he can make significant headway. The aspects are also most encouraging for those Dragons seeking work or wanting to change their present duties. They should follow up any opportunities they see and will find the months of February and March and from September to November significant times for work opportunities.

However, while considerable progress is indicated, there are still certain points the Dragon would do well to bear in mind. Although he is indeed capable and self-reliant, he would find progress easier if he were to join forces with others rather than retain too independent an attitude. Also, he should discuss his ideas and plans with others rather than keep them to himself. This way he will find support more forthcoming and will benefit from some of the advice and suggestions he is given. In particular, the Dragon should seek out the views of those who are experienced and have already achieved what he himself is aiming for. By doing so, he could learn much of value as well as be given some useful and pertinent advice.

The Dragon will also enjoy some financial success over the year and this could include receiving an additional and, in many cases, unexpected sum. However, despite this upturn in his financial situation, the Dragon still needs to exercise care with his financial undertakings. He should be wary of risky ventures – not pushing his Dragon luck too far! – and should check the terms and obligations of any large agreement he enters into. Without such vigilance, he could find he is spending more than is necessary. Also, if the Dragon has funds that he does not immediately need, he would do well to consider setting these aside for some future purpose or investing them in a savings scheme. Without financial planning and control over the year, he could find he is spending a lot on non-essential items or being just a little too extravagant. It is something all Dragons would do well to watch.

As far as the Dragon's relations with others are concerned, he will be on top form. Both his domestic and social life will be a source of much pleasure and he will delight in following the activities of those around him. His family, in particular, will be most encouraging and several times during the year he will have reason to be grateful for their support. However, in return, he does need to take their views into account and carefully bear in mind any advice they give. Those close to him do speak with his best interests at heart and sometimes think of aspects, ideas or potential problems that he might have overlooked. Similarly, the Dragon himself will do much to assist others over the year and his reassuring and supportive manner, together with his sound judgement, will be appreciated by both young and old alike.

The Dragon will particularly enjoy any joint family activities he arranges, and any holidays or outings he is able to take will go well and be enjoyed by all. Also, with travel favourably aspected, the Dragon would do well to consider visiting an area he may have wanted to see for some time and, if he is interested in extending his language skills or work experience, consider the possibility of working in another country.

The Dragon's social life will also go well and he can look forward to some pleasing times with his friends. For those Dragons seeking romance or hoping to extend their circle of friends, the year will hold many excellent opportunities. Indeed, over the year the Dragon should aim to go out more and, for the unattached, a chance meeting in the first few months of the year could develop in a meaningful way. Any Dragon whose personal or social life may not have gone as well as he would have liked in recent times should also look on the year as the start of a brighter and happier time. Rather than dwell too much on what has gone before, these Dragons should concentrate their energies on the present and take positive steps to improve their social life. Anything they can do, such as joining a local group or society, would be well worth their while.

Overall, the Tiger year will be a constructive one for the Dragon and he can achieve much in most aspects of his life. However, to take advantage of the beneficial trends, the

Dragon should promote himself and his ideas and go after the opportunities that the year will bring. This is a positive and progressive time for him and he can achieve much. Just how much rests with him.

As far as the different types of Dragon are concerned, this will be an important and satisfying year for the *Metal Dragon*. Although he will have achieved much in recent years, there will be many Metal Dragons who will feel they are not making the most of their potential and will have ideas they want to try out and objectives still to achieve. In 1998 they will have the chance. The Metal Dragon will find this a favourable time to commence projects, go after a new position in his work or proceed with some of his plans and ideas. He will find that positive and constructive action on his part will be rewarded and that he will be able to achieve results that have been eluding him in the past. In setting about his activities he will also find it helpful to seek out those who have relevant experience or are in a position offer practical assistance. By doing so, he will receive much useful guidance as well as be warned of possible pitfalls to avoid. Throughout the year the Metal Dragon will gain much from the input of others and will be heartened by the level of support he receives. In 1998 he can achieve much and realize some of his aspirations, but to make the most of the favourable aspects that prevail, he should set about his activities with commitment and resolve. He can also look forward to an improvement in his financial situation and, while he will enjoy this upturn, it would still be worth him setting a certain amount aside for his future. If he succumbs to too many extravagances, he could later regret his spending. Domestically, this will be an active and pleasing year. Many Metal Dragons will spend time on home and garden projects, while some will decide to move. Either way they will be satisfied with what they achieve, but the Metal Dragon does need to remember to allow himself time – and patience – to complete his tasks. He can also look forward to some enjoyable occasions with his family and will have every reason to feel proud of the achievements of someone very dear to him. Any further encouragement he feels able to give will be warmly appreciated. The Metal Dragon's social life is also well aspected and during the year he will be invited to several pleasurable and, in some cases, memorable events. For any Metal Dragon who may be feeling lonely or hoping to make additional friends, the early months of the year are an especially favourable time and a chance meeting in the spring could later develop into a meaningful friendship. With so much happening over the year, the Metal Dragon may sometimes feel he is not able to devote too much time to his hobbies and interests. However, it is important he does not neglect these. They do provide him with an important source of relaxation and he could even find it beneficial to extend his interests in some way, thereby giving himself new and fresh challenges. The Metal Dragon has a wealth of experience and many fine talents and in 1998 he really should aim to put these to good use. Overall, this will be a pleasing and constructive year for him.

This will be a year of progress for the *Water Dragon* and by using his talents wisely and drawing on past experience he can make substantial gains. Particularly favoured are work matters. Throughout the Tiger year the Water Dragon should consider ways in which he can make more effective use of his wide-ranging skills. In this he should reflect on what he has already accomplished, what he would like to achieve in the future and how he himself feels he would like to develop. He would also do well to discuss his thoughts with those around him and particularly seek out those with relevant experience. Then, as a result of his deliberations, he should actively follow up any openings he sees and, in some cases, try to create them. Positive and enterprising action on his part will certainly be rewarded. Also, if there are any plans he has been nurturing, this would be a good year to set them in motion. Those Water Dragons seeking work should continue to pursue any openings they see; many will find their efforts rewarded and a position they attain could lead to improved ones in the future. The Water Dragon will also enjoy good fortune in financial matters, although he still needs to be careful with his spending. Money spent on too many extravagances may not be as easy to replace as he might imagine. Where possible, the Water Dragon would do well to consider setting something aside for his longer-term future and an investment made during the year could, in time, build into a useful asset. His personal life will, however, go well and for any Water Dragon who may have had to bear some recent sadness or misfortune, the Tiger year is very much a time to put the past behind him and concentrate on the present and the future. Those around him will, in any case, prove most supportive and at all times the Water Dragon should be open in discussing his feelings and any problems he might have as well as be forthcoming with his ideas. As he will find throughout the year, the advice and assistance he is given will prove both constructive and helpful. The Water Dragon will also take much pride in the progress of those close to him and there could be cause for at least one family celebration over the year. Socially, too, the Water Dragon will be on good form and can look forward to some truly pleasurable occasions, with the summer months being well aspected. It is also a good year for him to get in contact with people he has not seen for some time and, if he has been meaning to visit a relation or friend living some distance away, this would be a good year to do so. Generally, 1998 will be a satisfying year for the Water Dragon. By giving of his best and promoting his talents he will make good progress. Added to which, both his domestic and social life will bring him a considerable amount of pleasure.

With his determined and enterprising nature the *Wood Dragon* is set to do well in the Tiger year. In his work he will be able to put his experience and ideas to good use and those around him, including some who hold much influence, will be appreciative of his undertakings. As a result, many Wood Dragons will be given additional duties, be promoted or be successful in obtaining a new and more challenging position. Also, the Wood Dragon will see several significant changes taking place around him and despite any initial misgivings he might have, he will find that fresh opportunities will occur. Throughout the year it would be very much in his interests to keep alert to all that is happening. Also, if he has any ideas he has been wanting to put into practice, this would be a good year to take those all-important initial steps. The Tiger year is one for positive action and with such favourable aspects, the Wood Dragon can achieve much. In addition to the advances he will make in his work, he will also enjoy an improvement in his financial situation. However, despite this upturn, it would still be in his interests to keep a watchful eye over his level of spending and put any spare money he might have towards a specific purpose rather than spend it too readily. Personally, the Tiger year is well aspected and the Wood Dragon will take much pleasure in following and encouraging the activities of those around him. He will also assist someone much older than himself over the year and while he may not wish to appear too interfering, any advice and practical support he is able to give will be much appreciated. Overall, his relations with others will go well and those around him will, as always, value his considerate nature, enterprising ways and incisive judgement. The Wood Dragon can also look forward to attending several interesting social occasions during the year and these will help him to extend his circle of friends and acquaintances. For those Wood Dragons who are unattached and are seeking additional friends or romance, the aspects are encouraging, with the spring being a most favourable time. In view of the generally active nature of the year, it is important that the Wood Dragon does not neglect his hobbies or interests; these do provide him with a valuable source of relaxation and help him unwind from his usual daytime activities. He will also very much enjoy the travelling that he undertakes over the year and any breaks or holidays will be most beneficial for him. In almost all respects this will be a satisfying year for the Wood Dragon and good fortune will accompany him.

However, to make the most of the aspects that prevail, he does need to set about his activities in a determined way and resolve to make the most of his considerable talents and abilities.

This will be both a pleasing and productive year for the *Fire Dragon*. Over the year there will be some excellent opportunities for him to advance his position and personally the year will hold some happy and memorable times. However, to maximize the favourable aspects that prevail, the Fire Dragon needs to have some idea of what he wants to achieve over the year and to set himself some priorities. With his ambitious nature and broad interests there could be the temptation for him to spread his energies too widely or attempt too many things all at the same time. In 1998 he will find the best results will come from concentrating his efforts on specific objectives. These can concern almost any area of his life, from his work or his accommodation to some personal aspiration, but to make the most of the year, he does need to plan and prioritize. In his work, the Fire Dragon can make considerable headway. Others will admire his determined and enthusiastic manner and many Fire Dragons will be given additional duties, be promoted or be transferred to another position. The Fire Dragon should also pursue any opportunities he sees, remembering that the Tiger year is one which favours enterprise. Similarly, those Fire Dragons seeking work should actively follow up any openings that they see and by considering different ways in which they can use their skills they could widen the range of openings available to them. Again, some enterprising thinking could bring pleasing results. As far as financial matters are concerned, this could prove an expensive year for the Fire Dragon and it would be in his interests to keep a close watch over his outgoings. Expenses connected with his accommodation could figure prominently over the year and he does need to make sure he is conversant with any obligations he might be placed under and that he makes adequate allowance for this in his budget. With care, he should avoid problems, but this is not a year in which he can be too extravagant or careless with his money. Personally, however, the year will go splendidly, with romance, new friendships and a pleasing social life all favourably aspected. The Fire Dragon will also have good reason for a personal celebration over the year, with the summer months being an active time. There will also be several opportunities for him to travel over the year and the journeys he goes on will prove both interesting and enjoyable, especially if they are to destinations he has not visited before. In 1998 the Fire Dragon can achieve much. With his determined and agreeable manner he has a lot in his favour and by channelling his energies wisely and going after specific objectives, he can turn this into a successful and personally fulfilling year.

Over the last few years the *Earth Dragon* will have thought of some ideas or plans that he would like to carry out but will not have been able to put them into practice. In the Tiger year, though, it would be worth him looking more closely at his ideas and talking them over in detail with others. Then, after considering their views and making sure he has sufficient support, he should start to set some of his plans in motion. These could concern moving, carrying out alterations to his home, travelling to a particular destination, taking up a new interest or pursuing a personal ambition, but whatever they are, this is a year for action. It is very much a positive and progressive time for the Earth Dragon. However, while so much will go well for him, he should not rush things unnecessarily or take undue risks. In 1998 he can and will accomplish much, but should let it be at a sensible pace. Also, if during the year he becomes involved in any particularly complicated matter, has important documents to complete or is worried about something, he should seek the advice and guidance of others rather than keep his concerns to himself. In many cases he could find his worries are unfounded or can be simply and effectively dealt with. The Earth Dragon will also obtain considerable satisfaction from his hobbies and interests over the year and he would do well to get in contact with fellow enthusiasts. This will not only enable him to further his interest but will also lead to some pleasurable social occasions. Any Earth Dragon who may be feeling lonely or would like to make some new and additional friends would find it really worth his while to go out more and maybe consider joining a local society or club. As with most things in 1998, positive action on his part will be rewarded and most Earth Dragons will make new and important friendships as the year progresses. For those Earth Dragons in education, this will prove an important year and while they may sometimes feel daunted by what is being asked of them, they will nevertheless accomplish a great deal. In many cases the young Earth Dragon will enjoy rising up to the challenges given him and will impress others with his diligence and alert mind. However, if he does have any problems with his schoolwork, he should tell others rather than keep his worries to himself. He should remember that those around him are prepared to help and support him and he should ask if he feels he needs further guidance. Generally, this will be a favourable year for the Earth Dragon. Both his domestic and social life will bring him much pleasure and he will also take satisfaction in putting into practice some of the ideas he has long been nurturing. The aspects will support him well in much of what he does.

FAMOUS DRAGONS

Clive Anderson, Moira Anderson, Maya Angelou, Jeffrey Archer, Roseanne Arnold, Joan Baez, Michael Barrymore, Count Basie, Bill Beaumont, Pat Benatar, St Bernadette, James Brown, Neneh Cherry, Kenneth Clarke, James Coburn, William Cohen, Bing Crosby, Roald Dahl, Salvador Dali, Charles Darwin, Neil Diamond, Bo Diddley, Matt Dillon, Christian Dior, Frank Dobson, Placido Domingo, Fats Domino, Stephen Dorrell, Faye Dunaway, Prince Edward, Adam Faith, Bruce Forsyth, Sigmund Freud, Michael Gambon, James Garner, Sir John Gielgud, Graham Greene, Che Guevara, Herbie Hancock, David Hasselhoff, Sir Edward Heath, Joan of Arc, Tom Jones, Imran Khan, Martin Luther King, Ian Lang, John Lennon, Abraham Lincoln, Queen Margrethe II of Denmark, Brian Mawhinny, Yehudi Menuhin, François Mitterrand, Bob Monkhouse, Hosni Mubarak, Florence Nightingale, Nick Nolte, Al Pacino, Elaine Paige, Gregory Peck, Pele, Esther

Rantzen, Sir Cliff Richard, Smokey Robinson, George Bernard Shaw, Martin Sheen, Mel Smith, Ringo Starr, Princess Stephanie of Monaco, Dave Stewart, Karlheinz Stockhausen, Shirley Temple, Raquel Welch, Mae West, Robin Williams, Frank Zappa.

4 FEBRUARY 1905 ∼ 24 JANUARY 1906	*Wood Snake*
23 JANUARY 1917 ∼ 10 FEBRUARY 1918	*Fire Snake*
10 FEBRUARY 1929 ∼ 29 JANUARY 1930	*Earth Snake*
27 JANUARY 1941 ∼ 14 FEBRUARY 1942	*Metal Snake*
14 FEBRUARY 1953 ∼ 2 FEBRUARY 1954	*Water Snake*
2 FEBRUARY 1965 ∼ 20 JANUARY 1966	*Wood Snake*
18 FEBRUARY 1977 ∼ 6 FEBRUARY 1978	*Fire Snake*
6 FEBRUARY 1989 ∼ 26 JANUARY 1990	*Earth Snake*

THE
SNAKE

THE PERSONALITY OF THE SNAKE

We always have time enough, if we will but use it aright.
                    – *Johann Wolfgang von Goethe: a Snake*

The Snake is born under the sign of wisdom. He is highly intelligent and his mind is forever active. He is always planning and always looking for ways in which he can use his considerable skills. He is a deep thinker and likes to meditate and reflect.

Many times during his life he will shed one of his famous Snake skins and take up new interests or start a completely different job. The Snake enjoys a challenge and he rarely makes mistakes. He is a skilful organizer, has considerable business acumen and is usually lucky in money matters. Most Snakes are financially secure in their later years provided they do not gamble – the Snake has the distinction of being the worst gambler in the whole of the Chinese zodiac!

The Snake generally has a calm and placid nature and prefers the quieter things in life. He does not like to be in a frenzied atmosphere and hates being hurried into making a quick decision. He also does not like interference in his affairs and tends to rely on his own judgement rather than listen to advice.

The Snake can at times appear solitary. He is quiet, reserved and sometimes has difficulty in communicating with others. He has little time for idle gossip and will certainly not suffer fools gladly. He does, however, have a good sense of humour and this is particularly appreciated in times of crisis.

The Snake is certainly not afraid of hard work and is thorough in all that he does. He is very determined and can occasionally be ruthless in order to achieve his aims. His confidence, will-power and quick thinking usually ensure his success, but should he fail it will often take a long time for him to recover. He cannot bear failure and is a very bad loser.

The Snake can also be evasive and does not willingly let people into his confidence. This secrecy and distrust can sometimes work against him and it is a trait which all Snakes should try to overcome.

Another characteristic of the Snake is his tendency to rest after any sudden or prolonged bout of activity. He burns up so much nervous energy that without proper care he can – if he is not careful – be susceptible to high blood pressure and nervous disorders.

It has sometimes been said that the Snake is a late starter in life and this is mainly because it often takes him a while to find a job with which he is genuinely happy. However, the Snake will usually do well in any position which involves research and writing and where he is given sufficient freedom to develop his own ideas and plans. He makes a good teacher, politician, personnel manager and social adviser.

The Snake chooses his friends carefully and, while he keeps a tight control over his finances, he can be particularly generous to those he likes. He will think nothing of buying expensive gifts or treating his friends or loved ones to the best theatre seats in town. In return he demands loyalty. The Snake is very possessive and he can become extremely jealous and hurt if he finds his trust has been abused.

The Snake is also renowned for his good looks and is never short of admirers. The female Snake in particular is most alluring. She has style, grace and excellent (and usually expensive) taste in clothes. A keen socializer, she is likely to have a wide range of friends and has a happy knack of impressing those who matter. She has numerous interests and her advice and opinions are often highly valued. She is generally a calm-natured person and while she involves herself in many activities, she likes to retain a certain amount of privacy in her undertakings.

The affairs of the heart are very important to the Snake and he will often have many romances before he finally settles down. He will find that he is particularly well suited to those born under the signs of the Ox, Dragon, Rabbit and Rooster. Provided he is allowed sufficient freedom to pursue his own interests, he can also build up a very satisfactory relationship with the Rat, Horse, Goat, Monkey and Dog, but he should try to steer clear of another Snake as they could very easily become jealous of each other. The Snake will also have difficulty in getting on with the honest and down-to-earth Pig, and will find the Tiger far too much of a disruptive influence on his quiet and peace-loving ways.

The Snake certainly appreciates the finer things in life. He enjoys good food and often takes a keen interest in the arts. He also enjoys reading and is invariably drawn to subjects such as philosophy, political thought, religion or the occult. He is fascinated by the unknown and his enquiring mind is always looking for answers. Some of the world's most original thinkers have been Snakes, and – although he may not readily admit it – the Snake is often psychic and relies a lot on intuition.

The Snake is certainly not the most energetic member of the Chinese zodiac. He prefers to proceed at his own pace and to do what he wants. He is very much his own master and throughout his life he will try his hand at many things. He is something of a dabbler, but at some time – usually when he least expects it – his hard work and efforts will be recognized and he will invariably meet with the success and the financial security which he so much desires.

THE FIVE DIFFERENT TYPES OF SNAKE

In addition to the 12 signs of the Chinese zodiac, there are five elements and these have a strengthening or moderating influence on the sign. The effects of the five elements on the Snake are described below, together with the years in which the elements were exercising their influence. Therefore all Snakes born in 1941 are Metal Snakes, those born in 1953 are Water Snakes, and so on.

Metal Snake: 1941

This Snake is quiet, confident and fiercely independent. He often prefers to work on his own and will only let a privileged few into his confidence. He is quick to spot opportunities and will set about achieving his objectives with an awesome determination. He is astute in financial matters and will often invest his money well. He also has a liking for the finer things in life and has a good appreciation of the arts, literature, music and good food. He usually has a small group of extremely good friends and can be generous to his loved ones.

Water Snake: 1953

This Snake has a wide variety of interests. He enjoys studying all manner of subjects and is capable of undertaking quite detailed research and becoming a specialist in his chosen area. He is highly intelligent, has a good memory, and is particularly astute when dealing with business and financial matters. He tends to be quietly spoken and a little reserved, but he does have sufficient strength of character to make his views known and attain his ambitions. He is very loyal to his family and friends.

Wood Snake: 1905, 1965

The Wood Snake has a friendly temperament and a good understanding of human nature. He is able to communicate well with others and often has many friends and admirers. He is witty, intelligent and ambitious. He has numerous interests and prefers to live in a quiet, stable environment where he can work without too much interference. He enjoys the arts and usually derives much pleasure from collecting paintings and antiques. His advice is often very highly valued, particularly on social and domestic matters.

Fire Snake: 1917, 1977

The Fire Snake tends to be more forceful, outgoing and energetic than some of the other types of Snake. He is ambitious, confident and never slow in voicing his opinions – and he can be very abrasive to those he does not like. He does, however, have many leadership qualities and can win the respect and support of many with his firm and resolute manner. He usually has a good sense of humour, a wide circle of friends and a very active social life. The Fire Snake is also a keen traveller.

Earth Snake: 1929, 1989

The Earth Snake is charming, amusing and has a very amiable manner. He is conscientious and reliable in his work and approaches everything he does in a level-headed and sensible way. He can, however, tend to err on the cautious side and never likes to be hassled into making a decision. He is extremely adept at dealing with financial matters and is a shrewd investor. He has many friends and is very supportive towards the members of his family.

PROSPECTS FOR THE SNAKE IN 1998

The Chinese New Year starts on 28 January 1998. Until then, the old year, the Year of the Ox, is still making its presence felt.

The Year of the Ox (7 February 1997 to 27 January 1998) will have been a reasonable one for the Snake and while not all his activities will have gone as well as he would have liked, he can still make modest progress in what remains of the year. During the Ox year he will have found that dedicated and determined effort on his part will have brought results and this will particularly apply to the last few months of the year. The Ox favours the worker and if the Snake is prepared to make the effort then he will be rewarded accordingly.

In his work the Snake can make some gains and in the closing months of the year he should remain alert to all that is going on around him. This way he could learn of some information that will be to his advantage or of some openings that might soon become available. Also, if he has the opportunity to take on additional duties which would help widen his experience, he should do so. Anything he can do to enhance his prospects at this time would be to his advantage.

In his relationships, whether with family, friends or colleagues, the Snake should aim to involve others more readily in his activities and be prepared to discuss his views and plans. While he might like to retain an independent stance, such an attitude could undermine his position and cause resentment. The Snake may be one of the more independent and self-reliant of the Chinese signs, but in the latter part of the Ox year it really would be in his interests to open up more. This warning apart, the Snake's relations with others will generally go well and he can look forward to some personally pleasing and gratifying times. November and December are two particularly favoured months, with some highly enjoyable social occasions indicated.

Generally, the Ox year is one that calls for care and commitment, and provided the Snake remains mindful of others and the conditions that prevail, he will not fare too badly. As he will find, the more effort that he puts into his activities – no matter what area of his life this might concern – the more he will achieve and the better the progress he will make.

The Year of the Tiger begins on 28 January 1998 and will be a variable one for the Snake. The Snake likes to conduct his activities at a measured pace and prefers to plan what he does rather than take immediate action. By nature he is cautious and careful. He will feel ill at ease with the bustle and changes that the Tiger year will bring and could find progress limited. So it will not be the easiest of years for him, but despite this, he can still get much of value from it and there will also be some aspects he will greatly enjoy.

As far as his work is concerned, the Snake should consolidate any recent gains he has made and concentrate on areas in which he has most experience. By doing so he will be able to make more effective use of his skills and his judgement will be better informed. At all times, though, the Snake should remain alert to all that is going on around him and be prepared to adapt to any new situations that arise. Admittedly, he may feel uneasy about some of what happens over the year, but new and interesting opportunities will emerge. In addition, some of what happens will enable the Snake to reassess his current position and will give him a clearer idea of his future aims and where he should be concentrating his efforts. The Snake may not always like change, but some of the consequences of the Tiger year will have a positive outcome and will help prepare him for the more successful times he is soon to enjoy.

In the Tiger year, though, the Snake should continue to set about his duties in his usual thorough manner and if required to adjust to new procedures or systems he should show himself adaptable rather than appear too resistant. This is not a year in which he can risk stepping out of line! The Snake also needs to exercise care in his relations with his colleagues and if he finds himself in any tense or fraught situation he should remain his usual tactful self. Again, with the variable trends that exist, this is not a year in which he can afford to impair his relations with those around him.

More positively, however, if the Snake considers that he needs additional training or new skills in order to progress, this would be an excellent year to obtain them. The Snake might enrol on an appropriate course or study privately, but either way he will find the acquisition of a further skill an absorbing and fulfilling use of his time. Similarly, those Snakes seeking work should also take advantage of any training courses they may be eligible for. What they learn and accomplish in the Tiger year will have a positive bearing on their future.

Those Snakes seeking work should also remain determined in their quest and actively follow up any openings they see. Many will find their efforts rewarded in a surprising and rather fortuitous manner, but it will take some persistence on their part.

The Snake's cautious nature will also be of help to him in his financial dealings. In 1998 he could face several large expenses, particularly involving his accommodation and transport, but with careful budgeting he should be able to avoid problems arising. However, throughout the year, he should remain wary of any dubious or speculative schemes that he may hear about; all is not as straightforward as it might appear and he should not allow himself to be caught off guard. This is not a year for taking risks or for entering into large commitments without checking the details and implications carefully. Similarly, the Snake should be careful when completing forms or dealing with important pieces of paperwork. If not, he could find himself involved in some tiresome and protracted correspondence which he could well do without. Again, as with so many aspects of his life, care is needed.

The Snake's personal life will, however, bring him much satisfaction and he will be reassured and heartened by the support he receives from those around him. In view of the variable nature of the year, he should not hesitate to speak to others about any concerns or worries he might have. Many a time he will find truth in the saying 'a worry shared is a worry halved'. Although the Snake does have a tendency to keep things to himself and relies a lot on his own judgement, in 1998 he really will gain much from the advice and input of others.

In addition to the pleasure his family and relations will bring, the Snake's social life will go well and he can look forward to attending several enjoyable, and in some cases, memorable events. If he is seeking new friends or romance, it would be worth him going out more and getting in contact with others, perhaps by joining in more group activities. Positive action on his part will be rewarded, but he does need to take the initiative. For the unattached Snake, a friendship made in the latter part of the year could develop in a meaningful way over the next year.

The Snake will also spend some of his spare time in carrying out accommodation and garden projects. In doing this, he should try to involve others rather than do too much single-handed. This way he will not only find the project quicker and easier to complete but also more satisfying for all concerned. Similarly, the Snake would do well to encourage activities all can enjoy, such as trips out or visits to places of interest. With some of the demands and pressures of the year there is a danger that, for some Snakes, the more pleasurable activities will be lost or put to one side. For his own good, and that of others, this is something the Snake would do well to watch. At busy times it is also important that he allows himself time to relax and unwind. The Snake does tend to burn up much nervous energy and in view of the demanding nature of the year he does need to take good care of himself. If not, he could feel tired, tense and not make as much of himself as he otherwise could. He could also find that regular and suitable exercise will do much for his well-being.

Generally, much will happen in 1998 – sometimes a little too much for the Snake's liking! However, he can truly benefit from the experience he gains, from reappraising his current situation and from making the most of the changes that occur. He will then find himself in an excellent position to make the headway he so much desires. The Tiger year is very much a preparation for the better times that await him in 1999.

As far as the different types of Snake are concerned, 1998 will be a variable year for the *Metal Snake*. Sometimes things will go well for him but overall he could find his progress not as easy or as substantial as he would like. For one so determined, the year will undoubtedly, in parts, be frustrating. However, the Metal Snake is both shrewd and astute, and he picks his moments to advance with care. For much of the year, he will settle for observing what happens around him and then, when an opportunity arises, will do his best to turn it to his advantage. This will be a year for patience and vigilance, but despite the frustrations, there will still be chances for the Metal Snake to advance his position. In his work he should remain watchful and be prepared to adjust to any changes that occur. Indeed, it will be out of these changes that the Metal Snake will find the best opportunities, with the spring and closing months of the year being important periods, particularly for work matters. Throughout the year the Metal Snake also needs to remain mindful of the views and opinions of his colleagues and should he find himself in any fraught situation he should remain his diplomatic self. Words said in haste could be regretted later! The Metal Snake will also need to exercise caution when dealing with financial matters. While many Metal

Snakes can look forward to receiving a sum of money for work which they have carried out in the past or from another source, they should use this carefully, either saving it or putting it towards a specific purpose. Speculative ventures should be avoided, along with engaging in too many expensive indulgences. Money acquired and spent in the Tiger year may not always be as easy to replace as the Metal Snake may think! His domestic life will, however, bring him considerable satisfaction and he can look forward to some pleasant and rewarding times with those around him, with the summer proving especially enjoyable. Throughout the year the Metal Snake should be forthcoming about his thoughts and ideas and remain mindful of any advice he is given. His family and close friends do speak with his best interests at heart and over the year he will learn much of value from others. With the demands of the year it is also important that the Metal Snake does not neglect his hobbies or interests. These do provide him with a valuable source of relaxation and if he wishes to extend them in some way, or even take up an additional interest, he will find that this will provide him with many hours of pleasure. He should also try to ensure that he takes a holiday or allows himself a proper break over the year; again, this will prove most beneficial for him and by visiting an area new to him he could find his travels will turn out particularly well. Although the Tiger year will contain some uncertainties, particularly with changes concerning his work, there will be much for the Metal Snake to enjoy, with his family, friends and interests all bringing him much pleasure. Life will gradually improve towards the end of the year, with mid October marking the start of a new and sustained upturn in the Metal Snake's fortunes.

The main successes that the *Water Snake* has enjoyed in the past have often been the result of long and hard endeavour. In 1998 he will need to continue this endeavour, but with the knowledge that further success and the realization of some of his more cherished aims are not far off. Late 1998 and 1999 will be a truly progressive time for him, but in the meantime the Water Snake will need to be patient and persevering. At the start of the Tiger year he would do well to look closely at his current situation and consider what he is hoping to achieve. If at all possible, he should discuss his aims with others, particularly seeking out the advice of those who have already achieved what he hopes to accomplish. By doing so he will obtain much useful advice and guidance. Admittedly the Water Snake may be something of a loner, but throughout the year it really would be in his interests to be forthcoming and involve others more readily in his plans. He should also be prepared to adjust to changing situations rather than remain intransigent or too set in his ways. Indeed, some of the events of 1998 will be instrumental in propelling him to new heights and towards the goals he seeks, but to make the most of these the Water Snake will need to show some flexibility in both his attitude and planning. Similarly, those Water Snakes seeking work should continue to pursue any openings that they see; although their quest for employment may not be easy, they will ultimately find their persistence rewarded and one opening they attain could lead to better positions in the future. It is also an excellent year for the Water Snake to add to his skills, especially those related to his current aspirations. Experience obtained and new skills learned in 1998 could prove valuable to him and again do much to help with the advances he is soon to make. The Water Snake is usually most careful when dealing with financial matters and in the Tiger year he should not be tempted by any scheme or risky venture without careful investigation. This is just not a year when he can afford to take risks or become too complacent in money matters. Without care, money could all too easily be squandered or lost. The Water Snake's family and friends will, as always, prove most important to him and he will greatly value their support and encouragement. He can also look forward to some particularly pleasing family occasions, with joint family activities, holidays and outings and the successes of a younger relation all bringing him much joy. The Water Snake will also spend some of his spare time in redecorating and making alterations to his home and should allow himself plenty of time for this. These projects could take him longer to complete than he first envisaged and to set an unrealistic deadline could place him under unnecessary pressure. Also, if he has to move any heavy or cumbersome objects, he should seek assistance. Without care, a strain could result in considerable discomfort. Water Snakes, be warned! Although there will be times in 1998 when the Water Snake may feel disappointed with his progress, he should not lose heart. All the time he will be preparing for the success and advances he is about to enjoy, and will find that from late 1998 circumstances will start to swing very much in his favour.

Although the Tiger year may not be without its difficulties, it will nevertheless be an important and significant one for the *Wood Snake*. In 1998 he could find that events cause him to modify some of his existing plans and prevent him from carrying out some of his activities in the way he would have liked. However, while this may prove frustrating at the time, in some cases the problems and delays could turn out to be blessings in disguise. Some of the events of the year will help the Wood Snake to re-evaluate his plans and his current situation and will lead him to new and better ideas. The year will also enable him to gain useful experience and by facing up to any problems that emerge, he will learn much which can be put to good use later. Indeed, often before a period of growth and success, there is a time of reflection, of setbacks and re-appraisal, and the Tiger year will be such a time for the Wood Snake. For many Wood Snakes it will represent the initial stages of a new period of growth, and as the year draws to a close, significant progress is indicated. In his work, however, it is important that the Wood Snake remains aware of all the changes and developments taking place around him over the year and is informed of the views of his colleagues. To adopt too independent an attitude could leave him isolated and prevent him from making the most of any openings that arise. Also, whether in work or seeking work, the Wood Snake could find it helpful to consider different ways in which he can use his many skills. Some enterprising thinking on his part could broaden the range of openings he can pursue. He will, however, need to exercise care when dealing with financial matters and should keep a close watch over his level of spending. If he is not careful he could find his outgoings are greater than he first thought or has allowed for. Wood

Snakes, be warned! Domestically, this will be a busy but satisfying year. Although there will be many calls upon his time, the Wood Snake will delight in the activities and progress of those around him and can look forward to some pleasurable family events and occasions. At busy times, though, he should not hesitate to ask for assistance rather than try to cope with too much single-handed. He will find help readily forthcoming, should he ask. For any Wood Snake who may find himself living in a new area, who may be unattached or would like to make new friends, it really would be in his interests to consider joining a local group or society, or just going out more. By taking the initiative, he can do much to improve his social life and a new friendship made over the year could, in time, become meaningful and long-lasting. Although this may not be the easiest of years for the Wood Snake, its long-term significance cannot be underestimated. The Tiger year is one in which he will gain much valuable experience and it will prepare the way for the considerably better times that he is soon and so deservedly to enjoy.

This will be an interesting year for the *Fire Snake*, bringing both change and challenges. However, it will teach him much and in both adversity and triumph he will be adding to his experience and learning from his successes and mistakes. In this respect, the Tiger year will be a highly instructive period for him and will do much to prepare him for the progress he will enjoy in succeeding years. Also, although he may hold very definite ideas about what he would like to achieve, in the Tiger year he would do well to show some flexibility. It is better for him to broaden his experience now rather than hold so rigidly to his plans that he misses out on opportunities to develop. Much will happen over the year and the Fire Snake needs to make the most of the situations in which he finds himself. Throughout the year he should also actively pursue any openings that arise; admittedly, not all his attempts to advance his position will be successful, but his perseverance will, in time, be rewarded and with every attempt he makes, he will gain further experience. In 1998 flexibility and perseverance should, as far as his work is concerned, be his watchwords. In financial matters, the Fire Snake should keep a close watch over his general level of spending; without care and some restraint, his outgoings could be greater than he thought and result in him having to make economies later. He should also avoid taking unnecessary financial risks – in 1998 he could find it is easier to spend or lose money than gain it! On a personal level the Tiger year will prove very active for him and he will find himself much in demand with others, with the spring and summer months being particularly favoured. However, to maintain the usually good relations he enjoys with so many, the Fire Snake does need to remain mindful of their views and if any differences should arise, seek an amicable solution rather than allow any ill-feeling to continue unchecked in the background. Sometimes the Fire Snake has a tendency to expect those around him to fall in line with plans without demur and if he is not careful, this could lead to some tensions. It is something he would do well to avoid. The Fire Snake will, however, enjoy any travelling that he undertakes over the year and if finances permit, should aim to go away at least once during the year. A break and change of scene will prove both beneficial and enjoyable for him. Overall, the Fire Snake will emerge from the year wiser and more experienced. What he achieves in the Tiger year will be of great value to him in the future. And from a personal angle, the year holds much promise.

The *Earth Snake* is both shrewd and perceptive and his inborn sense of caution will help him much over the year. When problems arise – and these are most likely to concern matters of a bureaucratic nature – he will be able to put them in perspective and deal with them with considerable skill. However, should there be any matter which arises over the year which he does not fully understand or feel experienced enough to deal with, the Earth Snake should seek appropriate advice rather than try to deal with it unaided. With important correspondence, official forms and matters of a financial nature he will need to proceed carefully. More positively, however, his family life will go well and the Earth Snake will delight in the successes and progress enjoyed by those close to him. As always, his opinions and assistance will be highly valued and any advice and encouragement he feels able to give to those around him will be truly valued, probably more so than he may realize at the time. His social life, too, will bring him much satisfaction and he can look forward to attending several enjoyable social events over the year; at one he could be asked to play an important and distinguished part. The Earth Snake will also enjoy the time he devotes to his interests and those of a creative nature, or which take him out of doors, will go especially well. For those Earth Snakes who are keen gardeners or walkers or who enjoy travel, the year will contain many satisfying moments. Those Earth Snakes born in 1989 will make pleasing progress in their education, although there may be times when they will feel under pressure or be worried about certain subjects or aspects of school. At these times the young Earth Snake would do well to speak of his anxieties rather than keep them to himself. Those around him are keen to help and by talking to others he could find his worries are misplaced or easily rectified. Although the Earth Snake will need to exercise caution in many of his undertakings, the year will still contain many rewarding times. In particular, his family, friends and interests will all bring him much pleasure, and he will find that by late summer the more troublesome aspects of the Tiger year will have passed and that a better and more fulfilling period is beginning to emerge.

FAMOUS SNAKES

Muhammad Ali, Ann-Margret, Yasser Arafat, Paddy Ashdown, Ronnie Barker, Kim Basinger, Benazir Bhutto, Bjork, Tony Blair, William Blake, Heinrich Böll, Michael Bolton, Betty Boothroyd, Brahms, Pierce Brosnan, Will Carling, Casanova, Chubby Checker, Tom Conti, Randy Crawford, Jim Davidson, Bob Dylan, Elgar, Sir Alexander Fleming, Henry Fonda, Mahatma Gandhi, Greta Garbo, Art Garfunkel, J. Paul Getty, Dizzy Gillespie, W. E. Gladstone, Goethe, Princess Grace of Monaco, Stephen Hawking, Nigel Hawthorne, Audrey Hepburn, Jack Higgins, Paul Hogan, Michael Howard, Howard Hughes, Isabelle Huppert, Liz Hurley, Rev. Jesse Jackson, Stacy Keach, Howard Keel, J. F. Kennedy, Carole King, James Last, Cindi Lauper, Courtney Love, Dame Vera Lynn, Linda McCartney, Craig McLachlan, Magnus Magnusson, Nigel Mansell, Mao Tse-tung, Robert Mitchum, Nasser, Bob Newhart, Mike Oldfield, Aristotle Onassis, Jacqueline Onassis, Ryan O'Neal, Dorothy Parker, Pablo Picasso, Mary Pickford, Michael Portillo, André Previn, Helen Reddy, Griff Rhys Jones, Franklin D. Roosevelt, Mickey Rourke, Jean-Paul Sartre, Franz Schubert, Brooke Shields, Nigel Short, Paul Simon, Delia Smith, John Thaw, Dionne Warwick, Charlie Watts, Ruby Wax, Oprah Winfrey, Victoria Wood, Virginia Woolf, Susannah York.

25 JANUARY 1906 ～ 12 FEBRUARY 1907   *Fire Horse*

11 FEBRUARY 1918 ～ 31 JANUARY 1919   *Earth Horse*

30 JANUARY 1930 ～ 16 FEBRUARY 1931   *Metal Horse*

15 FEBRUARY 1942 ～ 4 FEBRUARY 1943   *Water Horse*

3 FEBRUARY 1954 ～ 23 JANUARY 1955   *Wood Horse*

21 JANUARY 1966 ～ 8 FEBRUARY 1967   *Fire Horse*

7 FEBRUARY 1978 ～ 27 JANUARY 1979   *Earth Horse*

27 JANUARY 1990 ～ 14 FEBRUARY 1991   *Metal Horse*

THE

HORSE

THE PERSONALITY OF THE HORSE

Sometimes if you want to see a change for the better, you have to take things into your own hands.

– Clint Eastwood: a Horse

The Horse is born under the signs of elegance and ardour. He has a most engaging and charming manner and is usually very popular. He loves meeting people and likes attending parties and other large social gatherings.

He is a lively character and enjoys being the centre of attention. He has considerable leadership qualities and is much admired for his honest and straightforward manner. He is an eloquent and persuasive speaker and has a great love of discussion and debate. The Horse also has a particularly agile mind and can assimilate facts remarkably quickly.

He does, however, have a fiery temper and although his outbursts are usually short-lived, he can often say things which he will later regret. He is also not particularly good at keeping secrets.

The Horse has many interests and involves himself in a wide variety of activities. He can, however, get involved in so much that he can often waste his energies on projects which he never has time to complete. He also has a tendency to change his interests rather frequently and will often get caught up with the latest craze or 'in thing' until something better or more exciting turns up.

The Horse also likes to have a certain amount of freedom and independence. He hates being bound by petty rules and regulations and as far as possible likes to feel that he is answerable to no one but himself. But despite this spirit of freedom, he still likes to have the support and encouragement of others in his various enterprises.

Due to his many talents and likeable nature, the Horse will often go far in life. He enjoys challenges and is a methodical and tireless worker. However, should things work against him and he fail in any of his enterprises, it will take a long time for him to recover and pick up the pieces again. Success to the Horse means everything. To fail is a disaster and a humiliation.

The Horse likes to have variety in his life and he will try his hand at many different things before he settles down to one particular job. Even then, he will probably remain alert to see whether there are any new and better opportunities for him to take up. The Horse has a restless nature and can easily get bored. He does, however, excel in any position which allows him sufficient freedom to act on his own initiative or which brings him into contact with a lot of people.

Although the Horse is not particularly bothered about accumulating great wealth, he handles his finances with care and will rarely experience any serious financial problems.

The Horse also enjoys travel and he loves visiting new and far-away places. At some stage during his life he will be tempted to live abroad for a short period of time and due to his adaptable nature he will find that he will fit in well wherever he goes.

The Horse pays a great deal of attention to his appearance and usually likes to wear smart, colourful and rather distinctive clothes. He is very attractive to the opposite sex and will often have many romances before he settles down. He is loyal and protective to his partner, but, despite his family commitments, still likes to retain a certain measure of independence and have the freedom to carry on with his own interests and hobbies. He will find that he is especially well suited to those born under the signs of the Tiger, Goat, Rooster and Dog. The Horse can also get on well with the Rabbit, Dragon, Snake, Pig and another Horse, but he will find the Ox too serious and intolerant for his liking. The Horse will also have difficulty in getting on with the Monkey and the Rat – the Monkey is very inquisitive and the Rat seeks security, and both will resent the Horse's rather independent ways.

The female Horse is usually most attractive and has a friendly, outgoing personality. She is highly intelligent, has many interests and is alert to everything that is going on around her. She particularly enjoys outdoor pursuits and often likes to take part in sport and keep-fit activities. She also enjoys travel, literature and the arts, and is a very good conversationalist.

Although the Horse can be stubborn and rather self-centred, he does have a considerate nature and is often willing to help others. He has a good sense of humour and will usually make a favourable impression wherever he goes. Provided he can curb his slightly restless nature and keep a tight control over his temper, he will go through life making friends, taking part in a multitude of different activities and generally achieving many of his objectives. His life will rarely be dull.

THE FIVE DIFFERENT TYPES OF HORSE

In addition to the 12 signs of the Chinese zodiac, there are five elements and these have a strengthening or moderating influence on the sign. The effects of the five elements on the Horse are described below, together with the years in which the elements were exercising their influence. Therefore all Horses born in 1930 and 1990 are Metal Horses, those born in 1942 are Water Horses and so on.

Metal Horse: 1930, 1990

This Horse is bold, confident and forthright. He is ambitious and also a great innovator. He loves challenges and takes great delight in sorting out complicated problems. He likes to have a certain amount of independence and resents any outside interference in his affairs. The Metal Horse has charm and a certain charisma, but he can also be very stubborn and rather impulsive. He usually has many friends and enjoys an active social life.

Water Horse: 1942

The Water Horse has a friendly nature, a good sense of humour, and is able to talk intelligently on a wide range of topics. He is astute in business matters and quick to take advantage of any opportunities that arise. He does, however, have a tendency to get easily distracted and can change his interests – and indeed his mind – rather frequently, and this can sometimes work to his detriment. He is nevertheless very talented and can often go far in life. He pays a great deal of attention to his appearance and is usually smart and well turned out. He loves to travel and also enjoys sport and other outdoor activities.

Wood Horse: 1954

The Wood Horse has a most agreeable and amiable nature. He communicates well with others and, like the Water Horse, is able to talk intelligently on many different subjects. He is a hard and conscientious worker and is held in high esteem by his friends and colleagues. His opinions and views are often sought and, given his imaginative nature, he can quite often come up with some very original and practical ideas. He is usually widely read and likes to lead a busy social life. He can also be most generous and often holds high moral viewpoints.

Fire Horse: 1906, 1966

The element of Fire combined with the temperament of the Horse creates one of the most powerful forces in the Chinese zodiac. The Fire Horse is destined to lead an exciting and eventful life and to make his mark in his chosen profession. He has a forceful personality and his intelligence and resolute manner bring him the support and admiration of many. He loves action and excitement and his life will rarely be quiet. He can, however, be rather blunt and forthright in his views and does not take kindly to interference in his own affairs or to obeying orders. He is a flamboyant character, has a good sense of humour and will lead a very active social life.

Earth Horse: 1918, 1978

This Horse is considerate and caring. He is more cautious than some of the other types of Horse, but he is wise, perceptive and extremely capable. Although he can be rather indecisive at times, he has considerable business acumen and is very astute in financial matters. He has a quiet, friendly nature and is well thought of by his family and friends.

PROSPECTS FOR THE HORSE IN 1998

The Chinese New Year starts on 28 January 1998. Until then, the old year, the Year of the Ox, is still making its presence felt.

The Year of the Ox (7 February 1997 to 27 January 1998) will have been a relatively good year for the Horse and he will have made positive progress with many of his activities. The Ox year is very much one which rewards effort and the Horse – who is certainly a hard worker – will have risen up to the tasks and challenges given him and acquitted himself well. In what remains of the Ox year the Horse should continue to set about his duties in his usual spirited manner and look at ways in which he can put his skills and experience to best use. Some enterprising thinking could lead to him creating some interesting possibilities and ideas. Those Horses seeking work should also consider the various ways in which they could use their wide-ranging skills; by doing so they could discover some additional openings to pursue.

In addition to the favourable aspects concerning his work, the Horse will also enjoy an upturn in his financial situation, particularly in the last few months of the year. By remaining alert, he could acquire some items for himself and his home at most advantageous prices. There will also be some excellent bargains to be had in the post-Christmas sales and if there is an expensive item that the Horse has been wanting, this would be a good time to look around.

As far as his relations with others are concerned, however, the Horse does need to exercise care. Sometimes he has a tendency to become preoccupied with his own concerns at the expense of others. If he is not careful, tensions could occur which could undermine his relations with those around him. To prevent this, the Horse should make every effort to involve others in his own activities as well as take an active interest in all that is going on around him. He will find that positive input on his part will do much to ease any tensions. Social occasions at the end of the year would also be an ideal time to reconcile any differences that might have arisen. Indeed, the Christmas and New Year holidays are most favourably aspected and will give him a chance to rest and unwind after the pressures of the year as well as enjoy himself. The Horse can also be content in the knowledge that he will be able to build on what he has achieved in the next Chinese year.

The Year of the Tiger begins on 28 January 1998 and will be a time of opportunity for the Horse. In recent years the Horse will have achieved much and gained valuable experience as well as given thought to his future aims and aspirations. In 1998 he will be given the chance to put some of his ideas into practice and improve on his current situation. The Tiger year is very much one of positive change – some resulting from action that the Horse himself takes and some arising from circumstances outside his control. Out of these changes will arise new challenges and opportunities, many of which the Horse will be able to turn to his advantage.

The events of the year will also help to give the Horse a new incentive to make the most of himself. Any Horse who feels he is becoming staid or has not been making the progress of which he is capable will find the Tiger year will give him the chance to bring about the changes he has been desiring.

Throughout the year the Horse should set about his work with his customary resolve, determined that he can and will improve upon his position. He knows that he has it within him to do well and in 1998 his commitment and self-belief will be rewarded. To help his progress, though, he does need to remain alert to all that is going on around him. This way he will find himself better placed to spot any opportunities that are soon to arise or to assess how he can use his skills to the best advantage. He should also advance any ideas that he has as well as use any chance he gets to extend his experience. In 1998 his positive approach will find favour with others and this will do much to enhance his prospects.

When a promotion opportunity arises, or if the Horse sees any position or opening that interests him, he should actively follow it up. Indeed, the determined Horse can make great strides in his career and throughout the year will find much truth in the saying 'nothing ventured, nothing gained'. Those Horses seeking work should also remain undaunted in their quest for a position and many will find their persistence rewarded quite early on in the year. These Horses could also find that they will benefit from a twist of good fortune over the year and that one opening leads to another, better one in a comparatively short space of time.

To help his progress over the year, the Horse would, however, do well to concentrate his efforts on specific areas rather than engage in too many objectives all at the same time. If not, there is a risk that he could spread his energies too widely and not achieve as much as he otherwise might. His best results will come from dedicated and determined effort, and if he bears this in mind, his gains and progress over the year can be significant and far-reaching.

Academic matters are also well favoured and the Horse would do well to use any opportunity he gets to extend his skills and qualifications. He will find this will provide him with an interesting and absorbing challenge as well as be a satisfying use of his time. For those Horses in education, this will be a highly productive year and the time they devote to their studies will be rewarded with some pleasing results. Again, though, these Horses must remain disciplined – to get distracted or not be too systematic could undermine their efforts. This is something they would do well to watch.

As far as financial matters are concerned, this will be an expensive year for the Horse. Almost all areas of his life could involve him in some sizeable outlay, ranging from his accommodation to travel, to an active domestic and social life and to any personal items he may want to acquire. If he is his usual careful self and makes appropriate modifications to his budget at times of large expense, then he should be able to avoid problems. However, this is not a year when he can afford to spend without regard to his financial position, take undue risks or regard his savings as a bottomless pit. It is a year which calls for vigilance and skilful financial management. Horses, take note!

Domestically, this will be a busy but gratifying year. The Horse can look forward to some particularly rewarding times with his family and will delight in the personal successes that those around him enjoy. Joint activities, mutual interests and projects around the home will also work out well and give all concerned much satisfaction. In addition, any family outings and holidays the Horse is able to arrange will bring much pleasure.

However, while there is much to his domestic life that will bring him happiness, there will also be times of pressure for the Horse, particularly with numerous household tasks, chores and family matters requiring his attention. At busy times, he would be helped if he were to sort out his priorities and concentrate on these rather than try to deal with everything at once. This includes not starting new projects until existing ones are complete! The Horse should also not hesitate to ask those around him for assistance at particularly demanding times. However, despite the pressures and occasional fraught moment, these will still be meaningful times for him and he can look forward to many splendid occasions with those around him.

The Tiger year will also see an upturn in the Horse's social life and socially he will be more active than he has been for several years. There will be opportunities for him to add to his circle of friends and, for the unattached Horse, romance beckons. The summer, in particular, will be an active time, with several enjoyable parties and functions for him to attend. Any Horse who may be feeling lonely or who has had some recent sadness to bear will see a significant improvement in his fortunes over the year. By taking up new interests, getting in contact with others and joining in more with group activities he will find the year bringing new happiness and hope into his life.

Generally, the Tiger year holds much potential for the Horse and will give him a good chance to show his true worth and advance his position. It is a year of positive change and opportunity, and the Horse, with his enterprising spirit, is ideally placed to take advantage of the favourable aspects that prevail. Provided he exercises care with his financial dealings, this can be a truly successful year for him and one he will much enjoy.

As far as the different types of Horse are concerned, this will be a year of interesting possibilities for the *Metal Horse*. However, to take advantage of the positive aspects that prevail, he needs to show some flexibility in his approach, even if it means revising some of his existing plans. Events can work out very much in his favour in 1998, but to benefit from them he does need to adapt to new and changing situations. The changes that occur can apply to almost any area of the Metal Horse's life, from his accommodation to offers of assistance from others, to taking up new subjects, hobbies or learning new skills. By being adventurous in his outlook, the Metal Horse can achieve much and many of the year's events, unexpected though some might be, can work to his advantage. Rather than resist the changes the year will bring, the Metal Horse should look at the opportunities and the benefits that can arise from them. In all that happens, those around him will be keen to support and advise, and if there is any major decision the Metal Horse needs to take or any matter giving him misgivings, he should seek the opinions of others. In 1998 he will be considerably heartened by the encouragement and backing he is given. Domestically, this will be a pleasing year for the Metal Horse, with the achievements and progress of those close to him being a source of much pride. There will also be good cause for some family celebrations over the year and at one of these he could find himself taking centre stage. The Metal Horse should also use any opportunity he gets to visit relations or friends he has not seen for some time; such a meeting will prove most meaningful. His social life, too, will go well and he can look forward to attending several interesting parties and functions over the course of the year. For any Metal Horse who may have recently moved to a new area or is seeking additional friends, it really would be in his interests to get in contact with others and consider joining a local group or society. Positive input on his part will be rewarded and by making the effort he can do much to improve his social life and make what will become some very good and sound friend-ships. Another area which is favourably aspected concerns outdoor activities and for those Metal Horses who enjoy travel, gardening, exploring the countryside or following sport, there will be many pleasurable moments. Overall, the year will go well for the Metal Horse, but he does need to adapt to and make the most of the new situations that arise. He can achieve a considerable amount in 1998, but just how much rests on his attitude and approach.

This will be an active and generally favourable year for the *Water Horse*. In recent years he will have accom-plished much and the Tiger year will give him the chance to build on his successes and make further progress. However, to get the best from the year, the Water Horse would do well to consider what he would now like to accomplish and set himself some goals and objectives. Without this, there is a danger that he could drift through the year and not make the most of himself or the oppor-tunities that arise. In 1998 he can make great headway, but he does need to set about his activities in a purposeful and disciplined manner. In his work he should continue to give of his best but use any chance he gets to promote his ideas and pursue any openings he sees. His determination and resolve will be rewarded and several times he will be able to benefit from the new situations and opportunities that arise. For the enterprising and determined Water Horse, of which there are so many, the year holds much potential. Those Water Horses seeking work or wanting to change their current position should also actively follow up any interesting vacancies that occur. They will find their persistence rewarded, with the early months of the year being well aspected. This will, however, be a generally expensive year for the Water Horse and he would do well to watch his level of spending. With care, he should be able to avoid problems, but this is not a year for extravagance, over-indulgence or for taking financial risks. As far as the Water Horse's domestic and social life are concerned, this will be an interesting and eventful year. He will be much in demand with those around him and can look forward to many pleasurable family and social occasions. There will also be several parties and functions for him to enjoy, especially over the summer months, and these will allow him to add to his already wide circle of friends and acquaintances. Those close to the Water Horse will also be most supportive and, in view of some of the decisions he will need to take over the year, he should not hesitate to seek their views and advice. Many times he will have good reason to be thankful for the encouragement and support he is given and for the constructive suggestions he receives. It is also important that the Water Horse does not neglect his hobbies and interests over the year. These do provide a valuable source of relaxation for him and, if he is able to extend an interest in some way, such as learning about a new aspect or contacting fellow enthusiasts, he could find that it will make the interest all the more fulfilling. Generally, this will be a highly promising year for the Water Horse and by making the most of the opportunities that arise, he will accomplish much. Added to which, his domestic and social life will both be a source of much pleasure, making this one of the most satisfying years he has enjoyed for some time.

This will be a positive year for the *Wood Horse* and he will be able to make good progress in many of his activities. The Wood Horse possesses an enquiring mind and enterprising nature, and these two qualities will serve him well throughout the year. In 1998 he should actively promote his skills and ideas, and if he has any plans that he wishes to carry out, he should seek the opinion of others. If their reaction is favourable, he should then set them in motion. Positive action on his part will bring its rewards, but in all that he does he will fare better by acting in conjunction with others rather than retaining too independent an approach. Indeed, over the year the Wood Horse will greatly benefit from the input and advice of others, and should he have any uncertainties over any matter with which he is involved, he should seek out those who have the necessary experience to help and advise. This way he will receive many practical suggestions and some useful encouragement as well as be alerted to possible pitfalls to avoid. Over the year he will make considerable progress in his work and when changes and new situations arise, as they will several times, the Wood Horse should look positively upon them and explore ways in which he can turn them to his advantage. Again, his enterprising nature will be of much value. There will be many a time over the year when the Wood Horse will benefit from his imaginative approach, from being in the right place at the right time or from opportunities that unexpectedly arise. His progress and success will also be reflected by an improvement in his financial situation. However, while the Wood Horse will enjoy this upturn, there will be several large expenses that he will have to meet, especially involving his accommodation, and at these times he will need to make appropriate adjustments to his outgoings. This is not a year when he should be tempted to stretch his resources too far or let any financial improvement lull him into complacency or undue extravagance. Wood Horses, be warned! Domestically, this will, however, be a most satisfying year and the Wood Horse will take much pleasure in the progress and successes enjoyed by those around him. Several times over the year there will be good cause for family rejoicing and get-togethers. The Wood Horse will also find joint activities are favoured and if there are any projects that he wants to carry out on his home or garden he would do well to involve others rather than undertake the work on his own. As far as social matters are concerned, this will be one of the busiest years he has enjoyed for some time and he can look forward to attending a variety of events, parties and, in some cases, prestigious functions. For the lonely or unattached Wood Horse the prospects for making new friends are also most encouraging, especially in the spring and summer months. Overall, 1998 will be a pleasing and productive year for the Wood Horse and by setting about his activities with determination and resolve he will make excellent progress. He possesses many fine and admirable talents and in 1998 he will be able to put them to good use.

This will be an interesting year for the *Fire Horse* and one in which he will make considerable progress in many of his activities. Particularly well aspected are work matters, and over the year the Fire Horse will be given the chance to consolidate any recent gains he has made and build upon his skills and experience. As almost all Horses will find, the Tiger year will bring change, and for the Fire Horse this will mean new opportunities and the chance to move to different and more varied responsibilities. Admittedly, this will bring with it some daunting challenges and difficult decisions, but this often brings out the best in the Fire Horse and in 1998 he will rise up to all the tasks given him and considerably enhance his position and reputation. There will also be some positive developments for those Fire Horses seeking work and many will find their persistence rewarded, with the early months of the year being an active and encouraging time. As far as financial matters are concerned, this will prove an expensive year for the Fire Horse, particularly concerning items of furnishing and equipment that he may want for his home. At expensive times it would be very much in his interests to monitor his level of spending and, if necessary, make modifications to his regular outgoings, including cutting back on some costly indulgences! This is not a year in which he can spend without regard to his financial situation, take unnecessary risks or enter major transactions without making allowances for any obligations he may be placed under. Personally, this will prove a busy year for the Fire Horse and he will be much in demand with both family and friends. There will be many enjoyable occasions and social events to look forward to and the Fire Horse will take much satisfaction in following the activities of those around him. However, with the pressures that the year will bring, particularly with the likelihood of increased work responsibilities, it is important that he does not take out any anxieties that he has on those around him. Sharp words or a lost temper could undermine the good relations he enjoys. This is something the Fire Horse needs to watch. He should also remember that those close to him are keen to support him and see him succeed, and he should not hesitate to speak of any concerns he might have or to seek their advice. By doing so he will be considerably heartened by the obvious regard and affection others have for him and will be glad of the practical advice and support he is given. Another area which is also well aspected is travel and the Fire Horse will thoroughly enjoy and benefit from any journeys, holidays and breaks he is able to take over the year. Overall, this will be a positive year for the Fire Horse and while some of its changes will bring new challenges, he will find these will give him an added incentive to do well and make the most of himself. With his usual skill and enterprising disposition, he will indeed impress others and improve his position. Personally, too, the year will prove most enjoyable, making this both a successful and rewarding year for the Fire Horse.

This will be an eventful year for the *Earth Horse*, with many positive and significant changes taking place. On a personal level, the Tiger year will bring considerable happiness, with romance and the prospects of engagement or marriage well aspected. For any Earth Horse who is lonely or seeking new friends, the aspects are highly encouraging and it would very much be in the interests of these Earth Horses to go out more, visit places where they can meet others or consider joining a local society or interest group. Positive action on their part will be well rewarded and many Earth Horses will establish new and meaningful friendships during the course of the year. All Earth Horses will find the spring and summer months are

especially positive for social matters. In addition, many
Earth Horses will move and while this will cause some
disruption, being in a different area will bring opportunities and the chance to make new friends as well as the
fun of discovering the amenities and attractions that
the new location offers. However, with so much activity
indicated, this will be a costly year and the Earth Horse
needs to keep a close watch over his outgoings. If he
stretches his resources too far he could find he is having to
make cutbacks later in the year and deny himself things he
might want. As far as money matters are concerned, this is
a year that calls for considerable care. There will, however,
be some excellent opportunities for the Earth Horse in
his work and many Earth Horses will be successful in
obtaining new and more varied responsibilities. Throughout the year the Earth Horse should remain alert for
chances to pursue and for ways in which he can put his
talents and experience to best use. Also, if there are any
courses that he can attend that would enable him to add to
his skills, he should follow these up. Professionally and
academically, this will be a most progressive year and the
Earth Horse's determined and diligent approach will
impress others. However, while the aspects are so encouraging, he does need to be realistic in his expectations.
Although he may have some very definite aims, many of
these are for the longer term and can only be attained once
he has the necessary experience. At the moment he should
concentrate on getting that experience and keep his present
aspirations within reach. To attempt too much too soon or
aim for overly ambitious objectives will bring disappointment and could lead to less satisfactory results. The Earth

Horse would also do well to remember that time is very much on his side and in this and the next few years he should concentrate on getting experience and progressing at a sensible pace. Generally, however, the Tiger year will be a highly favourable one for the Earth Horse. On a personal level, these will be times of much activity and happiness and what the Earth Horse accomplishes in his work will stand him in excellent stead for the positive developments that await him in future years.

FAMOUS HORSES

Neil Armstrong, Rowan Atkinson, Margaret Beckett, Samuel Beckett, Ingmar Bergman, Leonard Bernstein, Sir John Betjeman, Karen Black, Cherie Blair, Helena Bonham-Carter, Leonid Brezhnev, Eric Cantona, Ray Charles, Chopin, Sean Connery, Billy Connolly, Catherine Cookson, Ronnie Corbett, Elvis Costello, Kevin Costner, Michael Crichton, James Dean, Les Dennis, Kirk Douglas, Clint Eastwood, Thomas Alva Edison, Britt Ekland, Chris Evans, Linda Evans, Harrison Ford, Michael Forsyth, Aretha Franklin, Sir Bob Geldof, Billy Graham, Gene Hackman, Susan Hampshire, Rolf Harris, Rita Hayworth, Jimi Hendrix, Bob Hoskins, Ted Hughes, Janet Jackson, Jermaine Jackson, Nikita Khrushchev, Robert Kilroy-Silk, Neil Kinnock, Calvin Klein, Dr Helmut Kohl, Lenin, Annie Lennox, Desmond Lynam, Paul McCartney, Norma Major, Nelson Mandela, Princess Margaret, Curtis Mayfield, Spike Milligan, Ben Murphy, Jimmy Nail, Sir Isaac Newton, Louis Pasteur, Ross Perot, Harold Pinter, David Platt, Stephanie Powers, J. B. Priestley, Puccini, Rembrandt, Ruth Rendell, Jean Renoir, Theodore Roosevelt, Helena Rubenstein, Peter Sissons, Lord Snowdon, Alexander Solzhenitsyn, Lisa Stansfield, Michaela Strachan, Barbra Streisand, Kiefer Sutherland, Patrick Swayze, John Travolta, Kathleen Turner, Mike Tyson, Vivaldi, Robert Wagner, Billy Wilder, Andy Williams, the Duke of Windsor, Steve Wright, Tammy Wynette, Boris Yeltsin, Michael York.

13 FEBRUARY 1907 ~ 1 FEBRUARY 1908	*Fire Goat*
1 FEBRUARY 1919 ~ 19 FEBRUARY 1920	*Earth Goat*
17 FEBRUARY 1931 ~ 5 FEBRUARY 1932	*Metal Goat*
5 FEBRUARY 1943 ~ 24 JANUARY 1944	*Water Goat*
24 JANUARY 1955 ~ 11 FEBRUARY 1956	*Wood Goat*
9 FEBRUARY 1967 ~ 29 JANUARY 1968	*Fire Goat*
28 JANUARY 1979 ~ 15 FEBRUARY 1980	*Earth Goat*
15 FEBRUARY 1991 ~ 3 FEBRUARY 1992	*Metal Goat*

THE
GOAT

THE PERSONALITY OF THE GOAT

If you don't have a dream, how are you going to make a dream come true?

— Oscar Hammerstein II: a Goat

The Goat is born under the sign of art. He is imaginative, creative and has a good appreciation of the finer things in life. He has an easy-going nature and prefers to live in a relaxed and pressure-free environment. He hates any sort of discord or unpleasantness and does not like to be bound by a strict routine or rigid timetable. The Goat is not one to be hurried against his will but, despite his seemingly relaxed approach to life, he is something of a perfectionist and when he starts work on a project he is certain to give of his best.

The Goat usually prefers to work in a team rather than on his own. He likes to have the support and encouragement of others and if left to deal with matters on his own he can get very worried and tends to view things rather pessimistically. Wherever possible he will leave major decision-making to others while he concentrates on his own pursuits. If, however, he feels particularly strongly about a certain matter or has to defend his position in any way, he will act with great fortitude and precision.

The Goat has a very persuasive nature and often uses his considerable charm to get his own way. He can, however, be rather hesitant about letting his true feelings be known and if he were prepared to be more forthright he would do much better as a result.

The Goat tends to have a quiet, somewhat reserved nature but when he is in company he likes he can often become the centre of attention. He can be highly amusing, a marvellous host at parties and a superb entertainer. Whenever the spotlight falls on him, his adrenalin starts to flow and he can be assured of giving a sparkling performance, particularly if he is allowed to use his creative skills in any way.

Of all the signs in the Chinese zodiac, the Goat is probably the most gifted artistically. Whether it is in the theatre, literature, music or art, he is certain to make a lasting impression. He is a born creator and is rarely happier than when occupied in some artistic pursuit. But even in this, the Goat does well to work with others rather than on his own. He needs inspiration and a guiding influence, but when he has found his true *métier*, he can often receive widespread acclaim and recognition.

In addition to his liking for the arts, the Goat is usually quite religious and often has a deep interest in nature, animals and the countryside. He is also fairly athletic and there are many Goats who have excelled in some form of sporting activity or who have a great interest in sport.

Although the Goat is not particularly materialistic or concerned about finance, he will find that he will usually be lucky in financial matters and will rarely be short of the necessary funds to tide himself over. He is, however, rather indulgent and tends to spend his money as soon as he receives it rather than make provision for the future.

The Goat usually leaves home when he is young but he will always maintain strong links with his parents and the other members of his family. He is also rather nostalgic and is well known for keeping mementoes of his childhood and souvenirs of places that he has visited. His home will not be particularly tidy but he knows where everything is and it will also be scrupulously clean.

Affairs of the heart are particularly important to the Goat and he will often have many romances before he finally settles down. Although he is fairly adaptable, he prefers to live in a secure and stable environment and will find that he is best suited to those born under the signs of the Tiger, Horse, Monkey, Pig and Rabbit. He can also establish a good relationship with the Dragon, Snake, Rooster and another Goat, but he may find the Ox and Dog a little too serious for his liking. Neither will he care particularly for the Rat's rather thrifty ways.

The female Goat devotes all her time and energy to the needs of her family. She has excellent taste in home furnishings and often uses her considerable artistic skills to make clothes for herself and her children. She takes great care over her appearance and can be most attractive to the opposite sex. Although she is not the most well organized of people, her engaging manner and delightful sense of humour create a favourable impression wherever she goes. She is also a good cook and usually gets much pleasure from gardening and outdoor pursuits.

The Goat can win friends easily and people generally feel relaxed in his company. He has a kind and understanding nature and although he can occasionally be stubborn, he can, with the right support and encouragement, live a happy and very satisfying life. The more he can use his creative skills, the happier he will be.

THE FIVE DIFFERENT TYPES OF GOAT

In addition to the 12 signs of the Chinese zodiac, there are five elements and these have a strengthening or moderating influence on the sign. The effects of the five elements on the Goat are described below, together with the years in which the elements were exercising their influence. Therefore all Goats born in 1931 and 1991 are Metal Goats, those born in 1943 are Water Goats, and so on.

Metal Goat: 1931, 1991

This Goat is thorough and conscientious in all that he does and is capable of doing very well in his chosen profession. Despite his confident manner, he can be a great worrier and he would find it a help to discuss his worries with others rather than keep them to himself. He is loyal to his family and employers and will have a small group of extremely good friends. He has good artistic taste and is usually highly skilled in some aspect of the arts. He is often a collector of antiques and his home will be very tastefully furnished.

Water Goat: 1943

The Water Goat is very popular and makes friends with remarkable ease. He is good at spotting opportunities but does not always have the necessary confidence to follow them through. He likes to have security both in his home life and at work and does not take kindly to change. He is articulate, has a good sense of humour and is usually very good with children.

Wood Goat: 1955

This Goat is generous, kind-hearted and always eager to please. He usually has a large circle of friends and involves himself in a wide variety of different activities. He has a very trusting nature but he can sometimes give in to the demands of others a little too easily and it would be in his own interests if he were to stand his ground a little more often. He is usually lucky in financial matters and, like the Water Goat, is very good with children.

Fire Goat: 1907, 1967

This Goat usually knows what he wants in life and he often uses his considerable charm and persuasive personality in order to achieve his aims. He can sometimes let his imagination run away with him and has a tendency to ignore matters which are not to his liking. He is rather extravagant in his spending and would do well to exercise a little more care when dealing with financial matters. He has a lively personality, many friends and loves attending parties and social occasions.

Earth Goat: 1919, 1979

This Goat has a very considerate and caring nature. He is particularly loyal to his family and friends and invariably creates a favourable impression wherever he goes. He is reliable and conscientious in his work but he finds it difficult to save and never likes to deprive himself of any little luxury which he might fancy. He has numerous interests and is often very well read. He usually gets much pleasure from following the activities of various members of his family.

PROSPECTS FOR THE GOAT IN 1998

The Chinese New Year starts on 28 January 1998. Until then, the old year, the Year of the Ox, is still making its presence felt.

The Year of the Ox (7 February 1997 to 27 January 1998) will not have been the easiest of years for the Goat; many Goats will have found progress difficult and had problems to overcome. The year will have contained times of uncertainty and worry and there will have been occasions when the Goat has been disappointed at how certain events have worked out. However, there are now good reasons for him to take heart.

By facing up to the problems and difficulties the year has brought, the Goat will have learned much and gained valuable experience. Indeed, it is often considered that problems and adversity are a good test of character and so it is for the Goat in the Ox year. He will have learned from any mistakes he has made and some of the more challenging situations will have helped him to focus his attention on his present position and future goals.

Also, the closing months of the Ox year are generally more positive than the earlier parts and from September onwards there will be a gradual improvement in the Goat's fortunes. It is at this time that he will begin to make the progress that has been eluding him and will find that some of the problems that have been troubling him begin to be resolved.

To assist this upturn the Goat should, however, take positive action to improve his situation. If, over the course of the year, his relations with some of those around him – be they family, friends or colleagues – have become strained, he should aim to resolve any differences. A positive and conciliatory approach on his part could do much good and, from November to the end of the Ox year, both his social and domestic life will bring him much happiness. He will also find it helpful to discuss any concerns he might have with those around him; sometimes the advice and input of others will do much to solve or ease his problems.

Also, if there are any matters the Goat may have put to one side, such as correspondence or household jobs, he should make a concerted effort to deal with them at this time. By doing so, he will be pleased with how much he is able to complete and will find himself better able to attend to and enjoy the festivities at the end of the year.

The Year of the Tiger begins on 28 January 1998 and will be an interesting year for the Goat. The Tiger year is very much one which brings change and while some of the changes may not always be to the Goat's liking, their long-term significance can be quite considerable. The nature of the year will also mean that the Goat will need to show some flexibility in his outlook, but provided that he remains positive and gives of his best, he will accomplish much.

In his work there will be several important developments. Almost all Goats will see a change in their duties over the year; sometimes this will arise through their being given new responsibilities, through changes in the company or organization they work for, or through new opportunities that they see and pursue. These will be interesting times for the Goat and he would do well to keep himself informed of any imminent changes that might create new opportunities for him. Even if some of these openings are different from the ones he has been hoping for, he would do well to follow them up. It is better for him to take action now and make the most of the situation in which he finds himself rather than wait for conditions that may still be far off. Also, what he accomplishes over the year will stand him in excellent stead for the more progressive and favourable times that await him in 1999.

The aspects are also encouraging for those Goats seeking work and there will be some interesting opportunities in the early part of the year, with March and April being two particularly favoured months. Many Goats will find that a new position they obtain, even though it may not be quite what they were originally seeking, will develop in a positive manner and lead to further opportunities in the future. As all Goats will find, in matters of employment the Tiger year will bring several surprises, some of which will, in the longer term, prove positive.

This is also an ideal year for the Goat to add to his skills and if there is a skill or qualification that he feels he needs in order to advance, or one that he has been considering learning for some time, this is an excellent year in which to begin. Again, anything that the Goat can do to enhance his prospects will be to his advantage.

Those Goats in education will also make pleasing progress. There may be many activities the young Goat would prefer to do rather than study, but it really would be in his interest to make the sacrifice and wholeheartedly apply himself to his work, particularly if there are important exams approaching. The time he devotes to his education will repay him handsomely in the future.

The Goat will, however, need to exercise care when dealing with financial matters. Several times during the year he will want to purchase some costly items, both for himself and his accommodation. At these times he should consider his purchases carefully and obtain prices from several different outlets before proceeding. To act on impulse or rush into any transaction without due consideration could leave him regretting his purchase and possibly involve him in more expense than is necessary. Similarly, the Goat should be wary of entering risky or speculative ventures; money committed to such schemes may not be easy to recover. Generally, if the Goat has any doubts over any financial matter, he should seek advice.

Domestically, this will be a busy but satisfying year for the Goat. As always, he will do much to assist and encourage those around him, but there will also be numerous household matters and projects that will require his attention. Indeed, with the activity and demands of the year there will be times when he will despair of all he has to do. At busy times the Goat would be helped if he were to decide upon his priorities and concentrate on these rather than commit himself to too much at any one time.

Also, he should resist the temptation of starting new projects – especially of a DIY nature or in the garden – until he has finished his current tasks. One job well done is better than lots started and left unfinished. However, despite the high level of activity in his home life, these will still be rich and rewarding times and the Goat can look forward to many pleasurable occasions with those around him. In particular, any mutual interests that he has with those close to him will prove most fulfilling, and any family holidays, breaks and outings he takes are also likely to go well. The Goat's family means much to him and the time spent on family activities, together with the support he gives and receives over the year, will do much to encourage and hearten him.

The Goat's social life will also be busier than usual and he can look forward to many enjoyable occasions with his friends and to attending a variety of interesting parties, functions and events. For the lonely or unattached Goat, the spring months will see a marked upturn in his social life and a friendship formed at this time could become significant over the next few years.

Generally, the Goat's relations with others will go well, but to preserve the harmony he so values, he does need to remain mindful of others' views and feelings. While those close to him will do much to please and assist him, the Goat cannot expect to have his ideas and plans prevailing all the time. To appear too unaccommodating or intransigent could cause some ill-feeling and is something all Goats should watch and strive to avoid. Similarly, if any differences occur, no matter how slight, discretion and a willingness to compromise will certainly not come amiss.

With the demands of the year it is also important that the Goat devotes time to his hobbies and interests and allows himself time to regularly relax and unwind. Many Goats will find creative activities an ideal tonic and for any Goat who has literary or artistic aspirations, a project started in the Tiger year will not only provide many hours of pleasure but could also have a successful outcome in 1999. The Goat will also find outdoor activities satisfying, particularly any that allow him the opportunity to get some additional exercise. Gardening, walking, cycling and similar pursuits can all be beneficial for the Goat over the year.

Although the Tiger year will bring pressures and change, particularly involving work activities, it will still be a constructive year for the Goat. In many cases the events will provide him with a greater incentive to make more of himself and his abilities, and what he accomplishes will serve him well in the future, particularly in the more favourable and progressive Year of the Rabbit.

As far as the different types of Goat are concerned, this will be a satisfying year for the *Metal Goat*. He can look forward to many rewarding and gratifying times with those around him and will have good reason to feel proud of their successes and progress. Any additional encouragement he feels able to give will be much valued and, as always, his views and advice will be held in high esteem. The Metal Goat will himself benefit from the input of others and should not hesitate to ask for help or advice with any project he is undertaking or if he has any matter concerning him. Support is readily available and the Metal

Goat should draw on this rather than carry on unaided or keep things too much to himself. Over the year he will obtain particular satisfaction from projects that he carries out on his home, especially those connected with decor. His fine artistic taste and eye for detail will be as good as ever and he will be delighted with what he achieves, although he should allow plenty of time for practical projects rather than rush them or set himself too tight a deadline. He will also take much pleasure in furthering his hobbies and interests, and again creative pursuits will be to the fore. For the Metal Goat who enjoys writing, it could be worth writing about one of his interests and, if appropriate, passing on his experiences and findings. He could find his work well received and this in itself could lead to another fulfilling occupation. Outdoor activities are also favoured and those Metal Goats who enjoy gardening, sport or exploring the countryside can look forward to some most gratifying occasions. The Metal Goat will also enjoy the travelling that he undertakes and should take advantage of any opportunity he gets to meet with friends or relations he has not seen for some time. For those Metal Goats who may be feeling lonely or hoping to make additional friends, the year will hold out many opportunities for socializing and meeting others; indeed, a new friendship could be formed while the Metal Goat is travelling or away on holiday. However, while there is much to the year he will enjoy, there are certain aspects the Metal Goat must watch. He needs to be careful in financial matters and if he has any doubts over any transaction or agreement he is considering, he should seek further clarification rather than take risks. Also, should he need to move heavy objects or undertake tasks of a hazardous nature, he must seek assistance rather than risk spraining or hurting himself. This is not a year for taking personal risks or ignoring safety precautions. Metal Goats, take note! Generally, though, this will be a satisfying year for the Metal Goat and by using his time wisely and putting his skills and talents to good use he will have every reason to feel pleased with what he is able to accomplish.

This will be a variable year for the *Water Goat*. Although there will be aspects he will greatly enjoy, the Tiger year will also bring times of upheaval and uncertainty and the Water Goat, who so values a settled existence, is never one who particularly enjoys this. However, worrying though some aspects of the year may be, many of the changes that occur will have a positive outcome. They will enable the Water Goat to reflect on his present position and his future aspirations and, in many cases, provide him with the stimulus to act on some of his ideas. The Water Goat knows he has it within him to achieve much, and the events of Tiger year will encourage him to set about his activities with a greater resolve and determination. As such, the year holds much potential for the Water Goat. The opportunities that it brings will herald the start of a new and interesting phase in his life. In his work, this will be an important year. For those Water Goats wanting to transfer to new duties or seeking work, there will be several openings to pursue and it really would be in their interests to actively promote their skills and past experience as much as possible. Determined and decisive action on their part will bring positive results. There will also be some Water Goats who are keen to set in motion some ideas they have, start up a business or pursue some long-held aspiration. Before taking any irrevocable action, though, these Water Goats do need to carefully consider the implications of their decision and seek the views of those close to them as well as those who can advise in a more professional capacity. What the Water Goat decides during the year will have a major bearing on his future and his decisions should not be taken lightly or hurriedly. It is better to proceed slowly and surely rather than commence something in an ill-conceived way. The Water Goat will also need to exercise care when dealing with financial matters and if he enters into any major transaction, he should make sure he is aware of – and makes allowances for – any obligations he might be placed under. It would also be in his interests to keep a close watch over his level of spending. Without care this could be greater than he thought and, unless watched, could result in him having to economize later. This is a year which calls for vigilance, a certain restraint and careful financial management. The Water Goat's domestic life will be generally busy, with many matters requiring his attention. However, while there may be moments of pressure, he will delight in following the activities of those around him and over the year there will be many family occasions, events and successes for him to enjoy. As always, he will be much in demand with others, and domestically and socially the year holds much promise. However, with the demands and pressures of the year, it is important that the Water Goat does not neglect his well-being. If he does not get much exercise during the day, he could find some additional walking or activities such as swimming or cycling beneficial for him and any breaks or holidays he is able to take will also do him much good. Overall, this will be an important year for the Water Goat and some of the decisions he takes, together with what he accomplishes, will do much to lay the foundations for the more favourable and stable times he will enjoy over the next few years.

Although 1998 may contain some challenging times for the *Wood Goat*, what he achieves will be very much to his long-term advantage. In his work he should consolidate any recent gains he has made but at the same time remain mindful of the situations that currently prevail. Changes are afoot and the Wood Goat needs to keep informed of all that is going on. If not, he could miss out on some interesting openings that could be to his advantage and would enable him to advance his position. He should also be prepared to adapt to new situations that arise rather than hold rigidly to set plans. It is those Wood Goats who are prepared to be more flexible and adventurous in their outlook that will make the best progress over the year. Admittedly, the Wood Goat is not one who particularly likes change or the uncertainty that it brings, but by giving of his best and pursuing any opportunities he sees he will make good progress as well as lay the foundations for the successes he will enjoy in succeeding years. The Wood Goat would also do well to consider learning a new skill over the year, either one that would help him in his present position or something different from anything he has done before. He will find this a constructive and satisfying use of his time as well as being of future benefit. The Wood Goat will fare reasonably well in financial matters in 1998, although he would do well to put any spare money he has towards a specific purpose rather than allow it to 'burn a hole' in his pocket. In particular, by remaining alert at sale times he could be fortunate in acquiring some items that would add to the comfort and decor of his home at most reasonable prices. The Wood Goat's domestic life will be generally demanding over the year, with many matters requiring his attention. However, while there will be times when he will despair of all he has to do, these will still be meaningful and happy times for him. He will take much satisfaction in the progress enjoyed by those around him and there will also be good cause for some family rejoicing over the year. At busy times, though, the Wood Goat should seek the assistance of others rather than try to do too much single-handed. He should also resist the temptation of starting too many household projects all at the same time and again, wherever possible, should involve others in his undertakings. Not only will he find joint activities more pleasurable, but by drawing on others' skills he will also find the tasks quicker and easier to complete. The Wood Goat should also make sure he goes away for a break or proper holiday over the year. He will greatly benefit from a change of scene and travel is generally well aspected. It is also important that he does not neglect his hobbies and interests as they do provide him with a valuable source of relaxation. Generally, the Tiger year will be a satisfying year for the Wood Goat. Admittedly, some of the events and changes that occur will bring increased pressures, but by rising up to all that is asked and making the most of the conditions that prevail he will accomplish much. Added to which, he will be preparing the way for the better and more successful times that he is soon to enjoy.

Over the last 12 months the *Fire Goat* will have gained much experience as well as impressed others with his enterprising nature and amiable personality. In 1998 he will be able to draw on this and make further progress. In his work there will be several openings for him to pursue and many Fire Goats will take on new and more varied responsibilities during the course of the year. The Fire Goat should remain active in promoting his ideas and, with a bold and enthusiastic approach, he will do much to enhance his reputation and prospects. However, while the Fire Goat will certainly make progress, he does need to be realistic in his expectations. To aim for positions for which he does not yet have the necessary experience could bring disappointment and he should aim to advance at a steady but positive pace – and ideally in areas where he has most experience. The early part of the Tiger year is, however, an especially favourable time for career matters, with the period from March to May being well aspected. It is also at this time that those Fire Goats seeking work should remain alert for opportunities, especially as they could learn of some openings by chance. The Fire Goat will, however, need to exercise care when dealing with financial matters. Several times over the year he will want to buy some costly items, particularly for his home, and he does need to make allowances for these in his budget, even if this involves him making some economies. To stretch his resources too far without regard to his current financial position could give rise to problems – problems which, with care, could be averted. The Fire Goat's domestic life will, however, be active, with many demands upon his time and matters requiring his attention. He will nevertheless obtain much satisfaction from the activities and progress of those around him, and the support and encouragement he is able to give will be much appreciated. Similarly, if the Fire Goat himself feels under pressure or is in a dilemma about what action to take, he should not hesitate to ask for assistance. This will be readily forthcoming and the Fire Goat will be much encouraged by the support he receives as well as heartened by the obvious affection and esteem that others have for him. He can also look forward to some enjoyable times with his friends over the year as well as to attending some interesting, and in some cases, memorable parties and functions. For any Fire Goat who is unattached or seeking new friends, the months of May and June could mark the beginning of a new and important friendship. Generally, the Fire Goat will have good reason to be satisfied with what he achieves in the Tiger year and by setting about his activities in a determined and yet realistic manner, he will make progress. Furthermore, his accomplishments will lead to even better and greater achievements next year.

This will be a memorable year for the *Earth Goat* and one which will contain much personal happiness. The young and unattached Earth Goat can look forward to a particularly active social life with romance and new friendships well aspected. There will be parties and plenty of other social occasions to attend and for those Earth Goats seeking friends or who find themselves living in a new area, it really would be in their interests to go out more, get in contact with others and consider joining in with more group activities, perhaps at a club or local society. Friendships made in the Tiger year could become important and long-lasting. However, with an active social life indicated, the Earth Goat does need to get things in perspective. If he has exams approaching or has other important activities to attend, he should not neglect these or find that he is not giving of his best because of other distractions. The year should not all be play, play, play, but a sensible balance – and if the Earth Goat can maintain this, then his progress will be creditable. For those Earth Goats in education, their results will amply repay them for the time they devote to their studies, while those in work or seeking work will have the chance to gain useful and valuable experience. The Earth Goat should actively pursue any openings he sees but needs to be realistic in the positions he seeks. At the moment, he would do best to concentrate on training and adding to his experience. Once he has this, he will find himself better able to make the progress he desires. As far as financial matters are concerned, this will be an expensive year, particularly in view of the active social life the Earth Goat will lead, plus other expenses he will have to meet. Throughout the year he should keep a close watch on his level of spending and avoid taking undue risks. This is a year for care and sensible control over his purse strings! More positively, however, the Earth Goat's interests and hobbies will bring him much pleasure. Travel and outdoor activities are well favoured and for the many Earth Goats who enjoy creative pursuits, it would certainly be in their interests to promote their talents and bring their work to the attention of others. They could find it favourably received and they may obtain some useful encouragement as a result. Overall, this will be a positive year for the Earth Goat. He can look forward to some happy and memorable times with those around him as well as gain much valuable experience in his work and work-related activities. Sometimes his progress may not be as swift or as easy as he would like, but all the time he will be adding to his experience and will be able to put it to effective use in succeeding years.

FAMOUS GOATS

Pamela Anderson, Isaac Asimov, W. H. Auden, Jane Austen, Anne Bancroft, Boris Becker, Cilla Black, Ian Botham, Elkie Brooks, George Burns, Lord Byron, Leslie Caron, John le Carré, Coco Chanel, Nat 'King' Cole, Harry Connick Jr, Angus Deayton, Catherine Deneuve, John Denver, Charles Dickens, Ken Dodd, Sir Arthur Conan Doyle, Umberto Eco, Douglas Fairbanks, Keith Floyd, Dame Margot Fonteyn, Anna Ford, Noel Gallagher, Paul Gascoigne, Bill Gates, Mel Gibson, Newt Gingrich, Paul Michael Glaser, Mikhail Gorbachev, John Grisham, George Harrison, Mary Higgins Clark, Sir Edmund Hillary, Hulk Hogan, John Humphrys, Billy Idol, Julio Iglesias, Mick Jagger, Ben Kingsley, David Kossoff, Doris Lessing, Peter Lilley, Franz Liszt, John Major, Michelangelo, Joni Mitchell, Iris Murdoch, Rupert Murdoch, Mussolini, Randy Newman, Leonard Nimoy, Robert de Niro, Greg Norman, Oliver North, Edna O'Brien, Des O'Connor, Sinead O'Connor, Lord Olivier, Michael Palin, Marcel Proust, Keith Richards, Mickey Rourke, Sir Malcolm Sargent, Mike Smith, Freddie Starr, Lord Tebbit, Leslie Thomas, Lana Turner, Desmond Tutu, Mark Twain, Rudolph Valentino, Vangelis, Terry Venables, Lech Walesa, Barbara Walters, John Wayne, Fay Weldon, Bruce Willis, Debra Winger, Tom Wolfe, Paul Young.

2 FEBRUARY 1908 ～ 21 JANUARY 1909   *Earth Monkey*

20 FEBRUARY 1920 ～ 7 FEBRUARY 1921   *Metal Monkey*

6 FEBRUARY 1932 ～ 25 JANUARY 1933   *Water Monkey*

25 JANUARY 1944 ～ 12 FEBRUARY 1945   *Wood Monkey*

12 FEBRUARY 1956 ～ 30 JANUARY 1957   *Fire Monkey*

30 JANUARY 1968 ～ 16 FEBRUARY 1969   *Earth Monkey*

16 FEBRUARY 1980 ～ 4 FEBRUARY 1981   *Metal Monkey*

4 FEBRUARY 1992 ～ 22 JANUARY 1993   *Water Monkey*

THE
MONKEY

THE PERSONALITY OF THE MONKEY

> The battle of life is, in most cases, fought uphill; and to win it without a struggle were perhaps to win it without honour. If there were no difficulties there would be no success; if there were nothing to struggle for, there would be nothing to be achieved.
>
> – *Samuel Smiles: a Monkey*

The Monkey is born under the sign of fantasy. He is imaginative, inquisitive and loves to keep an eye on everything that is going on around him. He is never backward in offering advice or trying to sort out the problems of others. He likes to be helpful and his advice is invariably sensible and reliable.

The Monkey is intelligent, well-read and always eager to learn. He has an extremely good memory and there are many Monkeys who have made particularly good linguists. The Monkey is also a convincing talker and enjoys taking part in discussions and debates. His friendly, self-assured manner can be very persuasive and he usually has little trouble in winning people round to his way of thinking. It is for this reason that the Monkey often excels in politics and public speaking. He is also particularly adept in PR work, teaching and any job which involves selling.

The Monkey can, however, be crafty, cunning and occasionally dishonest, and he will seize on any opportunity to make a quick gain or outsmart his opponents. He has so much charm and guile that people often don't realize what he is up to until it is too late. But despite his resourceful nature, the Monkey does run the risk of outsmarting even himself. He has so much confidence in his abilities that he rarely listens to advice or is prepared to accept help from anyone. He likes to help others but prefers to rely on his own judgement when dealing with his own affairs.

Another characteristic of the Monkey is that he is extremely good at solving problems and has a happy knack of extricating himself (and others) from the most hopeless of positions. He is the master of self-preservation.

With so many diverse talents the Monkey is able to make considerable sums of money, but he does like to enjoy life and will think nothing of spending his money on some exotic holiday or luxury which he has had his eye on. He can, however, become very envious if someone else has got what he wants.

The Monkey is an original thinker and, despite his love of company, he cherishes his independence. He has to have the freedom to act as he wants and any Monkey who feels hemmed in or bound by too many restrictions can soon become unhappy. Likewise, if anything becomes too boring or monotonous, the Monkey soon loses interest and turns his attention to something else. He lacks persistence and this can often hamper his progress. He is also easily distracted, a tendency which all Monkeys should try to overcome. The Monkey should concentrate on one thing at a time and by doing so will almost certainly achieve more in the long run.

The Monkey is a good organizer and, even though he may behave slightly erratically at times, he will invariably have some plan at the back of his mind. On the odd occasion when his plans do not quite work out, he is usually quite happy to shrug his shoulders and put it down to experience. He will rarely make the same mistake twice and throughout his life he will try his hand at many things.

The Monkey likes to impress and is rarely without followers or admirers. There are many who are attracted to him by his good looks, his sense of humour or simply because he instils so much confidence.

Monkeys usually marry young and for it to be a success their partner must allow them time to pursue their many interests and the opportunity to indulge in their love of travel. The Monkey has to have variety in his life and is especially well suited to those born under the sociable and outgoing signs of the Rat, Dragon, Pig and Goat. The Ox, Rabbit, Snake and Dog will also be enchanted by the Monkey's resourceful and outgoing nature, but he is likely to exasperate the Rooster and Horse, and the Tiger will have little patience for his tricks. A relationship between two Monkeys will work well – they will understand each other and be able to assist each other in their various enterprises.

The female Monkey is intelligent, extremely observant and a shrewd judge of character. Her opinions and views are often highly valued, and, having such a persuasive nature, she invariably gets her own way. She has many interests and involves herself in a wide variety of activities. She pays great attention to her appearance, is an elegant dresser and likes to take particular care over her hair. She can also be a most caring and doting parent and will have many good and loyal friends.

Provided the Monkey can curb his desire to take part in all that is going on around him and concentrate on one thing at a time, he can usually achieve what he wants in life. Should he suffer any disappointments, he is bound to bounce back. The Monkey is a survivor and his life is usually both colourful and very eventful.

THE FIVE DIFFERENT TYPES OF MONKEY

In addition to the 12 signs of the Chinese zodiac, there are five elements and these have a strengthening or moderating influence on the sign. The effects of the five elements on the Monkey are described below, together with the years in which the elements were exercising their influence. Therefore all Monkeys born in 1920 and 1980 are Metal Monkeys, those born in 1932 and 1992 are Water Monkeys, and so on.

Metal Monkey: 1920, 1980
The Metal Monkey is very strong-willed. He sets about everything he does with a dogged determination and often prefers to work independently rather than with others. He is ambitious, wise and confident, and is certainly not afraid of hard work. He is very astute in financial matters and usually chooses his investments well. Despite his somewhat independent nature, the Metal Monkey enjoys attending parties and social occasions and is particularly warm and caring towards his loved ones.

Water Monkey: 1932, 1992

The Water Monkey is versatile, determined and perceptive. He also has more discipline than some of the other Monkeys and is prepared to work towards a certain goal rather than be distracted by something else. He is not always open about his true intentions and when questioned can be particularly evasive. He can be sensitive to criticism but also very persuasive and usually has little trouble in getting others to fall in with his plans. He has a very good understanding of human nature and relates well to others.

Wood Monkey: 1944

This Monkey is efficient, methodical and extremely conscientious. He is also highly imaginative and is always trying to capitalize on new ideas or learn new skills. Occasionally his enthusiasm can get the better of him and he can get very agitated when things do not quite work out as he had hoped. He does, however, have a very adventurous streak in him and is not afraid of taking risks. He also loves travel. He is usually held in great esteem by his friends and colleagues.

Fire Monkey: 1956

The Fire Monkey is intelligent, full of vitality and has no trouble in commanding the respect of others. He is imaginative and has wide interests, although sometimes these can distract him from more useful and profitable work. He is very competitive and always likes to be involved in everything that is going on. He can be stubborn if he does not get his own way and he sometimes tries to indoctrinate those who are less strong-willed than himself. The Fire Monkey is a lively character, popular with the opposite sex and extremely loyal to his partner.

Earth Monkey: 1908, 1968

The Earth Monkey tends to be studious and well-read, and can become quite distinguished in his chosen line of work. He is less outgoing than some of the other types of Monkey and prefers quieter and more solid pursuits. He has high principles, a very caring nature and can be most generous to those less fortunate than himself. He is usually successful in handling financial matters and can become very wealthy in old age. He has a calming influence on those around him and is respected and well liked by those he meets. He is, however, especially careful about whom he lets into his confidence.

PROSPECTS FOR THE MONKEY IN 1998

The Chinese New Year starts on 28 January 1998. Until then, the old year, the Year of the Ox, is still making its presence felt.

The Year of the Ox (7 February 1997 to 27 January 1998) will have been a variable year for the Monkey and although he will have made some progress, this will not have been without considerable effort on his part. He could also have found that some of his ideas and plans have not worked out as well as he would have liked and in some parts of the year he could have found himself lacking his usual zest and drive.

However, despite its tribulations, the Ox year will still have been important for the Monkey and he can accomplish much in the closing stages. He should continue to set about his activities in his usual purposeful way and even if he feels his efforts are not bringing the response he desires, he should not let this diminish his resolve. All the time he will be adding to his experience and placing himself in a good position for when suitable opportunities do arise. This is also a favourable time for him to add to his skills and if he is able to go on any courses or take some additional training he will find this will be time well spent and will help improve his prospects.

As far as financial matters are concerned, the Monkey should avoid pushing his luck too far and being tempted by risky or speculative ventures. All is not as straightforward as it might at first appear and without care he could find himself losing money. More positively, however, the Monkey could be fortunate in the post-Christmas sales and acquire some excellent bargains both for himself and his home.

Domestically and socially, the closing months of the Ox year will be an active time and the Monkey will be much in demand with others. He can look forward to attending several enjoyable parties and functions and, on a personal level, November and December will be two busy and gratifying months. However, to preserve the normally good relations he enjoys with so many, the Monkey does need to remain aware of the feelings of others and cannot expect to have his own way all the time. To be inflexible about certain arrangements, particularly concerning domestic matters, could cause some moments of tension and is something all Monkeys should watch.

Although the Ox year will not have been the smoothest for the Monkey, provided he sets about his activities with care he will do much to negate some of the more awkward aspects that prevail. Also, there will be many occasions he will enjoy, especially in the latter part of the year.

The Year of the Tiger begins on 28 January 1998 and will be a mixed year for the Monkey. The Tiger year very much favours enterprise and innovation, and the Monkey is certainly enterprising, but he also likes to be in control and this will not always be possible during the Tiger year. He could find himself subject to events not entirely of his choosing or find that his plans are subject to change. So some of the year will prove unsettling and the Monkey will find his progress not always as great as he would like. However, disquieting though this may be, the Monkey will undoubtedly be helped by several factors. First and foremost, he is highly resourceful and once he has accepted any changes and new situations that arise he will, in his true inimitable way, look at how he can turn events to his advantage. And his enterprising spirit will certainly not let him down!

Secondly, the events of the year will help the Monkey to reassess his current situation and future aims, and in doing this he will come up with new and sometimes better plans. Also, the thought he gives to his future will help to give him a clearer idea of where he should be concentrating his efforts. As a result, he will find he is making more effective use of his time.

Finally, periods of growth and success often follow periods of change and challenge, and so it will be for the Monkey. While neither the Ox nor Tiger year may be easy for him, they will allow him to gain valuable experience and he will be able to put this to effective use in succeeding years. In many respects what the Monkey decides and achieves in 1998 will prepare the way for the excellent progress he is soon to make.

In the Tiger year, however, the Monkey will see several significant changes take place in his work. This could be through the introduction of new procedures, changes in personnel or by being given new duties. At such times, the Monkey should be prepared to adapt rather than appear too inflexible. He is a past master, though, at making the best out of sometimes challenging situations and this ability will serve him well over the year. Also, if he decides to launch any new venture or plan he should make sure he has sufficient support before starting and will find he will make better progress by acting in conjunction with others rather than maintaining too independent an approach.

Despite the sometimes tricky aspects that prevail, any Monkey wanting to change his present duties or seeking work should actively follow up any openings he sees. Although not all his applications may meet with success, determination and persistence will be rewarded and many Monkeys will find that one position they attain – even though it may not be what they were originally hoping for – will enable them to discover and develop new talents. All Monkeys will find that some of what occurs at work over the year will have important implications for the future.

As far as the Monkey's financial situation is concerned, he should aim to put his money to purposeful use rather than allow it to slip through his fingers. In 1998 there could be many temptations for him to spend on extravagances and indulgences and, without care, he could come to rue some of his purchases. In the Tiger year the Monkey would do better to save for specific items or his long-term future rather than spend his money too readily.

Another area which calls for some care is the Monkey's relations with others. In view of the demanding nature of the year there will be occasions when the Monkey feels under pressure or becomes preoccupied with his own concerns. At such times he should try not to bottle up his feelings and would find it helpful to speak to others about anything troubling him. By doing so, he will not only unburden himself of some of his concerns but also gain much from the assistance and advice he is given. Admittedly, the Monkey does tend to conceal his emotions well and likes to keep his own counsel, but in the Tiger year he really should try to avoid being too insular or independent. In addition, he should guard against taking out his anxieties on others – irritability on his part, or some sharp words, could undermine the normally good relations he enjoys with so many and this is something he should watch. Also, should the Monkey find himself in disagreement with someone over the year, he should try to resolve it as quickly as he can. If not, there is a danger that it could escalate and cause him additional and often unnecessary worry as well as distract him from more useful activities. Fortunately this only applies to a few Monkeys, but should difficulties with others emerge, these words of advice may prove helpful.

However, while the Monkey will need to exercise care in his relations, both his family and social life will still be a source of much pleasure. Indeed, he can look forward to many rewarding times with his family and will not only delight in the progress and success enjoyed by those dear to him but will also get much satisfaction from family activities. He will also devote some of his spare time to carrying out projects around his home and while these may sometimes prove more complicated than he envisaged, he will be well satisfied with the finished result. However, in carrying out projects of a hazardous nature, the Monkey should not compromise his personal safety or take risks when using potentially dangerous equipment.

On a social level, the Monkey can also look forward to some agreeable times with his friends, with the spring and summer being an active and positive time. In addition to enjoying their companionship, the Monkey would do well to listen to the advice his friends proffer, particularly any from those who speak with the benefit of experience. There will be much wisdom in their words and the Monkey should consider carefully all he is told.

Although this will be a busy year for the Monkey, it is important that he does not neglect his hobbies or interests, especially those that allow him to take additional exercise or provide him with a break from his usual daily activities. Over the year they will prove an important and valuable source of relaxation as well as bringing him much personal satisfaction. The Monkey will also benefit from any breaks or holidays he takes and should try to go away at least once over the year.

Provided he exercises care with his activities and is prepared to make the most of the new and changing situations that arise, this can prove a reasonable year for the Monkey. And what he learns and achieves in 1998 will go a long way towards assisting his progress in the more favourable Year of the Rabbit. From late October onwards the Monkey will notice a gradual upturn in his fortunes and this will gather pace as the next Chinese year approaches.

As far as the different types of Monkey are concerned, 1998 will be an important year for the *Metal Monkey*. He will learn and achieve much, but to get the best results he will need to proceed at a steady and sensible pace. Although he may possess many fine abilities and has a clear idea of what he would like to achieve, he should not be overambitious in what he attempts. To achieve some of his aims requires skills and experience he has not yet obtained, particularly as far as his work is concerned. Also, some of the conditions that prevail over the year may not be ideal for making the advances he desires. In 1998 the Metal Monkey should concentrate on getting as much vocational experience as he can and even if this is not in the area he later wishes to concentrate on, what he learns could still prove useful to him in the future. In the meantime, this is a year which calls for patience and for steady, persistent effort, with modest but creditable progress as a result. Metal Monkeys seeking work should continue to follow up any opportunities they see but also investigate types of work which they may not have fully considered before. By widening their search they will be increasing the openings available to them and this could make their quest for a position easier and ultimately more successful. Those Metal Monkeys in education will also make pleasing progress, although to obtain the results they desire they will need to set about their studies in a systematic and disciplined manner and avoid too many distractions or leaving revision to the last moment! Good planning will certainly be rewarded. As far as financial matters are concerned, the Metal Monkey would do well to watch his level of spending and particularly guard against making large purchases on the spur of the moment. By looking around he may be able to obtain better prices elsewhere and generally would do well to avoid impulse buying or being overly extravagant. On a personal level the year will generally go well. The Metal Monkey can look forward to an active (although sometimes expensive) social life and will be much in demand with those around him. The months from May to August will be a busy time socially and for the unattached, romance beckons! The many Metal Monkeys who will move over the year will enjoy settling into their new location and will quickly form some new, and in many cases, significant friendships. However, in his relations with others, be they family, friends or colleagues, the Metal Monkey must remain mindful of their views and feelings. Sometimes he can be a little too independent-minded or rigid in his views and such an attitude could cause moments of friction. This is something the Metal Monkey should watch. Over the year he may also have to assist an older relation who has an awkward problem to contend with and anything he can do to help and advise will be much appreciated, probably more so than he may realize at the time. Overall, this will be an interesting year for the Metal Monkey and while he may have to temporarily curb some of his greater ambitions, by adding to his experience he will be doing much to help his long-term prospects. From a personal point of view, this will be a fulfilling and pleasing year with good prospects for making new friends and for romance.

Although the Tiger year may not be an entirely problem-free year for the *Water Monkey*, by remaining his usual watchful self and acting in conjunction with others he will do much to minimize the more awkward aspects that prevail. To get the best from the year, however, he should give some thought to what he would like to achieve, discuss this with others and then set about achieving his objectives. By having such a plan – and with the support of others behind him – he will obtain far more satisfactory results than by drifting through the year without any specific tasks or aims in mind. The Water Monkey will get particular pleasure from projects that he carries out on his accommodation over the year, especially from redecorating or anything that would add to the decor and comfort of his home. Similarly, his hobbies and interests will provide him with many hours of pleasure, and if he is able to contact fellow enthusiasts he will find that this will not only add to his knowledge but also lead to some interesting social occasions. Family matters, too, will go well for the Water Monkey and those around him will offer much useful support and encouragement. In addition, he will take much personal satisfaction in the progress of family members, and any additional assistance and words of advice he feels able to give will be much appreciated. The Water Monkey will also enjoy any holidays or breaks that he takes and should take advantage of any opportunity to meet up with friends or relations he has not seen for some time. Such a meeting will prove memorable for all concerned. With care and by using his time well, much of what the Water Monkey undertakes over the year will go well, but there are certain aspects he does need to watch. Should he find himself in disagreement with someone he should try to sort this out as quickly and amicably as he can rather than allow it to continue unchecked and sour part of the year for him. Also, if there are any matters concerning him, particularly involving finance or matters of a bureaucratic nature, he would do well to speak to others and seek advice rather than keep his fears to himself. He will find that a worry shared is indeed a worry halved and that those around him will be able to do much to help, sometimes even resolving the problem for him. But for them to be able to do this the Water Monkey does need to be open and forthcoming. Fortunately, any awkward situations that occur are more likely to be nigglesome than serious, but the Water Monkey must not let them escalate or get out of proportion. Generally, however, he will be content with much of what he achieves over the year, with his family, hobbies and the projects he undertakes all bringing him considerable satisfaction and pleasure.

Among the *Wood Monkey*'s many fine qualities is a determined and adventurous streak and this will serve him well over the year. In 1998 several important changes will take place and, while sometimes unexpected, they will often work to the Wood Monkey's advantage. The events of the year will bring him new opportunities, especially in his work, and in his true inimitable style, the Wood Monkey will rise up and tackle the challenges before him. They will give him a new impetus to demonstrate his true worth and make the most of his many abilities. Admittedly, his progress may not be all that he would like, but the important thing is that he will set in motion plans and ideas that will lead him to better and brighter things in the future; indeed, what he accomplishes now will be instrumental in paving the way for his future success. Over the year almost all Wood Monkeys will find themselves with new responsibilities and duties, sometimes unlike anything they have done before. But daunting though some of this may be, it will offer the Wood Monkey a chance to show his versatility, gain further experience and in the process, much impress others. In his undertakings, though, the Wood Monkey should work in conjunction with others rather than be too independent in his actions. This way he will benefit from the input of others and will find support for his own activities that much more forthcoming. There could also be some financial good fortune over the year; some Wood Monkeys could receive money for some work they have carried out in the past or from an unexpected source. Either way, they should aim to put any spare or additional money towards a specific purpose rather than spend it too freely. The Wood Monkey would also do well to consider making some provision for his future, perhaps by investing or contributing to a savings scheme. In future years, this could become a worthwhile asset. He can also look forward to some enjoyable occasions with his family and friends, and will have every reason to feel proud of the achievements of a younger relation. However, while domestic matters will generally go well, to preserve domestic harmony the Wood Monkey should remain mindful of the views and feelings of those around him. While he may possess strong opinions, he cannot expect to prevail all the time and to be too stubborn on certain domestic matters could result in needless acrimony. This is something all Wood Monkeys would do well to watch. With the high level of activity over the year, it is also important that the Wood Monkey devotes time to his hobbies and interests, particularly those that allow him to unwind and provide a break from his usual daytime concerns. If there is something that has recently intrigued him, particularly an interest that would help him to develop his creative talents, this would be an excellent year in which to find out more. Although the Tiger year will bring change and challenge, the Wood Monkey will feel stimulated by the opportunities that arise and as a result will turn what could have been an awkward year into a constructive one. In the following and more favourable Year of the Rabbit, he will be able to enjoy the fruits of his labours – and what splendid fruits they will be!

The *Fire Monkey* can fare well in the Tiger year. However, to get the best from it, he should be realistic in what he attempts and not commit himself to too many activities all at the same time. Ideally, early on in the year, he should sort out his priorities and decide what he wishes to achieve. In his work he should consolidate any recent gains he has made and continue to set about his duties in his usual enterprising way. He should also keep a close watch on all that is going on around him and when changes are in the offing – something that will occur several times over the year – he should see how he can turn them to his advantage. Some ingenious thinking on his part could help him to advance his position as well as impress those around him. Similarly, any Fire Monkey seeking work or new challenges should actively follow up any opportunities he sees. He could also be helped by looking at his various skills and past experience and considering other ways in which he can put them to use. Again, some imaginative thinking could open up interesting possibilities for him. Although the Fire Monkey can, through his own efforts, make progress over the year, he should still be wary of taking unnecessary risks and, in all that he does, make sure he has the backing of others. Work-wise, this can be a constructive year for him and what he achieves will help to prepare him for the even more substantial progress he will make over the next few years. Also, if he gets any chance to extend his skills, he could find this will be very much to his advantage. The Fire Monkey will fare reasonably well in financial matters, but again this is not a year in which to take undue risks or be tempted into speculative ventures. It would also be in his interests to keep a watchful eye over his level of spending – without care and some restraint, this could be greater than he thought and involve him in having to make economies later. Personally, however, the year will prove most satisfying. The Fire Monkey will take much pride in the achievements of those around him and can look forward to several memorable family occasions, including some well-deserved celebrations. Domestically, the year generally goes well, but to preserve the good relations that he so much values, the Fire Monkey should avoid becoming so preoccupied with his own concerns that he inadvertently neglects the interests of others. To help prevent this, he would find it helpful to encourage activities all can enjoy and, at busy times, suggest an outing or some other pleasurable activity to relieve some of the pressure. Overall, this will be a reasonable year for the Fire Monkey, and by making effective use of his skills and taking advantage of the opportunities that the year will bring, he will place himself in an excellent position to make more substantial advances in the future.

The Tiger year will be a year of change for the *Earth Monkey* and, while some of this will not be of his choosing, the effects can be far-reaching and, in many cases, positive. Throughout the year the Earth Monkey must keep alert to all that is going on around him and when he finds himself in new or changing situations, look at ways in which he can turn them to his advantage. By being adaptable and adventurous in his outlook, he can gain much from the year, even though some parts could prove unsettling for him. Many Earth Monkeys will be given new duties at work or transfer to different positions, and although some of what is asked of them will be daunting, they will be well-equipped to rise up to the challenges and gain further experience as well as impress others. Also, as the Earth Monkey will find, by dealing with and facing up to the tasks given him he will learn more than if he had had everything too easy. As the Chinese proverb says, 'The gem cannot be polished without friction, nor man perfected without trials.' In 1998 the Earth Monkey will be given every chance to display his true worth and discover for himself the strength of his character and resolve. For those Earth Monkeys who are discontent with their present position or are seeking work, there will be some excellent opportunities to pursue. These Monkeys could find it helpful to consider other ways in which they can draw on their skills and past experience, and also to approach companies or organizations they may wish to work for. Enterprising action on their part could produce results or yield some useful information. Financially, this will be an expensive year for the Earth Monkey, particularly concerning his accommodation and transport. In meeting these expenses, the Earth Monkey could be helped by carrying out a review of his financial position. This way he could discover some regular outgoings that are no longer necessary and which could represent, over time, considerable savings. With careful budgeting the Earth Monkey should be able to avoid problems, but throughout the year he should watch his level of expenditure and avoid too much extravagance or any undue risks. His personal life, too, will need careful handling. There will be many demands upon his time and occasions when he will feel under pressure, especially with the many household chores and duties he will have to do. At these times, he would do well to ask those around to assist rather than cope with too much single-handed. Help will be forthcoming, although sometimes the Earth Monkey may have to prompt others into action! However, while there will be busy times in his home life, there will also be much to enjoy. The Earth Monkey will delight in watching and encouraging the activities of those around him and will also take satisfaction in carrying out some creative projects on his home and garden. Again, however, he would do well to enlist the help of others rather than take on too much himself. In view of the activity of the year, he should also make sure he sets a regular time aside for his own personal interests and allows himself the chance to rest and unwind. To drive himself too hard could leave him feeling tired and anxious and prevent him giving of his best. Although 1998 will be a demanding year, by adjusting to the changes that it will bring and rising up to the opportunities given him, the Earth Monkey will do much to prepare himself for the splendid gains and progress he will make in the next few years. This is very much a year of preparation for the far, far better times that lie ahead.

FAMOUS MONKEYS

Gillian Anderson, Francesca Annis, Michael Aspel, Mike Atherton, Sue Barker, J. M. Barrie, David Bellamy, Jacqueline Bisset, Victor Borge, Julius Caesar, Princess Caroline of Monaco, Johnny Cash, Chelsea Clinton, Joe Cocker, Colette, John Constable, Alistair Cooke, David Copperfield, Joan Crawford, Timothy Dalton, Bette Davis, Danny De Vito, Bo Derek, Jonathan Dimbleby, Jason Donovan, Michael Douglas, Mia Farrow, Michael Fish, Carrie Fisher, F. Scott Fitzgerald, Ian Fleming, Dick Francis, Fiona Fullerton, Gauguin, Arthur Hailey, Jerry Hall, Tom Hanks, Stephen Hendry, Harry Houdini, P. D. James, Pope John Paul II, Lyndon B. Johnson, Edward Kennedy, Nigel Kennedy, Don King, Gladys Knight, Patti LaBelle, Leo McKern, Walter Matthau, Princess Michael of Kent, Kylie Minogue, Martina Navratilova, Jack Nicklaus, Derek Nimmo, Peter O'Toole, Charlie Parker, Chris Patten, Anthony Perkins, Robert Powell, Debbie Reynolds, Tim Rice, Little Richard, Mary Robinson, Mickey Rooney, Diana Ross, Boz Scaggs, Michael Schumacher, Tom Selleck, Omar Sharif, Wilbur Smith, Rod Stewart, Jacques Tati, Elizabeth Taylor, Dame Kiri Te Kanawa, Harry Truman, Leonardo da Vinci, the Duchess of Windsor, Bobby Womack.

22 JANUARY 1909 〜 9 FEBRUARY 1910 *Earth Rooster*

8 FEBRUARY 1921 〜 27 JANUARY 1922 *Metal Rooster*

26 JANUARY 1933 〜 13 FEBRUARY 1934 *Water Rooster*

13 FEBRUARY 1945 〜 1 FEBRUARY 1946 *Wood Rooster*

31 JANUARY 1957 〜 17 FEBRUARY 1958 *Fire Rooster*

17 FEBRUARY 1969 〜 5 FEBRUARY 1970 *Earth Rooster*

5 FEBRUARY 1981 〜 24 JANUARY 1982 *Metal Rooster*

23 JANUARY 1993 〜 9 FEBRUARY 1994 *Water Rooster*

THE
ROOSTER

THE PERSONALITY OF
THE ROOSTER

Perhaps the most valuable result of all education is the ability to make yourself do the thing you have to do, when it ought to be done, whether you like it or not. It is the first lesson that ought to be learned.

— *Thomas H. Huxley: a Rooster*

The Rooster is born under the sign of candour. He has a flamboyant and colourful personality and is meticulous in all that he does. He is an excellent organizer and wherever possible likes to plan his various activities well in advance.

The Rooster is highly intelligent and usually very well read. He has a good sense of humour and is an effective and persuasive speaker. He loves discussion and enjoys taking part in any sort of debate. He has no hesitation in speaking his mind and is forthright in his views. He does, however, lack tact and can easily damage his reputation or cause offence by some thoughtless remark or action. The Rooster also has a very volatile nature and he should always try to avoid acting on the spur of the moment.

The Rooster is usually very dignified in his manner and conducts himself with an air of confidence and authority. He is adept at handling financial matters and, as with most things, he organizes his financial affairs with considerable skill. He chooses his investments well and is capable of achieving great wealth. Most Roosters save or use their money wisely, but there are a few who are the reverse and are notorious spendthrifts. Fortunately, the Rooster has great earning capacity and is rarely without sufficient funds to tide himself over.

Another characteristic of the Rooster is that he invariably carries a notebook or scraps of paper around with him. He is constantly writing himself reminders or noting down important facts lest he forgets – the Rooster cannot abide inefficiency and conducts all his activities in an orderly, precise and methodical manner.

The Rooster is usually very ambitious, but can be unrealistic in some of the things that he hopes to achieve. He occasionally lets his imagination run away with him and, while he does not like any interference in the things he does, it would be in his own interests if he were to listen to the views of others a little more often. He also does not like criticism and if he feels anybody is doubting his judgement or prying too closely into his affairs, he is certain to let his feelings be known. He can also be rather self-centred and stubborn over relatively trivial matters, but to compensate for this he is reliable, honest and trustworthy, and this is very much appreciated by all who come into contact with him.

Roosters born between the hours of five and seven (both at dawn and sundown) tend to be the most extrovert of their sign, but all Roosters like to lead an active social life and enjoy attending parties and big functions. The Rooster usually has a wide circle of friends and is able to build up influential contacts with remarkable ease. He often belongs to several clubs and societies and involves himself in a variety of different activities. He is particularly interested in the environment, humanitarian affairs and anything affecting the welfare of others. The Rooster has a very caring nature and will do much to help those less fortunate than himself.

He also gets much pleasure from gardening and, while he may not always spend as much time in the garden as he would like, his garden is invariably well kept and extremely productive.

The Rooster is generally very distinguished in his appearance and, if his job permits, he will wear an official uniform with great pride and dignity. He is not averse to publicity and takes great delight in being the centre of attention. He often does well at PR work or any job which brings him into contact with the media. He also makes a very good teacher.

The female Rooster leads a varied and interesting life. She involves herself in many different activities and there are some who wonder how she can achieve so much. She often holds very strong views and, like her male counterpart, has no hesitation in speaking her mind or telling others how she thinks things should be done. She is supremely efficient and well organized and her home is usually very neat and tidy. She has good taste in clothes and usually wears smart but very practical outfits.

The Rooster usually has a large family and as a parent takes a particularly active interest in the education of his children. He is very loyal to his partner and will find that he is especially well suited to those born under the signs of the Snake, Horse, Ox and Dragon. Provided they do not interfere too much in the Rooster's various activities, the Rat, Tiger, Goat and Pig can also establish a good relationship with him, but two Roosters together are likely to squabble and irritate each other. The rather sensitive Rabbit will find the Rooster a bit too blunt for his liking, and the Rooster will quickly become exasperated by the ever-inquisitive and artful Monkey. He will also find it difficult to get on with the anxious Dog.

If the Rooster can overcome his volatile nature and exercise more tact, he will go far in life. He is capable and talented and will invariably make a lasting – and usually favourable – impression almost everywhere he goes.

THE FIVE DIFFERENT TYPES OF ROOSTER

In addition to the 12 signs of the Chinese zodiac, there are five elements and these have a strengthening or moderating influence on the sign. The effects of the five elements on the Rooster are described below, together with the years in which the elements were exercising their influence. Therefore all Roosters born in 1921 and 1981 are Metal Roosters, those born in 1933 and 1993 are Water Roosters, and so on.

Metal Rooster: 1921, 1981
The Metal Rooster is a hard and conscientious worker. He knows exactly what he wants in life and sets about everything he does in a positive and determined manner. He can

at times appear abrasive and he would almost certainly do better if he were more willing to reach a compromise with others rather than hold so rigidly to his firmly held beliefs. He is very articulate and most astute when dealing with financial matters. He is loyal to his friends and often devotes much energy to working for the common good.

Water Rooster: 1933, 1993

This Rooster has a very persuasive manner and can easily gain the co-operation of others. He is intelligent, well read and gets much enjoyment from taking part in discussions and debates. He has a seemingly inexhaustible amount of energy and is prepared to work long hours in order to secure what he wants. He can, however, waste much valuable time worrying over minor and inconsequential details. He is approachable, has a good sense of humour and is highly regarded by others.

Wood Rooster: 1945

The Wood Rooster is honest, reliable and often sets himself high standards. He is ambitious, but also more prepared to work in a team than some of the other types of Rooster. He usually succeeds in life, but does have a tendency to get caught up in bureaucratic matters or attempt too many things all at the same time. He has wide interests, likes to travel and is very considerate and caring towards his family and friends.

Fire Rooster: 1957

This Rooster is extremely strong-willed. He has many leadership qualities, is an excellent organizer and is most efficient in his work. Through sheer force of character he often secures his objectives, but he does have a tendency to be very forthright and not always consider the feelings of others. If the Fire Rooster can learn to be more tactful he can often succeed beyond his wildest dreams.

Earth Rooster: 1909, 1969

This Rooster has a deep and penetrating mind. He is extremely efficient, very perceptive and is particularly astute in business and financial matters. He is also persistent and once he has set himself an objective, he will rarely allow himself to be deflected from achieving his aim. The Earth Rooster works hard and is held in great esteem by his friends and colleagues. He usually gets much enjoyment from the arts and takes a keen interest in the activities of the various members of his family.

PROSPECTS FOR THE ROOSTER IN 1998

The Chinese New Year starts on 28 January 1998. Until then, the old year, the Year of the Ox, is still making its presence felt.

The Year of the Ox (7 February 1997 to 27 January 1998) will have been a positive year for the Rooster and the aspects remain favourable right to the end. The Rooster will feel comfortable with the ordered and structured nature that prevails in the Ox year and this will have allowed him to make progress with many of his activities and develop his ideas as well as lead a satisfying personal life.

In the remaining months of the year the Rooster can do particularly well in his work. He should continue to set about his duties in his usual efficient way but at the same time use any opportunity he gets to promote his ideas or further his position. This is the time for advance and the Rooster would do well to remember the proverb 'nothing ventured, nothing gained'. The bold and enterprising Rooster – of which there are so many – can make great headway in the Ox year and it rests with him to give of his best. Similarly, those Roosters seeking employment should remain alert for openings to pursue. Persistence on their part will bring results, sometimes in a most unexpected and fortuitous manner.

Financial matters, too, are well aspected and most Roosters will have enjoyed an upturn in their financial position over the Ox year. However, the Rooster should aim to put any spare money he has towards a specific purpose, or invest it, rather than spend it too readily. Also, he would do well to make some provision for Christmas and the holiday period at the end of the year; this could prove a more expensive time than he anticipated, although, to compensate for this, December and early January will be especially happy.

Personally, the Rooster will have enjoyed the Ox year and will have had some pleasant times with both his family and friends. He should, however, listen carefully to any advice he is given by those around him; they do speak with his best interests at heart and towards the end of the year he could be provided with some information or given ideas which will prove helpful to him over the next 12 months.

For the lonely or unattached Rooster, the aspects are positive for establishing new friendships and for romance. However, to take advantage of these trends, the Rooster would do well to go out more and join in group activities. By taking action and making the initial effort, he will do much to improve his social life and make some new and meaningful friends.

Overall, the Ox year is a highly encouraging time for the Rooster and by setting about his activities in a purposeful manner, he can achieve much.

The Year of the Tiger begins on 28 January 1998 and will be demanding for the Rooster. Tiger years are periods of change and activity, and while the Rooster is not averse to change, he likes it to be at his instigation and pace. This will not always be possible in 1998. Much will happen and the Rooster will not have the luxury of laying elaborate plans or of being fully in control of events. Accordingly, some of the year will be stressful for him, but despite this, the Rooster can take heart. Many of the events of the year can work in his favour. Furthermore, he will not only gain experience and learn much, but will also find new opportunities arising – opportunities that he can turn to his advantage. So this will be a busy and, at times, challenging year for the Rooster, but it will also be a significant one.

One area in which there will be considerable change is in the Rooster's work. Although many Roosters will have made excellent progress in recent times, further upheaval is indicated and this could involve the Rooster taking on yet more responsibilities, transferring to another position or changing jobs. At times, he will feel daunted by what is happening or being asked of him, but he will acquit himself well. He is, after all, blessed with a most determined and resolute nature and this, together with his efficient manner, will help him considerably over the year as well as impress others.

The Rooster should also look at the opportunities that any changes bring. If colleagues move on, there could be openings there or, if new procedures are introduced, perhaps he could make a positive contribution. He should also actively advance any ideas he has; some of these could be well received and again help to enhance his position. The Tiger year is, after all, a year for enterprise and by being forward with his ideas and positive in his outlook, the Rooster will be able to make good gains over the year.

For those Roosters wanting to change their present position or seeking employment, the aspects are also encouraging. Admittedly, to gain the type of position they seek will require much effort and determination on their part, but their persistence will pay off. Also, if in order to make the progress they desire they feel they need an additional skill or qualification, they should consider the Tiger year an ideal time to obtain this. Similarly, if there are any ideas that the Rooster has been nurturing and not yet had the chance to put into practice, now would be a good time to seek the opinions of others and take those all-important first steps. As the Rooster will find in 1998, positive action on his part will produce results, but the initiative to take that action rests with him.

However, while the Rooster can improve his position over the year there are certain points he does need to watch. He should avoid being too independent in his actions or starting any new venture without making sure he has the backing of others. To do so could affect his level of success. Also, the Rooster should be prepared to make the most of any new situations that arise, even though this may mean he has to revise existing plans. To appear too inflexible could undermine his position and prevent him from making the most of the opportunities that occur.

As far as financial matters are concerned, many Roosters will enjoy a pleasing upturn in their financial situation over the year. This could be through a salary increase, a gift, receiving funds from another source or the fruition of an investment. However, as with last year, if the Rooster finds he has spare funds at his disposal he would do well to save part and put the rest to a specific purpose. Without certain care and planning, he could find he has spent a considerable amount with little to show for his outlay. In addition to any financial upturn the Rooster will enjoy, he could have several strokes of luck over the year and should enter any competition that catches his eye.

Another area which is favourably aspected is travel and the Rooster should aim to go away at least once over the year. He will find a change of scene and the break any holiday gives him most beneficial. Out-of-door activities will also be especially pleasurable and for the many Roosters who enjoy gardening, walking or sport, the year will hold many enjoyable moments.

In addition to the activity indicated in the Rooster's professional life, his domestic and social life will also be busy. Domestically, there will be many calls upon his time, with many household matters requiring his attention. Sometimes the Rooster may feel fraught or despair at all he has to do, but by setting about his activities in his usual methodical manner and tackling one job at a time, he will accomplish much. Also, while there will be occasions when he will feel tired or under pressure, he should make every effort not to take out any tension or feelings of irritability on others. To do so could undermine the good relations he enjoys with those around him and take the edge off what will be a generally harmonious year.

Despite the busy nature of the year the Rooster can, however, look forward to some truly pleasurable family and social occasions, with the spring and summer months being favourably aspected. For the unattached Rooster, new friendships and romance will figure prominently, although the Rooster would do well to let any new romance develop gradually and in its own time rather than rush too hastily into a commitment. This way the relationship is likely to be based upon a more secure and stable foundation.

There will also be many Roosters who will move over the year and while the moving process will take up much of their time, they will be well satisfied with their new accommodation and location. Not only will they enjoy discovering the amenities and attractions their new area has to offer, but also by joining clubs, societies and getting in contact with others, they will quickly establish a new and interesting social life.

Overall, the Tiger year is one which offers considerable potential for the Rooster. Admittedly, some of the changes that occur will cause pressure and uncertainty, but out of all this will arise new openings and possibilities. And the Rooster, with his diligent and keen manner, will indeed benefit from much of what takes place. But to get the best from the year, he does need to be adventurous in his outlook and be prepared to make the most of the new situations that arise.

As far as the different types of Rooster are concerned, this will be a significant year for the *Metal Rooster*. The Metal Rooster has many admirable qualities and possesses a fine sense of purpose. He knows what he wants to achieve in life and is prepared to strive long and hard for his goal. Over the years, these attributes will serve him well and bring him considerable success, but there will be times when his progress will not be so easy or his plans work out as well as he would like. This will be such a year and it will involve the Metal Rooster in taking some far-reaching decisions as well as adjusting to new and changing situations. It will not be an easy time for him but, for all its challenges, will still prove important. Indeed, the events of 1998 will do much to help shape the Metal Rooster's future and give him a chance to evaluate his present position and his more immediate goals as well as teach him much about himself. In this respect the long-term effects of the Tiger year can be considerable. However, throughout the year the Metal Rooster will need to continue to set about his activities in his usual conscientious manner. For those Metal Roosters in education, good progress is certainly possible and the time they devote to their studies will be rewarded with some pleasing results. These Metal Roosters would also do well to consider any vocational skills they feel they might need and investigate the options and openings available to them. In this they would do well to approach those in a position to give expert guidance and consider carefully all they are told. Also, if they are offered the chance to gain additional experience, even though this may not quite be in the sphere they were hoping for, they should take advantage of it. Time is very much on their side and the more they learn now and the more experience they can get, the more this will help them in the future. The main thing for the Metal Rooster in 1998 is to be flexible in his undertakings rather than hold so rigidly to his existing plans that he misses out on the chance to progress. Personally, the Tiger year will, however, contain some very pleasurable occasions and the Metal Rooster can look forward to attending several enjoyable parties and functions. There will also be many opportunities for him to make new friends, especially over the summer months, with the prospects for romance particularly promising. The Metal Rooster will also obtain much satisfaction from his hobbies and interests, particularly those that take him out of doors, allow him to meet others or offer him the opportunity to travel. Generally, 1998 will be a busy year for him and while he may have to modify some of his existing plans and ideas to fit in with new situations, he will gain much of value. The Metal Rooster has good prospects ahead of him and what he learns and experiences over the Tiger year will stand him in excellent stead for the future.

This will be an interesting and varied year for the *Water Rooster*. Over the last few years he will have accomplished much and seen many changes taking place. Although some further changes will occur in the Tiger year, it will generally mark the start of a more settled and positive phase for him. Indeed, 1998 will, in some respects, mark the closing of one chapter in the Water Rooster's life and the opening of another – and early in 1998 he should consider what he would like to do in that chapter. Many Water Roosters will find that they now have more spare time for leisure pursuits and that this could be an excellent year in which to learn a new skill or take up another interest, perhaps something they have been meaning to do for some time but never had the opportunity of taking up. Alternatively, they could consider extending a current hobby in some way, either by learning about another aspect or, with their fine gift for communication, writing about their interest and experience. Anything positive and constructive they can do will bring them considerable satisfaction and be time well spent. Travel, too, is favourably aspected and the Water Rooster will greatly enjoy any holidays or breaks that he takes, especially when visiting areas new to him. As far as domestic matters are concerned, this will be a busy and generally pleasing year. The Metal Rooster can look forward to some pleasurable occasions with those around him, including some memorable family get-togethers, and will also take much pride in the progress of those close to him. As always, any advice and assistance he feels able to pass on will be highly valued and appreciated. In addition, he will take much satisfaction in carrying out projects on his home and garden and while these may sometimes be more involved and time-consuming than he originally thought, he will be pleased with what he achieves. One word of warning, though – the Water Rooster does need to exercise care when lifting or moving heavy objects. A strain could cause him considerable discomfort. His social life will, however, be more active than it has been for a long time and he can look forward to attending some enjoyable parties and functions over the year. For any Water Rooster who may have had some adversity to bear in recent years or is feeling lonely, it really would be in his interests to regard the Tiger year as the time to turn his attention firmly to the present and future. Among the positive steps such Water Roosters could take would be to start new and different pursuits, get in contact with others and join in more with local activities. Anything constructive they can do will certainly help, but the initiative does rest with them. Most of the year will go well for the Water Rooster but, as with any year, problems can and will arise. In particular, bureaucratic matters could prove troublesome and if the Water Rooster has important forms to complete or is involved in any complicated correspondence, he should proceed carefully. This is not a year for taking risks or being too complacent with important paperwork; to do so could prove problematic and even lead to additional expense. For the most part, 1998 will be a fulfilling year for the Water Rooster, and by using his time wisely and constructively he will have every reason to feel content with his achievements.

This will be a generally pleasing and positive year for the *Wood Rooster*, but to get the best from it he needs to be adaptable in his outlook. When changes are in the offing or he finds himself in new situations, he should look positively at what is happening and see how he can turn events to his advantage. For the determined and enterprising Wood Rooster these are important and significant times. Throughout the year the Wood Rooster will be helped by his discerning nature, and while he may have to accept that not all his immediate goals are possible, others are, including some newer ones, and by pursuing these he can make substantial gains. In his work the Wood Rooster needs to pay particular attention to all that is happening. He could find new schemes being introduced or restructuring taking place and by keeping himself informed he will be better able to assess his situation and take advantage of any openings that might arise. Similarly, he should advance any ideas he has and show himself willing to take on new responsibilities. His diligence and commitment will certainly be recognized and by giving of his best he will impress others, including those who hold much influence. For those Wood Roosters who are seeking employment or wishing to move to another position, there will also be some excellent opportunities, particularly in the months from March to June. These Wood Roosters could also find it helpful to consider other ways in which they could put their skills and past experience to good use; enterprising and innovative thinking on their part could lead to some interesting possibilities. The Wood Rooster will also fare well in financial matters; many Wood Roosters will now find themselves in a position to carry out improvements or projects concerning their accommodation that they have been considering for some time. However, before proceeding with any major work it would be in their interests to get full and written details of all the costs involved. This may be a favourable year for finance, but it is still not one for complacency. The Wood Rooster's domestic life will be generally busy over the year, with many calls upon his time. However, despite the often high level of activity, there will be many occasions he will greatly enjoy, including some memorable family gatherings. With the demands of the year it is, however, important that the Wood Rooster does not neglect his interests and he should aim to set a regular time aside for these, particularly those that provide him with a complete break from his everyday concerns. In addition, if he does not get much exercise during the day, some physical activity such as walking, cycling or swimming could be to his advantage. The Wood Rooster should also try to go away for at least one proper break or holiday over the year; again, he will greatly benefit from the rest this will give him. Overall, this will be a positive year for the Wood Rooster and while it will bring its pressures and changes, it will also contain some excellent opportunities for progress. By being adaptable and rising up to the challenges and new situations, the Wood Rooster can and will do well.

This will be a constructive year for the *Fire Rooster* and, with his irrepressible and determined nature, he will greatly enjoy the challenges and opportunities it will bring. He will make considerable progress and go a long way towards securing some of his more cherished ambitions. However, to get the best from the year, he should aim to consolidate any recent gains he has made and consider what he would like to achieve next. In this he would be helped by talking to those in a position to give expert guidance and should be open about his future aspirations. By doing so, and by taking the initiative, he could be given some valuable advice as well as information that had not been available to him before. Also, if the Fire Rooster feels he needs to further his skills in order to make the progress he desires, he should use the Tiger year to do this, either by going on courses or by private study. By considering his future in this way, he will gain a better sense of direction as well as prepare himself for the opportunities that will become available over the course of the year. For those Fire Roosters seeking work or wishing to change their present position there will be some excellent openings to pursue, with the spring and early summer months being an active and favourable time. This will also be a positive year for financial matters, although it would be in the Fire Rooster's interests to watch his general level of spending. Without care this could prove greater than he thought and, unless checked, could result in him having to make economies later. Despite the favourable aspects for financial matters, this is still a year which requires careful financial management. The Fire Rooster's domestic life will, however, bring him considerable satisfaction. He will take much pleasure in the progress of those around him and, as always, others will set great store by his assistance, advice and judgement. The Fire Rooster himself will be heartened by the encouragement he receives and throughout the year will gain much by involving others in his own activities. He can also look forward to a pleasurable social life and to attending several enjoyable parties and functions, with the summer months being an auspicious time. Travel, too, is well aspected and many Fire Roosters will journey far over the year, with prospects of visiting interesting and, in some cases, unusual destinations. Generally, 1998 will be a positive year for the Fire Rooster and by making the most of the opportunities that it will bring he will make good and well-deserved progress.

The Tiger year will be an active one for the *Earth Rooster* and while it will contain times of pressure and uncertainty, it will also offer opportunities and allow him to improve on his current situation. Indeed, over the last few years the Earth Rooster will have impressed many with his diligent and careful manner as well as gained much useful experience; in 1998 he will be able to draw on this and make further headway, particularly in his work. Many Earth Roosters will take on new and additional duties over the year and while these may not always be quite what was hoped for, they will enable the Earth Rooster to learn different aspects of his work as well as provide him with some interesting challenges which he will much enjoy tackling. Indeed, the events of the year will give the Earth Rooster an added impetus to make the most of himself and his abilities and, as a result, he will do well. Those Earth Roosters seeking work, or wanting to change their present position, will also make positive progress and will find their persistence and enterprise rewarded. The Earth Rooster will also enjoy a considerable improvement in his financial situation over the year. While he will naturally be pleased with this upturn, he could, however, face some large expenses, particularly involving his accommodation. Some Earth Roosters will move over the year while others will decide to have improvements carried out on their home. In either case, it would be worth the Earth Rooster keeping a close watch over all the costs involved, otherwise he could find himself having to spend more than is necessary. Financially, 1998 can be a favourable year, but it is still a time for care. As far as domestic matters are concerned, this will be a busy year for the Earth Rooster, with many matters requiring his attention. Again, his efficient and orderly manner will do much to help – indeed, others will marvel at just how much he actually does do – but at times of pressure he should not hesitate to ask for assistance rather than try to do too much single-handed. However, despite the demands of the year, his home life will still bring him considerable pleasure and he will take much delight in following the progress and achievements of those around him. He will also enjoy the travelling that he undertakes over the year and a holiday that he is able to take in the summer could turn out to be one of the best he has had for some time. In addition, the Earth Rooster will get much satisfaction from his hobbies, especially those of a more artistic and creative nature. He will find these will not only be fulfilling but will also help him to unwind and to put aside some of the pressures that he might be under. Although this will be a busy year for the Earth Rooster, he will enjoy rising to the challenges it will bring and will acquit himself well. With his many capabilities and strength of character, he has a fine future ahead of him and in 1998 he will be preparing himself for the success that awaits him. Overall, a constructive and enjoyable year for the Earth Rooster.

FAMOUS ROOSTERS

Adamski, Kate Adie, Francis Bacon, Danny Baker, Dame Janet Baker, Severiano Ballesteros, Enid Blyton, Sir Dirk Bogarde, Richard Briers, Michael Caine, Jasper Carrott, Enrico Caruso, Christopher Cazenove, Jean Chrétien, Eric Clapton, Joan Collins, Rita Coolidge, Cathy Dennis, Sasha Distel, the Duke of Edinburgh, Ernie Els, Gloria Estefan, Nick Faldo, Bryan Ferry, Errol Flynn, Benjamin Franklin, Dawn French, Stephen Fry, Sir James Goldsmith, David Gower, Steffi Graf, Melanie Griffith, Richard Harris, Goldie Hawn, Katherine Hepburn, Michael Heseltine, Glenn Hoddle, Quincy Jones, Alain Juppé, Diane Keaton, Dean Koontz, Bernhard Langer, Brian Lara, D. H. Lawrence, Martyn Lewis, David Livingstone, Ken Livingstone, Jayne Mansfield, Steve Martin, James Mason, W. Somerset Maugham, Paul Merton, Bette Midler, Van Morrison, Willie Nelson, Paul Nicholas, Barry Norman, Kim Novak, Yoko Ono, Dolly Parton, Michelle Pfeiffer, Nancy Reagan, Joan Rivers, Paul Scofield, Jenny Seagrove, Sir Harry Secombe, George Segal, Carly Simon, Johann Strauss, Barbara Taylor Bradford, Jayne Torvill, Sir Peter Ustinov, Richard Wagner, Neil Young.

10 FEBRUARY 1910 ～ 29 JANUARY 1911	*Metal Dog*
28 JANUARY 1922 ～ 15 FEBRUARY 1923	*Water Dog*
14 FEBRUARY 1934 ～ 3 FEBRUARY 1935	*Wood Dog*
2 FEBRUARY 1946 ～ 21 JANUARY 1947	*Fire Dog*
18 FEBRUARY 1958 ～ 7 FEBRUARY 1959	*Earth Dog*
6 FEBRUARY 1970 ～ 26 JANUARY 1971	*Metal Dog*
25 JANUARY 1982 ～ 12 FEBRUARY 1983	*Water Dog*
10 FEBRUARY 1994 ～ 30 JANUARY 1995	*Wood Dog*

THE
DOG

THE PERSONALITY OF THE DOG

> A strong passion for any object will ensure success, for
> the desire of the end will point out the means.
>
> – *William Hazlitt: a Dog*

The Dog is born under the signs of loyalty and anxiety. He usually holds very firm views and beliefs and is the champion of good causes. He hates any sort of injustice or unfair treatment and will do all in his power to help those less fortunate than himself. He has a strong sense of fair play and will be honourable and open in all his dealings.

The Dog is very direct and straightforward. He is never one to skirt round issues and speaks frankly and to the point. He can also be stubborn, but he is more than prepared to listen to the views of others and will try to be as fair as possible in coming to his decisions. He will readily give advice where it is needed and will be the first to offer assistance when things go wrong.

The Dog instils confidence wherever he goes and there are many who admire him for his integrity and resolute manner. He is a very good judge of character and he can often form an accurate impression of someone very shortly after meeting them. He is also very intuitive and can frequently sense how things are going to work out long in advance.

Despite his friendly and amiable manner, the Dog is not a big socializer. He dislikes having to attend large social functions or parties and much prefers a quiet meal with friends or a chat by the fire. The Dog is an excellent conversationalist and is often a marvellous raconteur of amusing stories and anecdotes. He is also quick-witted and his mind is always alert.

He can keep calm in a crisis and although he does have a temper, his outbursts tend to be short-lived. The Dog is loyal and trustworthy, but if he ever feels badly let down or rejected by someone, he will rarely forgive or forget.

The Dog usually has very set interests. He prefers to specialize and become an expert in a chosen area rather than dabble in a variety of different activities. He usually does well in jobs where he feels that he is being of service to others and is often suited to careers in the social services, the medical and legal professions and teaching. The Dog does, however, need to feel motivated in his work. He has to have a sense of purpose and if ever this is lacking he can quite often drift through life without ever achieving very much. Once he has the motivation, however, very little can prevent him from securing his objective.

Another characteristic of the Dog is his tendency to worry and to view things rather pessimistically. Quite often these worries are totally unnecessary and are of his own making. Although it may be difficult, worrying is a habit which the Dog should try to overcome.

The Dog is not materialistic or particularly bothered about accumulating great wealth. As long as he has the necessary money to support his family and to spend on the occasional luxury, he is more than happy. However, when he does have any spare money he tends to be rather a spendthrift and does not always put his money to its best use. He is also not a very good speculator and would be advised to get professional advice before entering into any major long-term investment.

The Dog will rarely be short of admirers, but he is not an easy person to live with. His moods are changeable and his standards high, but he will be loyal and protective to his partner and will do all in his power to provide a good and comfortable home. He can get on extremely well with those born under the signs of the Horse, Pig, Tiger and Monkey, and can also establish a sound and stable relationship with the Rat, Ox, Rabbit, Snake and another Dog, but will find the Dragon a bit too flamboyant for his liking. He will also find it difficult to understand the creative and imaginative Goat and is likely to be highly irritated by the candid Rooster.

The female Dog is renowned for her beauty. She has a warm and caring nature, although until she knows someone well she can be both secretive and very guarded. She is highly intelligent and despite her calm and tranquil appearance she can be extremely ambitious. She enjoys sport and other outdoor activities and has a happy knack of finding bargains in the most unlikely of places. She can also get rather impatient when things do not work out as she would like.

The Dog usually has a very good way with children and can be a loving and doting parent. He will rarely be happier than when he is helping someone or doing something that will benefit others. Providing he can cure himself of his tendency to worry, he will lead a very full and active life – and in that life he will make many friends and do a tremendous amount of good.

THE FIVE DIFFERENT TYPES OF DOG

In addition to the 12 signs of the Chinese zodiac, there are five elements and these have a strengthening or moderating influence on the sign. The effects of the five elements on the Dog are described below, together with the years in which the elements were exercising their influence. Therefore all Dogs born in 1910 and 1970 are Metal Dogs, those born in 1922 and 1982 are Water Dogs, and so on.

Metal Dog: 1910, 1970

The Metal Dog is bold, confident and forthright, and sets about everything he does in a resolute and determined manner. He has a great belief in his abilities and has no hesitation about speaking his mind or devoting himself to some just cause. He can be rather serious at times and can get anxious and irritable when things are not going according to plan. He tends to have very specific interests and it would certainly help him to broaden his outlook and also become more involved in group activities. He is extremely loyal and faithful to his friends.

Water Dog: 1922, 1982

The Water Dog has a very direct and outgoing personality. He is an excellent communicator and has little trouble in persuading others to fall in with his plans. He does, however, have a somewhat carefree nature and is not as disciplined or as thorough as he should be in certain matters. Neither does he keep as much control over his finances as he should, but he can be most generous to his family and friends and will make sure that they want for nothing. The Water Dog is usually very good with children and has a wide circle of friends.

Wood Dog: 1934, 1994

This Dog is a hard and conscientious worker and will usually make a favourable impression wherever he goes. He is less independent than some of the other types of Dog and prefers to work in a group rather than on his own. He is popular, has a good sense of humour and takes a very keen interest in the activities of the various members of his family. He is often attracted to the finer things in life and can get much pleasure from collecting stamps, coins, pictures or antiques. He also prefers to live in the country rather than the town.

Fire Dog: 1946

This Dog has a lively, outgoing personality and is able to establish friendships with remarkable ease. He is an honest and conscientious worker and likes to take an active part in all that is going on around him. He also likes to explore new ideas, and providing he can get the necessary support and advice, he can often succeed where others have failed. He does, however, have a tendency to be stubborn. Providing he can overcome this, the Fire Dog can often achieve considerable fame and fortune.

Earth Dog: 1958

The Earth Dog is very talented and astute. He is methodical and efficient and is capable of going far in his chosen profession. He tends to be rather quiet and reserved but has a very persuasive manner and usually secures his objectives without too much opposition. He is generous and kind and is always ready to lend a helping hand when it is needed. He is also held in very high esteem by his friends and colleagues and he is usually most dignified in his appearance.

PROSPECTS FOR THE DOG IN 1998

The Chinese New Year starts on 28 January 1998. Until then, the old year, the Year of the Ox, is still making its presence felt.

The Year of the Ox (7 February 1997 to 27 January 1998) will not have been the smoothest of years for the Dog. He could have found progress difficult and not all his plans will have worked out as well as he would have liked. Added to this, he could have encountered some problems in his relations with others and this too could have caused him some worry.

However, life for the Dog is about to improve and from September onwards he will notice a gradual upturn in his situation. This will gather pace as the more favourable Tiger year approaches.

In what remains of the Ox year, the Dog will need to proceed carefully. In particular, he should avoid taking unnecessary risks in financial matters and be wary of speculative ventures or of stretching his resources too far. The closing stages of the year will be an expensive time for him and he needs to deal with money matters with care. Also, if he has experienced any difficulties in his relations with others, particularly colleagues, he should try to resolve them, either by sorting out the difference, seeking a compromise or just agreeing to disagree. To let impaired relations continue unchecked, without any attempt at reconciliation, may only cause them to get worse as well as give the Dog additional worry. The Dog would do well to use the more positive closing stages of the Ox year to sort out any problems and differences he has. He will find a constructive approach will do much to help and that others will appreciate his efforts and respond accordingly.

The Dog would also do well to try and complete any outstanding matters that he has at this time, including any correspondence he might have been putting off. With a concerted effort he will be able to accomplish much and this will leave him freer to enjoy the holiday period and start the new year reasonably up to date.

By nature, the Dog tends to be a worrier and takes things very much to heart. The events of the Ox year may not have been easy for him, but he will have gained considerable experience, learned more about himself and, although he may not fully realize it, have done much to prepare the way for the progress he will enjoy in the Tiger year. As the Ox year closes, it is time for the Dog to become more positive in his outlook and to give some thought to his future plans.

The Year of the Tiger starts on 28 January 1998 and, after the tribulations of the last 12 months, will be a much happier and more successful time for the Dog. Most aspects of his life are favourably aspected and he will now be able to make the progress that may have been eluding him of late.

However, to get the best from the Tiger year, the Dog would do well to consider just what he would like to accomplish. Although some changes will occur which may cause him to modify some of his plans, at least he will then know the direction he is heading in and will have some objectives to aim for. Also, with this positive upturn, the Dog should not allow himself to dwell over past mistakes or setbacks – these have happened and the Dog will have learned much from them, but now is very definitely the time to concentrate on the present and future and, in some cases, start afresh. The Tiger year will mark a new and more positive phase for the Dog and he should go forward with optimism and a determination to make the most of himself and his considerable abilities.

In his work the Dog can achieve much. Many Dogs will be given increased responsibilities over the year or have the opportunity to widen their skills and in both cases the Dog should rise up to the offers and challenges given him. This is a year in which he can show his true worth and he will impress others greatly with his tenacity, commitment and integrity. There will also be some excellent opportunities for promotion and for furthering his position and the Dog should actively pursue any openings he sees. He should also advance any ideas he has and, if there is a project he has been nurturing for some time, this would be a favourable year to discuss it with others and consider setting it in motion.

Similarly, those Dogs seeking work should remain committed in their quest. Admittedly, some may have become disheartened by previous disappointments, but they should not allow this to diminish their resolve. These Dogs should make every effort to lift themselves up, re-establish belief in themselves, tell themselves, 'I can do it!' and then go forth with renewed resolve. The Dog possesses a very determined nature and when committed to a certain objective, his sense of purpose and drive will propel him towards his goals. This will certainly be the case in 1998 and positive action on his part will be rewarded.

The Dog will fare reasonably well in financial matters over the year, although it would be in his interests to keep a watch over his level of spending. Sometimes, without a certain restraint, his outgoings could be greater than he thought and result in him having to make cutbacks later. Also, if he enters into any large agreement he should make sure he is aware of the implications and any obligations he may be placed under. This is not a year for undue complacency in financial matters, or for taking risks.

The Dog's family and social life is, however, well aspected and he can look forward to having some meaningful times with those around him. He will take much satisfaction in the progress and activities of family members and any encouragement and advice he feels able to give will be greatly appreciated. There will also be good reason for some family rejoicing over the year and this again will give the Dog much pleasure. At one of these occasions, he could even find himself the focus of attention!

The Dog will draw much strength from the support he is given for his own undertakings and at all times he should feel free to discuss his thoughts and any concerns he might have with those around him. In 1998 he will get much value from the advice and ideas of others, as well as be heartened by the obvious affection they have for him.

The Dog will also devote some of his time over the year to carrying out projects to his home. In particular, many Dogs will undertake extensive redecoration. In this, the Dog should enlist the assistance of others. This will not only make the project easier to complete but will also bring a sense of satisfaction to all involved. Similarly, the Dog will find it beneficial to encourage activities that all can enjoy – perhaps an occasional outing, a special meal or inviting friends round. By making the effort, the Dog will find his personal and home life will bring him and those around him considerable pleasure and contentment.

His social life, too, will go well. For the unattached Dog, romance is well aspected and a chance meeting could well blossom over the year. This is also a year in which many Dogs will decide to get engaged or married and personally, 1998 will be a time of much joy. For any Dog whose social life may not have been as active as he would have liked, or who has had some recent sadness or adversity to bear, it really would be in his interests to turn his attention to the present and the future. Ideally, these Dogs should aim to go out more and get involved in societies or group activities. By taking the time and effort they will enjoy a pleasing upturn in their social life. For all Dogs, young and old, the summer months in particular will be a happy and pleasant time.

Another area which is favourably aspected is the Dog's own interests and despite the many demands upon him he should aim to set a regular time aside for these. They do provide him with a good source of relaxation as well as being personally fulfilling. The many Dogs who devote some of their energies to charitable causes or who help those in difficulty will also find their efforts much appreciated. The Tiger, who rules the year, is a great supporter of humanitarian causes and will support the Dog's efforts all the way.

Naturally no year is without its problems, but fortunately for the Dog, any that do arise are more likely to be niggling than serious. Also, some could be partly self-inflicted. In 1998 the Dog should be wary of taking on too many commitments at the same time, thereby putting himself under unnecessary pressure. If he does have any matters concerning him, he should speak to others rather than brood. In some cases he could find he is worrying unnecessarily or making a mountain out of a molehill. Also, while he might consider any important forms or official items of correspondence he receives a nuisance or intrusion on his time, he should not be dilatory in completing them. Without care, bureaucratic matters could, if not properly dealt with, prove troublesome and take up much of his spare time.

Generally, though, the Dog will fare well in the Tiger year. He should set about his activities in a positive spirit and be determined to make the most of himself. The Dog possesses many worthy attributes and the Tiger year will give him every opportunity to progress and show his true worth.

As far as the different types of Dog are concerned, 1998 will be a satisfying year for the *Metal Dog*. In recent times he may have become disheartened by his lack of progress. However, in 1998, the aspects will swing very much in his favour and almost all Metal Dogs will be able to improve upon their present situation. Indeed, almost as soon as the Tiger year begins, the Metal Dog will start to feel more positive in his outlook and sense that this is 'his year'. Indeed, this will be the year in which he will make the headway he has so long been desiring, and his increased resolve and determination will certainly help him to make advances. In his work the Metal Dog will be able to draw on his many skills and past experience and seek a better and more responsible position. He should also pursue any openings that interest him and if he has been considering a switch to a different type of job, this would be a good year to do so. Similarly, many of the Metal Dogs seeking work will be successful in their quest and again their committed and enthusiastic nature will be noticed and rewarded. The months from February to April and October and November will, in particular, be an active time for career matters. The Metal Dog will also enjoy an upturn in his financial situation over the year and this will enable him to buy some items or carry out some projects on his home that he has been wanting to do for some time. However, before going ahead with any large purchase or committing himself to a major financial transaction, it would be in his interests to check the options and prices available before proceeding; this way he could make a noticeable saving. He would also do well to set some money aside for a holiday or break. Travel is generally well aspected and the Metal Dog will greatly enjoy his time away, especially if it allows him to visit areas new to him. Domestically, this will be an active year, with many matters requiring the Metal Dog's attention. However, at busy times, especially if household chores are mounting up, he would find it in his interests to set himself priorities and avoid starting or committing himself to too many projects all at the same time. Also, he should not hesitate to ask for assistance from those around him; he will find help and support readily forthcoming. However, despite the active nature of his domestic life, there will be many family and social occasions he will greatly enjoy and generally his personal life will go well. For the unattached Metal Dog or for those seeking new friends, there will be many splendid opportunities to meet others and affairs of the heart are certainly well aspected. Another area which will also give the Metal Dog much pleasure is outdoor activity and for those Metal Dogs who enjoy gardening or sport or who are keen travellers, the year will contain many special moments. Overall the Tiger year will be a positive one for the Metal Dog and by setting about his activities with determination and resolve he will make excellent progress.

This will be a good year for the *Water Dog* and one which will hold many happy and memorable times. Over the year he will find himself much in demand with both family and friends and, on a personal level, the year will go extremely well. Those close to him will be most supportive and several times during the year he will feel heartened by the practical support and encouragement he is given. While most of his activities will go well, if the Water Dog does have any matter concerning him, he should not hesitate to seek the views of others rather than keep the problem to himself. Also, for those Water Dogs in education, if there is

any subject or matter causing problems, they should ask
for further guidance rather than struggle on unaided.
Others will only be too pleased to help. These Water Dogs
would also do well to set about their studies in an
organized and systematic way and, if there are important
exams approaching, avoid leaving revision to the last
moment. In 1998 the young Water Dog can make excellent
progress and will cover much important material. As far as
the Water Dog's domestic and social life is concerned, this
will be a most gratifying year. As always, his family means
much to him and their affection and love for him will be
amply demonstrated during the year. Socially, too, this will
be a meaningful time and there will be many enjoyable
parties and social occasions for the Water Dog to attend.
There will also be opportunities to make new friends and
strong indications of romance. Indeed, in 1998 matters of
the heart will bring the Water Dog much joy, as well as
occasional anguish, but generally this will be a time of
great happiness. For any Water Dog, whether born in 1922
or 1982, who may be feeling lonely or seeking new friends,
it would be very much in his interests to make every effort
to go out more and get in contact with others. The aspects
that prevail in the Tiger year are well disposed towards
him and by making the initial effort, he can bring about a
considerable improvement in his social life. The Water Dog
will also obtain much satisfaction from his hobbies and
interests and, if possible, he would do well to extend them
in some way, perhaps by learning about another aspect or
by getting in contact with fellow enthusiasts. For the Water
Dog who has a creative interest or aspiration, it would
certainly be in his interests to promote and further his

talents. With positive input on his part he can learn and achieve much. The Water Dog will also enjoy any travelling that he undertakes, although he will find his journeys all the more rewarding by reading about his destination before he leaves and, if visiting a country with a climate differing from his own, he must take sensible precautions. Overall, though, any holidays or breaks he takes will prove enjoyable and beneficial for him. While most of the Tiger year will go well for the Water Dog, one area in which he does need to exercise care is finance. He should avoid entering into risky ventures and be dubious about any 'get rich quick' schemes he may hear about. If he has any doubts or uncertainties about any financial matter, he should check. However, this warning apart, this will be a fulfilling and rewarding year for the Water Dog and with a positive attitude, he will achieve much as well as enjoy the pleasing times the Tiger year will bring.

This will be a rewarding year for the *Wood Dog*. However, to take advantage of the favourable aspects that prevail he would do well to give some thought to what he would like to accomplish over the next 12 months. In this, he should consider any places he would like to visit, different ways in which he could spend his leisure time and also any projects that he might like to carry out on his home and garden. Then, with some ideas in mind, he can start putting them into practice. With careful planning and good use of his time, the Wood Dog can accomplish a good deal as well as enjoy much of the year. He will also be helped by the encouraging attitude of those around him and at all times he should be forthcoming about any plans he is considering. As far as his personal interests are concerned, these too will bring him much satisfaction and any Wood Dog who is able to demonstrate a skill or interest, or who can bring his work to the attention of others, maybe even by writing about it, will be gratified by the response. In addition to the pleasure his existing interests will bring, if the Wood Dog is able to teach himself a new skill – perhaps one he has been contemplating for some time – he will find this too will lead to many fulfilling hours and be a stimulating challenge for him. He will also enjoy outdoor activities and for those Wood Dogs who are keen travellers and like exploring new areas, the year will contain some memorable moments. The Wood Dog's domestic and social life will also be most pleasurable. Those close to him will be a source of much pride and he will draw considerable satisfaction from following and encouraging their activities. There will also be good cause for some family celebrations over the year and at some of these the Wood Dog can look forward to playing a major part. His social life, too, will go well and during the year he will have the opportunity to attend several interesting parties and events. The late spring and early summer will be especially active for social matters and for those Wood Dogs who may be feeling lonely or hoping to make new friends, this will be a time of many social opportunities. Generally, this will be a positive year for the Wood Dog, but there are a few areas which could prove problematical. Important paperwork and large financial transactions need particular care and if the Wood Dog has any doubts about what is being asked or the implications of any agreement he is about to enter into, he should check rather than take risks. Also, if he has to take any major decisions over the year, he should not allow himself to be persuaded into taking any irrevocable action until he is certain in his own mind that it is the right course to take. This especially applies to those Wood Dogs who choose to move over the year; they will get what they want, but it may call for some patience on their part. Generally, this will be a successful and pleasurable year for the Wood Dog and he will have every reason to be pleased with his accomplishments. What he achieves now will also have a favourable bearing over the next few years.

In recent years many *Fire Dogs* will have felt that they have not been achieving as much as they would have liked; progress will have been limited and plans beset with delays and obstacles. This year will, however, mark a major upturn in the Fire Dog's fortunes and he will enjoy considerably greater success than he has experienced of late. In the Tiger year the Fire Dog should set about his activities with renewed vigour, determined to make the most of his skills and many fine talents. He knows he has it within him to achieve much and the Tiger year will give him the chance to realize his potential. At the start of the year, however, the Fire Dog would do well to consider just what it is he would like to accomplish in 1998 and to sort out his priorities accordingly. This way he will fare much better and achieve more than if he were to allow himself just to drift through the year. His plans could involve pursuing a personal ambition, projects at work or improvements at home, but formulating his ideas and giving himself objectives will help him to gain a sense of direction for the year. Much is possible in 1998 and it rests with the Fire Dog to plan and use his time wisely. In his work there will be several excellent opportunities to pursue, some of which he could have been waiting for for some time, and these will enable him to advance his position. Also, if the Fire Dog has a talent or skill he wishes to promote, particularly of a creative nature, he should do so. His work will be favourably received and this could lead to further opportunities. The Fire Dog's domestic and social life will also go well and he can look forward to many happy and meaningful times with those close to him. He will also take much personal satisfaction in the successes enjoyed by a younger relation and any advice or assistance he feels able to give will be greatly valued. Financially, too, the year will see an improvement in the Fire Dog's situation and if he has any spare funds at his disposal he would do well to consider making provision for his long-term future. A savings scheme started or investment made now could develop into a useful asset in later years. Also, with the aspects so favourable, it would be worth the Fire Dog entering any competition that catches his eye. In almost all respects the Tiger year will be a positive and rewarding one for him. For any Fire Dogs who may have been feeling low or dissatisfied with their current position or who have experienced recent unhappiness, this is a year for positive change and an upturn in their fortunes. For many, 1998 will represent the start of a new and positive phase and it rests with the Fire Dog to give of his best and show others just what he can do.

This will be a constructive year for the *Earth Dog* and he will make good progress in many of his activities. Over the last 12 months he will have impressed many with his tenacity and self-discipline as well as have gained much useful experience. In the Tiger year he will be able to draw on this and make further headway. Others will support him and if there are any ideas or plans he has been considering, this would be a good year to advance his proposals and take action. The enterprising Earth Dog can achieve much in 1998, but to take advantage of the positive aspects that prevail, he does need to take the initiative. For the determined and committed Earth Dog, this is a year that holds considerable potential. In his work the Earth Dog should consolidate any gains he has made but at the same time actively pursue any openings that arise. Over the year several changes are likely which will give rise to further opportunities and, in many cases, the Earth Dog will be well placed to take advantage of these and assume greater responsibilities. He could also be helped by discussing his aspirations with those senior to him or by approaching those currently in the type of position he seeks. By taking positive action he could be given some useful suggestions and obtain some unexpected assistance; again, though, it rests with him to act. This too applies to the Earth Dog seeking work – a direct approach to companies or organizations he would like to work for could produce some helpful advice and alert him to possible opportunities. It would also be in the Earth Dog's interests to consider learning a new skill over the year. This could either be one that he has been meaning to acquire for some time or something unrelated to anything he has done before. The Earth Dog will find his new interest a satisfying use of his time as well as of possible benefit to him in the future. He will fare well in financial matters over the year and will be well pleased with some furnishings and equipment he is able to purchase for his home. By keeping alert he could spot some excellent bargains, especially during sale times. The Earth Dog's domestic life will, though, be busy, with many demands upon his time. However, despite the pressures and occasional fraught moment, his fine organizational skills and ability to prioritize will help him accomplish much; indeed, others will marvel at, as well as appreciate, all that he manages to do. Busy though some of the Earth Dog's domestic life may be, it will still contain many happy moments and he will take much pride in the progress and success enjoyed by those around him. His social life, too, will be satisfying and many Earth Dogs will have the opportunity to add to their circle of friends and acquaintances over the year. For the unattached Earth Dog, a new friendship made in the early spring could become meaningful during the course of the Tiger year. Travel, too, is well aspected and a holiday or break taken during the summer will be one of the most enjoyable the Earth Dog has had for a long time. Generally, this will be a fulfilling year for the Earth Dog, but to make the most of the favourable aspects that prevail, he needs to be positive in his undertakings and determined to take any opportunities. The aspects will support him well and he should aim to take full advantage of them.

FAMOUS DOGS

André Agassi, Jane Asher, Brigitte Bardot, Dr Christiaan Barnard, Candice Bergman, Dr Boutros Boutros-Ghali, David Bowie, Kate Bush, Max Bygraves, Naomi Campbell, Mariah Carey, King Carl Gustaf XVI of Sweden, Belinda Carlisle, José Carreras, Paul Cézanne, Cher, Sir Winston Churchill, Petula Clark, Bill Clinton, Leonard Cohen, Robin Cook, Charles Dance, Daniel Day-Lewis, Christopher Dean, Claude Debussy, Frankie Dettori, Donovan, John Dunn, Sally Field, Robert Frost, Ava Gardner, Judy Garland, George Gershwin, Lenny Henry, O. Henry, Patricia Hodge, Victor Hugo, Barry Humphries, Michael Jackson, Felicity Kendal, Sue Lawley, Jamie Lee Curtis, Maureen Lipman, Sophia Loren, Joanna Lumley, Sandy Lyle, Shirley MacLaine, Madonna, Norman Mailer, Winnie Mandela, Barry Manilow, Rik Mayall, Golda Meir, Freddie Mercury, Hayley Mills, Liza Minnelli, David Niven, Gary Numan, Sydney Pollack, Elvis Presley, Priscilla Presley, The Artist formerly known as Prince, Anneka Rice, Malcolm Rifkind, Paul Robeson, Linda Ronstadt, Gabriela Sabatini, Sade, Carl Sagan, Susan Sarandon, Jennifer Saunders, Claudia Schiffer, Norman Schwarzkopf, Dr Albert Schweitzer, Alan Shearer, Clare Short, Sylvester Stallone, Robert Louis Stevenson, Sharon Stone, Jack Straw, David Suchet, Donald Sutherland, Chris Tarrant, Mother Teresa, Ben Vereen, Voltaire, Paul Weller, Timothy West, Prince William, Shelley Winters, Ian Woosnam.

30 JANUARY 1911 ～ 17 FEBRUARY 1912   *Metal Pig*

16 FEBRUARY 1923 ～ 4 FEBRUARY 1924   *Water Pig*

4 FEBRUARY 1935 ～ 23 JANUARY 1936   *Wood Pig*

22 JANUARY 1947 ～ 9 FEBRUARY 1948   *Fire Pig*

8 FEBRUARY 1959 ～ 27 JANUARY 1960   *Earth Pig*

27 JANUARY 1971 ～ 14 FEBRUARY 1972   *Metal Pig*

13 FEBRUARY 1983 ～ 1 FEBRUARY 1984   *Water Pig*

31 JANUARY 1995 ～ 18 FEBRUARY 1996   *Wood Pig*

THE
PIG

THE PERSONALITY OF THE PIG

Singleness of purpose is one of the chief essentials for success in life, no matter what may be one's aim.
— *John D. Rockefeller Jr: a Pig*

The Pig is born under the sign of honesty. He has a kind and understanding nature and is well known for his abilities as a peace-maker. He hates any sort of discord or unpleasantness and will do all in his power to sort out differences of opinion or bring opposing factions together.

He is an excellent conversationalist and speaks truthfully and to the point. He dislikes any form of false-hood or hypocrisy and is a firm believer in justice and the maintenance of law and order. In spite of these beliefs, however, the Pig is reasonably tolerant and often prepared to forgive others for their wrongs. He rarely harbours grudges and is never vindictive.

The Pig is usually very popular. He enjoys other people's company and likes to be involved in joint or group activities. He will be a loyal member of any club or society and can be relied upon to lend a helping hand at functions. He is also an excellent fund-raiser for charities and often a great supporter of humanitarian causes.

The Pig is a hard and conscientious worker and is particularly respected for his reliability and integrity. In his early years he will try his hand at several different jobs, but he is usually happiest where he feels that he is being of service to others. He will unselfishly give up his time for the common good and is highly valued by his colleagues and employers.

The Pig has a good sense of humour and invariably has a smile, joke or some whimsical remark at the ready. He loves to entertain and to please others, and there are many Pigs who have been attracted to careers in show business or who enjoy following the careers of famous stars and personalities.

There are, unfortunately, some who take advantage of the Pig's good nature and impose upon his generosity. The Pig has great difficulty in saying 'No' and, although he may dislike being firm, it would be in his own interests to say occasionally, 'Enough is enough.' The Pig can also be rather naïve and gullible; however, if at any stage in his life he feels that he has been badly let down, he will make sure that it will never happen again and will try to become self-reliant. There are many Pigs who have become entrepreneurs or forged a successful career on their own after some early disappointment in life. And although the Pig tends to spend his money quite freely, he is usually very astute in financial matters and there are many Pigs who have become wealthy.

Another characteristic of the Pig is his ability to recover from setbacks reasonably quickly. His faith and his strength of character keep him going. If he thinks that there is a job he can do or has something that he wants to achieve, he will pursue it with a dogged determination. He can also be stubborn and, no matter how many may plead with him, once he has made his mind up he will rarely change his views.

Although the Pig may work hard, he also knows how to enjoy himself. He is a great pleasure-seeker and will quite happily spend his hard-earned money on a lavish holiday or an expensive meal – for the Pig is a connoisseur of good food and wine – or taking part in a variety of recreational activities. He also enjoys small social gatherings and, if he is in company he likes, can very easily become the life and soul of the party. He does, however, tend to become rather withdrawn at larger functions or when among strangers.

The Pig is also a creature of comfort and his home will usually be fitted with all the latest in luxury appliances. Where possible, he will prefer to live in the country rather than the town and will opt to have a big garden, for the Pig is usually a keen and successful gardener.

The Pig is very popular with the opposite sex and will often have numerous romances before he settles down. Once settled, however, he will be loyal and protective to his partner and he will find that he is especially well suited to those born under the signs of the Goat, Rabbit, Dog and Tiger, and also to another Pig. Due to his affable and easy-going nature he can also establish a satisfactory relationship with all the remaining signs of the Chinese zodiac, with the exception of the Snake. The Snake tends to be wily, secretive and very guarded, and this can be intensely irritating to the honest and open-hearted Pig.

The female Pig will devote all her energies to the needs of her children and her partner. She will try to ensure that they want for nothing and their pleasure is very much her pleasure. Her home will either be very clean and orderly or hopelessly untidy. Strangely, there seems to be no in-between with Pigs – they either love housework or detest it! The female Pig does, however, have considerable talents as an organizer and this, combined with her friendly and open manner, enables her to secure many of her objectives.

She can also be a caring and conscientious parent and has very good taste in clothes.

The Pig is usually lucky in life and will rarely want for anything. Provided he does not let others take advantage of his good nature and is not afraid of asserting himself, he will go through life making friends, helping others and winning the admiration of many.

THE FIVE DIFFERENT TYPES OF PIG

In addition to the 12 signs of the Chinese zodiac, there are five elements and these have a strengthening or moderating influence on the sign. The effects of the five elements on the Pig are described below, together with the years in which the elements were exercising their influence. Therefore all Pigs born in 1911 and 1971 are Metal Pigs, those born in 1923 and 1983 are Water Pigs, and so on.

Metal Pig: 1911, 1971

The Metal Pig is more ambitious and determined than some of the other types of Pig. He is strong, energetic and likes to be involved in a wide variety of different activities. He is very open and forthright in his views, although he can be a little too trusting at times and has a tendency to accept things at face value. He has a good sense of humour and loves to attend parties and other social gatherings. He has a warm, outgoing nature and usually has a large circle of friends.

Water Pig: 1923, 1983

The Water Pig has a heart of gold. He is generous and loyal and tries to remain on good terms with everyone. He will do his utmost to help others, but sadly there are some who will take advantage of his kind nature and he should, in his own interests, be a little more discriminating and be prepared to stand firm against anything that he does not like. Although he prefers the quieter things in life, he has a wide range of interests. He particularly enjoys outdoor pursuits and attending parties and social occasions. He is a hard and conscientious worker and invariably does well in his chosen profession. He is also gifted in the art of communication.

Wood Pig: 1935, 1995

This Pig has a friendly, persuasive manner and is easily able to gain the confidence of others. He likes to be involved in all that is going on around him and can sometimes take on more responsibility than he can properly handle. He is loyal to his family and friends and he also derives much pleasure from helping those less fortunate than himself. The Wood Pig is usually an optimist and leads a very full, enjoyable and satisfying life. He also has a good sense of humour.

Fire Pig: 1947

The Fire Pig is both energetic and adventurous and he sets about everything he does in a confident and resolute manner. He is very forthright in his views and does not mind taking risks in order to achieve his objectives. He can, however, get carried away by the excitement of the moment and ought to exercise more caution with some of the enterprises in which he gets involved. The Fire Pig is usually lucky in money matters and is well known for his generosity. He is also very caring towards the members of his family.

Earth Pig: 1959

This Pig has a kindly nature. He is sensible and realistic and will go to great lengths in order to please his employers and to secure his aims and ambitions. He is an excellent organizer and is particularly astute in business and financial matters. He has a good sense of humour and a wide circle of friends. He also likes to lead an active social life, although he does sometimes have a tendency to eat and drink more than is good for him.

PROSPECTS FOR THE PIG IN 1998

The Chinese New Year starts on 28 January 1998. Until then, the old year, the Year of the Ox, is still making its presence felt.

The Year of the Ox (7 February 1997 to 27 January 1998) will have been a constructive year for the Pig and he will have made good progress with many of his activities. Indeed, the Pig often thrives in the ordered nature of the Ox year and as it draws to a close there is still much that he can achieve.

However, to make the most of the trends that prevail, the Pig would do well to decide upon his priorities and set about achieving these in his usual illustrious style. As he will have found over the year, positive and applied effort on his part does produce results, and he should continue to advance his plans and ideas as well as actively pursue any openings he sees. The months from November to January will bring some interesting possibilities for him and many Pigs will find their recent endeavours will lead them to new responsibilities and duties. With determination, all Pigs can make good headway at this time.

The Pig will also have enjoyed good fortune in financial matters during the Ox year, although it would be in his interests to keep a watch over his level of outgoings. Much socializing is indicated and with December being a traditionally expensive month, the Pig will be involved in considerable outlay. However, despite the costs, the Pig will enjoy himself (socially he will be on top form!) and will have the chance of meeting some friends and relations he has not seen for some time. In addition, there could be the opportunity to make some interesting journeys in December and early January, some of which could be arranged at short notice and come as something of a surprise.

Overall, the Ox year will have been satisfying for the Pig and by setting about his activities in an organized and positive manner he will have accomplished much. In addition, the year will have contained many personally pleasing times for him, with the latter part being especially well aspected for social and family matters.

The Year of the Tiger begins on 28 January 1998 and will be a more variable year for the Pig. Over the year he will face some changes and find that his level of progress may not always be as great as he would like. However, despite some difficulties, there will still be aspects of the year that the Pig will enjoy and, with care, he can emerge in an excellent position to make more substantial gains in the near future.

In his work, though, the Pig will need to proceed carefully. He would do well to consolidate any gains he has made over the last 12 months and if he has recently been given new duties or taken a new position, he should concentrate his efforts on this. In 1998 it would be best for him to remain in areas where he has most experience rather than get involved in ambitious new ventures or schemes.

Many Pigs will, however, see changes connected with their work and will need to keep themselves informed of developments and show some readiness to adapt to any new procedures or systems that may be introduced. Although some may not be to the Pig's liking, he will need to show some flexibility in his approach and a willingness to adapt to new situations. Failure to do so could undermine his position and also reduce his chances when opportunities do become available. However, while the Pig will need to proceed with some caution, he can still gain much from the year. If he is offered the opportunity to extend his experience or go on courses, he should do so. Anything he can do to add to his skills – even if this is just through personal study – will certainly help his prospects. Also, if the Pig sees any openings that interest him, he should pursue them. Admittedly, progress in 1998 may not always be easy or immediate, but it is still possible, particularly in the last quarter of the year. Similarly, those

Pigs wanting to transfer to another position or seeking work should remain undaunted in their quest. Their perseverance will be rewarded and in the Tiger year this can often be in a rather unexpected manner! All Pigs would also do well to take note of some advice a more senior colleague or friend gives them. There will be much wisdom in their words and it would be in the Pig's interests to follow up any suggestions he is given. By doing so he could find it will greatly advance his prospects.

Another area which requires care is finance. This will prove an expensive year for the Pig, with some large costs connected with his accommodation. Fortunately his keen financial sense will help him much over the year, but it would be in his interests to keep a tight control over his purse strings and make modifications to his budget at times of expense. Also, if the Pig has to authorize any work to be carried out on his accommodation, he should obtain several quotations and a breakdown of all the costs involved before proceeding. Without such vigilance, he could find himself spending more than is necessary. Many Pigs will decide to move over the year and again it is essential for them to watch the costs involved as well as be aware of any obligations they might be placed under. Some aspects of the Tiger year can prove tricky, and finance, major transactions and important paperwork all need to be handled with care. Pigs, be warned!

With some of the pressures that the Tiger year will bring, there will be occasions when the Pig will feel a little on edge or preoccupied with events. At such times, he would find it helpful to discuss his concerns with others rather than keep them to himself. By being forthcoming in this way, he is likely to feel much better in himself and will gain from the assistance and advice of others. Also, if the Pig finds himself in disagreement with someone over the year, he should aim to sort it out as quickly and amicably as he can. If not, he runs the risk of the matter escalating or becoming an unwelcome distraction. Fortunately, the Pig is usually adept at defusing awkward situations and he will find this skill of considerable value over the year.

Another area which calls for care concerns rumours or 'too good to be true' offers the Pig might hear about. All is not as straightforward as it might first appear and the Pig should remain circumspect about anything he may learn from dubious sources.

Although much of the foregoing has been of a negative nature, with good sense the Pig will be able to overcome many of the more challenging aspects of the year and will find many occasions to enjoy himself. In particular, his domestic life, although busy, will prove most satisfying, and the Pig will take great pleasure in following and encouraging the activities of those around him. The successes of a younger relation will be a source of especial pride. The Pig will also enjoy any family outings or holidays he takes, particularly those arranged on the spur of the moment and as something of a surprise and treat. The Pig has a great fondness for the finer and more agreeable things in life and his talent for seeking out activities all can enjoy will certainly be appreciated by others. In his home life there will, however, be times of great activity. This may concern projects being undertaken on his home, members of his family moving or the Pig himself being involved in a move. At these and other demanding times it would be very much in his interests to share the burden and responsibilities rather than try to deal with too much single-handed. By asking, he will find assistance readily forthcoming.

The Pig's social life will also provide him with some enjoyable times and he can look forward to attending several interesting parties and functions over the year. Some of these will allow him to extend his already wide circle of friends and acquaintances, and for the unattached Pig, a chance meeting in the first half of 1998 could develop in a meaningful way.

In addition, the Pig will obtain much satisfaction from his hobbies and interests and will find them a welcome diversion from his usual daily concerns. Indeed, he should aim to set a regular time aside for his pastimes and could find it useful to contact fellow enthusiasts; this could help him to further his interests as well as lead to some pleasurable social occasions. Those Pigs who have hobbies of a creative nature, especially involving the arts, would also do well to bring their work to the attention of others and perhaps even enter an appropriate competition. By doing so they could find their talent encouraged in a most positive manner.

Although the Tiger year will not be without its difficulties, it will also contain some very positive elements for the Pig. Throughout, he will be usefully adding to his experience and at the same time greatly impressing others. Indeed, even when facing challenges, the Pig's sterling qualities will become evident and all this will do much to enhance his reputation and help his prospects, especially with the upturn he will enjoy in the more auspicious Year of the Rabbit.

As far as the different types of Pig are concerned, 1998 may not be the easiest of years for the *Metal Pig* but it will still prove an important one. He will be able to make reasonable progress in many of his activities, but it will require considerable effort on his part. In his work he needs to be realistic in his expectations and show some readiness to adapt to new and changing situations. Admittedly, as a Metal Pig he may hold some very definite ideas about what he wants to achieve – which in itself is a commendable asset – but to attain many of his aspirations requires patience, persistence and experience. In 1998, he should concentrate on building up that experience rather than trying to achieve too much too soon. In particular he would be greatly helped by adding to his skills and if there is a skill or qualification he feels he will need in the future, the Tiger year would be an excellent time to obtain it. Similarly, for those Metal Pigs seeking work, if there are any courses they can attend or ways in which they can further their skills, they should follow these up. These Pigs could also be helped by making direct approaches to companies and organizations they may wish to work for rather than waiting for openings to occur. Enterprising action could produce some useful pieces of information or interesting results. The Metal Pig will, however, need to exercise care when dealing with financial matters. In 1998 he could face several large expenses, particularly involving moving, new furnishings or equipment for his accommodation. To avert problems, he will need to keep a close watch over his outgoings and make sure he makes allowances for any new obligations he may be placed under. Domestically, this will be a busy but rewarding year.

The Metal Pig will take much satisfaction in following the activities of those around him and can look forward to some particularly happy family occasions. However, there will also be times of pressure for the Metal Pig, with many demands upon him and household tasks requiring his attention, even more so for those who move. At busy times the Metal Pig would find it helpful to set himself priorities and concentrate on these rather than spread his energies too widely. He should also not hesitate to ask for assistance from others rather than try to cope with too much single-handed. Similarly, if there are any matters causing him concern, he will find it better to discuss them openly than keep them to himself. Busy though the year may be, on a personal and domestic level, these will still be rewarding times for the Metal Pig and he will take much satisfaction in what he achieves. It is also important he does not neglect his hobbies and interests over the year, particularly those that provide him with a break from his usual daily activities. If he is rather sedentary during the day, he could find some additional exercise or taking part in out-of-door activities will prove beneficial for him as well. Although the year will not be without its problems and challenges, what the Metal Pig is able to achieve will stand him in excellent stead for the future.

This will be an important year for the *Water Pig* and while some of it will be demanding, sometimes even stressful, it will have a significant bearing on the next few years. The Water Pig will need to make several decisions; for those in education this could concern the choice of subjects to study or deciding which vocational skills they may need in the future, while those Water Pigs born in

1923 may consider changing their accommodation or carrying out some important alterations. In all cases, when decisions have to be made, the Water Pig should consider his options carefully, discuss them with those close to him and, if need be, seek professional advice. Some of what he decides will have far-reaching consequences and it is therefore important he chooses wisely. Two things he should guard against are being pressurized into taking action against his better judgement and rushing decisions. Time is on his side and with care and forethought he will be generally pleased with how events work out for him. Those Water Pigs in education will cover much useful material over the year and the time they devote to their studies will be rewarded with some encouraging results. Admittedly, some of the year they will feel under pressure, but they will be helped by planning their work (rather than leaving everything to the last moment!) and will learn more by rising to the challenges given them than they would by finding things too easy. The young Water Pig has a grand future ahead of him and what he learns now will be of much help to him in years to come. Those Water Pigs born in 1923 could, however, have some niggling problems to contend with, particularly concerning accommodation. Rather than keep any worry or problem to themselves they should not hesitate to seek the assistance and views of others. Sometimes the Water Pig makes the mistake of thinking that those around him do not want to be troubled by his concerns; such is not the case, and by being open and forthcoming he will receive much useful assistance. Those Water Pigs who move will, after the upheaval, take much pleasure in settling into their new location, finding out about the amenities on offer and establishing a new social life – indeed, by involving himself in group activities the Water Pig will soon make some new and good friends. All Water Pigs, whether born in 1923 or 1983, will obtain considerable satisfaction from their hobbies and interests, and should make sure they set a regular time aside for them. Outdoor activities will prove particularly enjoyable and for those Water Pigs who like gardening, walking or travelling, the year will contain some fulfilling times. Although 1998 will not be without its pressures or problems, its lasting effects will herald the start of a new and more settled phase in the Water Pig's life. And from a personal angle, the year will hold some pleasant and satisfying times.

This will be a mixed year for the *Wood Pig*, with some parts going well for him but others proving more troublesome. However, there is much that the Wood Pig can do to counter some of the more awkward aspects that prevail. At the start of the year he would find it helpful if he were to give some thought to what he would like to accomplish over the next 12 months and plan his activities accordingly. His aims could concern personal projects, hobbies, household tasks or something connected with his work, but by planning the Wood Pig will find he is making more constructive use of his time than if he were to allow himself to drift without any particular objective in mind. However, he should avoid setting himself tight deadlines – which could result in him being placed under unnecessary pressure – or getting involved in risky undertakings. He would also do well to discuss his plans with those around him and throughout the year he will find he gains much from the input and advice of others. One particular area which could prove especially satisfying concerns creative projects and if the Wood Pig has any interior decorating that he wishes to carry out or his hobbies are of a creative nature, he should make sure he devotes ample time to them. It is also a favourable year for him to consider broadening his interests in some way, perhaps by taking up something that has intrigued him for some time but which he has never had the chance to do before. In particular, something connected with photography, music, literature or art could prove particularly satisfying. The Wood Pig will also obtain much pleasure from both his family and social life. However, should he find himself with any uncertainties or problems, he should not hesitate to ask for help or advice. He should remember that those around him hold him in great affection and will only be too pleased to assist, should he ask. In particular those Wood Pigs who may be feeling lonely or have had some recent adversity to contend with should try to adopt a positive approach over the year and aim to go out more and involve themselves in a wide range of different activities. Positive action on their part will certainly help and by the end of the year these Wood Pigs will find their prospects considerably improved. The Wood Pig will also enjoy any travelling that he undertakes and all Wood Pigs should aim to go away at least once during the year. A change of scene will be most beneficial and the destination likely to surpass expectations. While many aspects of the Wood Pig's life will go well, as with every year problems will emerge. In the Tiger year these are most likely to concern matters of a bureaucratic nature and where form filling, financial transactions and ordering large items are concerned, considerable care and vigilance are needed. If the Wood Pig has doubts over any such matter, he should seek advice rather than take risks. This warning apart, there will be much to the Tiger year that the Wood Pig will enjoy and by using his time constructively he will accomplish much and help prepare the way for the more settled and favourable period that will be with him later in 1998 and throughout the Year of the Rabbit.

This will be a significant year for the *Fire Pig* with some important changes indicated. However, to make the most of it, he will need to adapt to new situations that arise, even if this means modifying some of his existing plans. With the right approach, the year will hold out several interesting possibilities for him and, in some cases, mark the beginning of a new phase in his life. The changes that occur, particularly involving his work, will bring new challenges and opportunities, challenges the Fire Pig will tackle and surmount and which will help give him a renewed incentive to make the most of himself. Indeed, for any Fire Pig who is dissatisfied with his present position or feels in a rut, 1998 will bring the changes he has long been desiring. Admittedly, some of the Tiger year will be tough and require important decisions, but the Fire Pig will emerge from it in a much improved position and, more importantly, well placed to take advantage of the more progressive times that await him in 1999. Indeed, as he will have found in the past, a period of growth and progress is often preceded by a time of change and reappraisal, and the Tiger year is such a time. As far as financial matters are concerned, this will prove an expensive year for the Fire Pig and he will spend much on items of furnishing and equipment for his home. To avoid problems, he will need to budget accordingly. This is just not a year in which he can take risks with his money or spend large sums without regard to his current financial position. The Fire Pig's domestic life will be busy – sometimes hectic! – but despite the pressures, those around him will be a source of much joy. The Fire Pig will delight in following the activities of others and there will be several family occasions that will bring him much pride and personal satisfaction. Similarly, he will be heartened by the support he receives from those close to him and would do well to bear in mind any advice he is given. The Fire Pig will also enjoy the travelling that he undertakes over the year and a holiday or break during the summer is likely to be particularly pleasurable. His interests, too, will bring him much satisfaction, particularly those that allow him to meet others and are in complete contrast to his usual daytime activities. Generally, this will be an interesting year for the Fire Pig and by rising up to its changes and challenges, he will be preparing the way for the considerable progress he is soon to enjoy. Also, from a personal angle, the Tiger year will contain some pleasing and rewarding times.

This will be a busy and varied year for the *Earth Pig*. In recent times he will have accomplished much as well as made pleasing progress in many of his activities. However, the changes that the Tiger year so often brings will cause him to reflect on his current position and just what he would like to accomplish in the future. In this respect, the year will prove highly significant. In considering his future the Earth Pig would find it instructive to approach those who are currently engaged in what he himself hopes to do one day. This way he could obtain some useful advice and assistance. It would also be helpful for him to consider any skills and qualifications he might need and to take steps to obtain these. For many Earth Pigs, what they decide and set in motion in the Tiger year will have far-reaching implications. However, while he will give much thought to his future, the Earth Pig should continue to set about his current activities in his usual disciplined manner and give of his best. Again, what he achieves and the impression he creates will stand him in good stead for the future. Those Earth Pigs seeking work should also remain active in their quest and could find it helpful to extend the range of positions they are considering. The Earth Pig does, after all, possess many diverse talents and some enterprising thinking on his part could help him to come up with some interesting possibilities. He will, however, need to exercise considerable care in financial matters. Many Earth Pigs will spend much on their home over the year and to help pay for this will need to make some modifications to their regular outgoings, including cutting back on some extravagances. Without a certain vigilance, the Earth Pig could find he is having to dip deeply into his savings over the year and these may not always be so easy to replenish as he first thought. His domestic life will be pleasant but busy and he will take delight in encouraging the activities of those around him. The progress of a younger relation will be a source of particular pride. The Earth Pig will also take much satisfaction in carrying out practical projects on his home and garden, although when using potentially dangerous tools or equipment, he does need to take all the precautions necessary; this is not a year in which to compromise his personal safety. He will, however, greatly enjoy the travelling that he undertakes over the year and will get much benefit from any holidays and breaks. With his many capabilities, the Earth Pig has a bright future ahead of him and what he accomplishes in the Tiger year will do much to prepare him for it.

FAMOUS PIGS

Russ Abbot, Bryan Adams, Woody Allen, Julie Andrews, Fred Astaire, Sir Richard Attenborough, Lucille Ball, Hector Berlioz, David Blunkett, Humphrey Bogart, James Cagney, Maria Callas, Dr George Carey, Richard Chamberlain, Jack Charlton, Hillary Clinton, Glenn Close, David Coultard, Sir Noël Coward, Oliver Cromwell, Billy Crystal, the Dalai Lama, Bobby Davro, Phil Donahue, Richard Dreyfuss, Sheena Easton, Ben Elton, Ralph Waldo Emerson, David Essex, Farrah Fawcett, Henry Ford, Emmylou Harris, Chesney Hawkes, William Randolph Hearst, Ernest Hemingway, Henry VIII, Alfred Hitchcock, King Hussein of Jordan, Elton John, C. G. Jung, Stephen King, Nastassja Kinski, Henry Kissinger, Kevin Kline, Hugh Laurie, David Letterman, Jerry Lee Lewis, Marcel Marceau, Johnny Mathis, Dudley Moore, Patrick Moore, Morrissey, John Mortimer, Wolfgang Amadeus Mozart, Michael Parkinson, Luciano Pavarotti, Prince Rainier of Monaco, Maurice Ravel, Ronald Reagan, Ginger Rogers, Nick Ross, Salman Rushdie, Baroness Sue Ryder of Warsaw, Pete Sampras, Arantxa Sanchez, Carlos Santana, Arnold Schwarzenegger, Steven Spielberg, Emma Thompson, Tracey Ullman, Michael Winner, the Duchess of York.

APPENDIX

The relationship between the 12 animal signs – both on a personal level and business level – is an important aspect of Chinese horoscopes and in this appendix the compatibility between the signs is shown in the two tables that follow. Also included are the names of the signs ruling the hours of the day and from this it is possible to find your ascendant and discover yet another aspect of your personality.

PERSONAL RELATIONSHIPS

KEY

1 Excellent. Great rapport.
2 A successful relationship. Many interests in common.
3 Mutual respect and understanding. A good relationship.
4 Fair. Needs care and some willingness to compromise in order for the relationship to work.
5 Awkward. Possible difficulties in communication with few interests in common.
6 A clash of personalities. Very difficult.

	Rat	Ox	Tiger	Rabbit	Dragon	Snake	Horse	Goat	Monkey	Rooster	Dog	Pig
Rat	1											
Ox	1	3										
Tiger	4	6	5									
Rabbit	5	2	3	2								
Dragon	1	5	4	3	2							
Snake	3	1	6	2	1	5						
Horse	6	5	1	5	3	4	2					
Goat	5	5	3	1	4	3	2	2				
Monkey	1	3	6	3	1	3	5	3	1			
Rooster	5	1	5	6	2	1	2	5	5	5		
Dog	3	4	1	2	6	3	1	5	3	5	2	
Pig	2	3	2	2	2	6	3	2	2	3	1	2

BUSINESS RELATIONSHIPS

KEY
1 Excellent. Marvellous understanding and rapport.
2 Very good. Complement each other well.
3 A good working relationship and understanding can be developed.
4 Fair, but compromise and a common objective are often needed to make this relationship work.
5 Awkward. Unlikely to work, either through lack of trust, understanding or the competitiveness of the signs.
6 Mistrust. Difficult. To be avoided.

	Rat	Ox	Tiger	Rabbit	Dragon	Snake	Horse	Goat	Monkey	Rooster	Dog	Pig
Rat	2											
Ox	1	3										
Tiger	3	6	5									
Rabbit	4	3	3	3								
Dragon	1	4	3	3	3							
Snake	3	2	6	4	1	5						
Horse	6	5	1	5	3	4	4					
Goat	5	5	3	1	4	3	3	2				
Monkey	2	3	4	5	1	5	4	4	3			
Rooster	5	1	5	5	2	1	2	5	5	6		
Dog	4	5	2	3	6	4	2	5	3	5	4	
Pig	3	3	3	2	3	5	4	2	3	4	3	1

YOUR ASCENDANT

The ascendant has a very strong influence on your personality and, together with the information already given about your sign and the effects of the element on your sign, it will help you gain even greater insight into your true personality according to Chinese horoscopes.

The hours of the day are named after the 12 animal signs and the sign governing the time you were born is your ascendant. To find your ascendant, look up the time of your birth on the table below, bearing in mind any local time differences in the place you were born.

11 p.m.	to	1 a.m.	The hours of the Rat
1 a.m.	to	3 a.m.	The hours of the Ox
3 a.m.	to	5 a.m.	The hours of the Tiger
5 a.m.	to	7 a.m.	The hours of the Rabbit
7 a.m.	to	9 a.m.	The hours of the Dragon
9 a.m.	to	11 a.m.	The hours of the Snake
11 a.m.	to	1 p.m.	The hours of the Horse
1 p.m.	to	3 p.m.	The hours of the Goat
3 p.m.	to	5 p.m.	The hours of the Monkey
5 p.m.	to	7 p.m.	The hours of the Rooster
7 p.m.	to	9 p.m.	The hours of the Dog
9 p.m.	to	11 p.m.	The hours of the Pig

RAT: The influence of the Rat as ascendant is likely to make the sign more outgoing, more sociable and also more careful with money. A particularly beneficial influence for those born under the sign of the Rabbit, Horse, Monkey and Pig.

OX: The Ox as ascendant has a restraining, cautionary and steadying influence which many signs will benefit from. This ascendant also promotes self-confidence and will-power and is an especially good ascendant for those born under the signs of the Tiger, Rabbit and Goat.

TIGER: This ascendant is a dynamic and stirring influence which makes the sign more outgoing, more action-orientated and more impulsive. A generally favourable ascendant for the Ox, Tiger, Snake and Horse.

RABBIT: The Rabbit as ascendant has a moderating influence, making the sign more reflective, serene and discreet. A particularly beneficial influence for the Rat, Dragon, Monkey and Rooster.

DRAGON: The Dragon as ascendant gives strength, determination and an added ambition to the sign. A favourable influence for those born under the signs of the Rabbit, Goat, Monkey and Dog.

SNAKE: The Snake as ascendant can make the sign more reflective, more intuitive and more self-reliant. A good influence for the Tiger, Goat and Pig.

HORSE: The influence of the Horse will make the sign more adventurous, more daring and, on some occasions, more fickle. Generally a beneficial influence for the Rabbit, Snake, Dog and Pig.

GOAT: This ascendant will make the sign more tolerant, easy-going and receptive. The Goat could also impart some creative and artistic qualities to the sign. An especially good influence for the Ox, Dragon, Snake and Rooster.

MONKEY: The Monkey as ascendant is likely to impart a delicious sense of humour and fun to the sign. He will make the sign more enterprising and outgoing – a particularly good influence for the Rat, Ox, Snake and Goat.

ROOSTER: The Rooster as ascendant helps to give the sign a lively, outgoing and very methodical manner. Its influence will increase efficiency and is good for the Ox, Tiger, Rabbit and Horse.

DOG: The Dog as ascendant makes the sign more reasonable and fair-minded as well as giving an added sense of loyalty. A very good ascendant for the Tiger, Dragon and Goat.

PIG: The influence of the Pig can make the sign more sociable, content and self-indulgent. It is also a caring influence and one which can make the sign want to help others. A good ascendant for the Dragon and Monkey.

HOW TO GET THE BEST FROM YOUR CHINESE SIGN AND THE YEAR

To supplement the earlier chapters on the personality and horoscope of the signs, I have included in this appendix a guide on how you can get the best out of your sign and the year.

Each of the 12 Chinese signs possesses its own unique strengths and by identifying them you can use them to your advantage. Similarly, by becoming aware of possible weaknesses you can do much to rectify them and in this respect I hope the following sections will be useful. Also included are some tips on how you can get the best from this most interesting of Chinese years. The areas covered are general prospects, career prospects, finance and relations with others.

THE RAT

The Rat is blessed with many fine talents but his undoubted strength lies in his ability to get on with others. He is sociable, charming and a good judge of character. He also possesses a shrewd mind and is good at spotting opportunities.

However, to make the most of himself and his abilities, the Rat does need to impose some discipline upon himself. He should resist the temptation (sometimes very great!) of getting involved in too many activities all at the same time and decide upon his priorities and objectives. By concentrating his energies on specific matters he will fare much better as a result. Also, given his personable manner, he should seek out positions where he can use his personal relations skills to good effect. For a career, sales and marketing could prove ideal.

The Rat is also astute in dealing with finance but, while often thrifty, he can sometimes give way to moments of indulgence. Although he deserves to enjoy the money he has so carefully earned, it may sometimes be in his interests to exercise more restraint when tempted to satisfy too many extravagant whims!

The Rat's family and friends are also most important to him and while he is loyal and protective towards them, he does tend to keep his worries and concerns to himself. He would be helped if he were more willing to discuss any anxieties he has. Those around the Rat think highly of him and are prepared to do much to help him, but for them to do this he does need to be less secretive and guarded.

With his sharp mind, keen imagination and sociable manner, the Rat does, however, have much in his favour. First, though, he should decide what he wants to achieve and then concentrate upon his chosen objectives. When he has commitment, the Rat can be irrepressible and, given his considerable charm, he can often be irresistible as well! Provided he channels his energies wisely he can make much of his life.

Advice for the Rat's Year Ahead

GENERAL PROSPECTS

The Tiger year may bring its challenges but the resourceful Rat will, as ever, be able to make something of it. True, he may have to forsake some of his existing plans and will have to adapt to the changes that occur but, out of these, new and exciting possibilities will emerge. The long-term effects and benefits of the Tiger year are, for the Rat, often significant. A good year for travel.

CAREER PROSPECTS

The Tiger year is one which favours enterprise and by rising to the challenges given him the Rat can do well. However, progress will not always be easy or automatic – the Rat will need to work hard and make the most of new situations as they arise. Over the year many Rats will see changes in their duties and these will help broaden their experience as well as be to their future benefit.

FINANCE

Although the Rat is careful with his money, this is a year for caution. He should avoid taking undue risks or being overly extravagant and must check the terms and obligations of any important agreement he enters into. This is just not a year in which he can afford to be complacent or push his luck too far.

RELATIONS WITH OTHERS

Domestically, this will be a busy year with many demands on the Rat's time. However, his family and friends will be most supportive and when facing decisions or problems he would do well to seek their views and advice. Similarly, the assistance he is able to give to others in 1998 will be much appreciated. Those Rats seeking new friends or who move to a new area should aim to go out more and get in contact with others. Positive effort on their part will prove well worth their while.

THE OX

Strong-willed, determined and resolute, the Ox certainly has a mind of his own! He is also persistent and sets about achieving his objectives with a dogged determination. In addition, he is reliable and tenacious and is often a source of inspiration to others. The Ox is a doer and an achiever and in life he often accomplishes much. However, for him to really excel, he would do well to try and correct his weaknesses.

Being so resolute and having such a strong sense of purpose, the Ox can be inflexible and narrow-minded. He can be resistant to change and prefers to set about his activities in his own way rather than be too dependent on others. He should aim to be more outgoing and adventurous in his outlook. His dislike of change can sometimes be to his detriment and if he were prepared to be more adaptable he could find his progress both easier and smoother.

The Ox would also be helped if he were to broaden his range of interests and become more relaxed in his approach. At times he can be so preoccupied with his own activities that he is not always as mindful of others as he should be and his demeanour can sometimes be studious and serious. There are times when he would benefit from a lighter touch.

However, the Ox is true to his word and loyal to his family and friends. He is admired and respected by others and his tremendous will-power usually enables him to secure much in life.

Advice for the Ox's Year Ahead

GENERAL PROSPECTS

With the bustle, activity and change that the Tiger year will bring, the Ox will sometimes feel ill at ease. However, to get the best from the year, he will need to watch developments closely and be prepared to adapt to the changing situations in which he finds himself. The year will also give him the opportunity to consider his present position and future aims. The plans he draws up and experience he obtains now will serve him well and lay the foundation for the better times he is soon to experience.

CAREER PROSPECTS

In 1998 the Ox will impress others with his careful and thorough approach, but throughout the year he must keep himself informed of all that is happening around him. This is not a year in which he can adopt a 'go it alone' attitude or appear too inflexible. He should take advantage of training opportunities and ways to extend his experience. Anything he can do to improve his prospects and add to his skills will be of considerable help to him.

FINANCE

Several large expenses are indicated and the Ox would do well to watch his level of outgoings carefully. He should also make sure that he checks the terms and obligations of any agreement he enters into.

RELATIONS WITH OTHERS

The Ox will greatly enjoy the company of his family and friends over the year and will delight in joining in with and encouraging their various activities. At busy times, or when facing any problems or uncertainties, he should seek the advice and assistance of others rather than pressing on single-handed. Despite the many demands upon his time, he should also make sure he does not neglect his hobbies and interests. These too will bring him much satisfaction.

THE TIGER

Lively, innovative and enterprising, the Tiger is one who enjoys an active lifestyle. He has a wide range of interests, an alert mind and a genuine liking of others. He likes to live life to the full. However, despite his enthusiastic and well-meaning ways, he does not always make the most of his considerable potential.

By being so versatile, the Tiger does have a tendency to jump from one activity to another or dissipate his energies by trying to do too much at any one time. To make the most of himself he should try to exercise a certain amount of self-discipline. Ideally, he should decide how best he can use his abilities, give himself some objectives and stick with these. If he can overcome his restless tendencies and persist in what he does, he will find he will accomplish much more.

Also, in spite of his sociable manner, the Tiger likes to retain a certain independence in his actions and while few begrudge him this, he would sometimes find life easier if he were more prepared to work in conjunction with others. His reliance upon his own judgement does sometimes mean that he excludes the views and advice of those around him, and this can be to his detriment. The Tiger may possess an independent spirit, but he must not let his independence go too far!

The Tiger does, however, have much in his favour. He is bold, original and quick-witted. If he can keep his restless nature in check he can enjoy considerable success. In addition, his engaging personality makes him one who is much admired and well-liked.

Advice for the Tiger's Year Ahead

GENERAL PROSPECTS

This is the Tiger's own year and one which holds much promise. He should set about his activities with renewed determination and vigour, putting past disappointments behind him and resolving to show everybody his true and wonderful worth. For the committed and determined Tiger these are auspicious times.

CAREER PROSPECTS

There will be many chances for the Tiger to improve his position in 1998. He should pursue any opportunities he sees as well as explore new avenues for his talents. He should also promote his ideas and continue to set about all he does in his usual enterprising and earnest way. These are progressive times and he should aim to make the most of them.

FINANCE

The Tiger can look forward to an improvement in his financial situation over the year. However, he should put any additional money he has to good use rather than be too lavish with his spending. Without care, he could find he is spending much on comparatively little! With this financial upturn, this is also a good time for the Tiger to consider making provision for his long-term future.

RELATIONS WITH OTHERS

The Tiger's family and friends will bring him considerable joy over the year and he can look forward to many pleasurable family and social occasions. Those around him will also give him much useful support and he would do well to heed any advice he is given. For those Tigers who are unattached, there will be many opportunities to meet others and build up new friendships. The prospects for romance and marriage are excellent. A year the Tiger will greatly enjoy.

THE RABBIT

The Rabbit is certainly one who appreciates the finer things in life. With his good taste, companionable nature and wide range of interests, he knows how to live well – and usually does!

However, for all his finesse and style, the Rabbit does possess traits he would do well to watch. His desire for a settled lifestyle makes him err on the side of caution. He dislikes change and as a consequence can miss out on opportunities. Also, there are many Rabbits who will go to great lengths to avoid difficult and fraught situations, and again, while few may relish these, sometimes in life it is necessary to take risks or stand your ground just to get on. At times it would certainly be in the Rabbit's interests to be bolder and more assertive in going after whatever he desires.

The Rabbit also attaches great importance to his relations with others and while he has a happy knack of getting on with most, he can be sensitive to criticism. In this, difficult though it may be, he should really try to develop a thicker skin. He should recognize that criticism, as well as some of the problems that occur in life (and which he strives so much to avoid), can be constructive and provide valuable learning opportunities.

The Rabbit, though, with his agreeable manner, keen intellect and shrewd judgement, does have much in his favour and invariably makes much of his life – and usually enjoys it too!

Advice for the Rabbit's Year Ahead

GENERAL PROSPECTS

An active year ahead – sometimes too active for the Rabbit's liking! The year will bring change and some uncertainties, but in the long run much of what happens will work to the Rabbit's advantage. He should pursue the opportunities that the year will bring, be prepared to adapt to the changes that occur and plan for the future. Excellent times await the Rabbit in 1999 and what he accomplishes in the Tiger year will help prepare him for the success he is soon to enjoy.

CAREER PROSPECTS

The Rabbit could feel uneasy about some of the changes that take place, although sometimes these will herald new opportunities for him. However, by setting about his duties in his usual thorough way and showing some willingness to adapt to new situations, he will impress others and this will help his progress. He should also give serious thought to his objectives for the next few years and if he feels he needs additional skills or experience, he should take steps to obtain these. This is very much a preparatory year for the significant advances the Rabbit will make in the future.

FINANCE

The Rabbit is usually careful and skilled when dealing with financial matters and in 1998 must not let his vigilance slip. This is not a year for risks or complacency. Rabbits, take note!

RELATIONS WITH OTHERS

The Rabbit can look forward to many pleasurable occasions with both family and friends and will get much satisfaction from his personal life. However, with some of the pressures of the year there may be occasions when he will feel edgy. At these times, the Rabbit should make every effort not to take out any feelings of irritability on others. If not, some relations could become temporarily strained. At times of pressure the Rabbit really would find it helpful to speak to others rather than keep his concerns to himself.

THE DRAGON

Enthusiastic, enterprising and honourable, the Dragon possesses many admirable qualities and his life is often full and varied. He is always one who gives of his best and even though not all his endeavours may meet with success, he is nonetheless resilient and hardy. As a person, he is much admired and respected.

However, for all his many qualities, the Dragon can be blunt and forthright and, through sheer strength of character, sometimes domineering. It would certainly be in his interests to listen more closely to others rather than be so self-reliant. Also, his enthusiasm can sometimes get the better of him and he can be impulsive. To make the most of his abilities, he should set himself priorities and set about his activities in a disciplined and systematic way. More tact and diplomacy might not come amiss either!

However, with his lively and outgoing manner, the Dragon is popular and well-liked. With good fortune on his side (and the Dragon is often lucky), his life is almost certain to be eventful and fulfilling. He has many talents and if he uses them wisely he will enjoy much success.

Advice for the Dragon's Year Ahead

GENERAL PROSPECTS

This is a year which offers the Dragon considerable scope and he should pursue his activities with vigour and resolve. It is a time for starting new projects, setting in motion long-held ideas and going after his objectives. For the bold and enterprising Dragon, this can be a positive and fulfilling year.

CAREER PROSPECTS

Considerable progress is possible. In 1998 the Dragon should remain alert for ways in which he can promote himself, his talents and ideas. His enterprise and enthusiasm will be noticed and rewarded and most Dragons will be able to significantly advance their position. For those Dragons seeking work or looking for fresh challenges, the year will contain many opportunities. Throughout the Tiger year the Dragon has much in his favour.

FINANCE

This year will mark an upturn in the Dragon's financial position. However, he should not allow his good fortune to lead him to too many extravagances or careless spending. In 1998 it would be worth him planning his purchases, saving for specific items and also making some provision for the future.

RELATIONS WITH OTHERS

A highly favourable year. The Dragon's domestic and social life will go well and he will find himself in great demand with others. He will obtain encouragement and useful support for his activities, but should listen carefully to any advice he is given, particularly from those who speak with the benefit of experience. The year also favours new friendships and romance and on a personal level will be a year the Dragon will much enjoy.

THE SNAKE

The Snake is blessed with a keen intellect. He has wide interests, an enquiring mind and good judgement. He tends to be quiet and thoughtful and plans his activities with considerable care. With his fine abilities he often does well in life, but he does possess traits which can undermine his progress.

The Snake is often guarded in his actions and sometimes loses out to those who are more action-oriented and assertive. He can also be a loner and likes to retain a certain independence in his actions, and this too can hamper his progress. It would be in his interests to be more forth-coming and involve others more readily in his plans. The Snake has many talents and possesses a warm and rich personality but there is a danger that this can remain concealed behind his often quiet and reserved manner. It really would be in his interests to aim to be more outgoing and show others his true worth.

However, the Snake is very much his own master. He invariably knows what he wants in life and is often prepared to journey long and hard to achieve his objectives. He does, though, have it in his power to make that journey easier. Lose some of that reticence, Snake, be more open, be more assertive and do not be afraid of the occasional risk!

Advice for the Snake's Year Ahead

GENERAL PROSPECTS

The Snake could well feel uneasy with the change and activity that the Tiger year will bring. However, he is wise enough to realize that change is necessary and that out of it can come new chances and opportunities. The patient Snake will, for the most part, content himself with observing (and adapting) to events, but when an opportunity presents itself, he will strike. And although this is essentially a year for care, there will still be opportunities to pursue. It is also an excellent year for the Snake to add to his experience and to prepare himself for the better times that await him in 1999.

CAREER PROSPECTS

Although the Snake is often a loner, it is essential that he does not distance himself too much from events or ignore the views of those around him this year. Many changes are possible and by observing what is happening the Snake will spot some excellent opportunities that he can turn to his advantage. This will not be an easy year, but by using his initiative the Snake can make progress or set in motion plans that will take him to better things in the future.

FINANCE

Although the Snake is often so careful when dealing with money, in 1998 he must not let his vigilance slip. He needs to keep a close watch over his outgoings, check the small print of any agreement he enters into and avoid risky or speculative ventures. Without care, it could be easy for the Snake to overspend or lose money in 1998. Snakes, take note!

RELATIONS WITH OTHERS

This is one of the more favourably aspected areas of the Snake's life this year and he will take much comfort from the support and encouragement he is given by those around him. Although this will be a busy year domestically, his family will be a source of much happiness. Socially, too, the year will contain some pleasurable occasions for the Snake and a new and important friendship could well be formed over the year.

THE HORSE

Versatile, hard-working and sociable, the Horse makes his mark wherever he goes. He has an eloquent and engaging manner and makes friends with ease. He is quick-witted, has an alert mind and is certainly not averse to taking risks or experimenting with new ideas.

The Horse possesses a strong and likeable personality but he does also have his weaknesses. With his wide interests he does not always finish everything he starts and he would do well to be more persevering. He has it within him to achieve considerable success but when he has made his plans he should stick with them. To make the most of his talents he does need to overcome his restless tendencies.

The Horse loves company and values both his family and friends. However, there will have been many a time when he has spoken in haste and regretted his words or lost his temper. Throughout his life, the Horse needs to keep his temper in check and learn to be diplomatic in tense situations. If not, he could risk jeopardizing the respect and good relations he so much values by a thoughtless remark or action.

The Horse, though, has a multitude of talents and a lively and outgoing personality. If he can overcome his restless and volatile nature, he can lead a rich and highly fulfilling life.

Advice for the Horse's Year Ahead

GENERAL PROSPECTS

Great times ahead. This is a year of considerable progress and the Horse should set about his activities with fresh resolve, determined to make the most of himself and his abilities. Personally, this will also be a rewarding and most enjoyable year.

CAREER PROSPECTS

A year of many interesting possibilities. New chances, new situations and new opportunities – great things await the Horse and he can make considerable headway in his work. This is a year when he should go after his goals and aspirations and actively follow up the many chances that the year will bring. This is a progressive and significant time and all Horses should aim to advance and improve on their position over the year. Their talents and efforts will be recognized and rewarded.

FINANCE

This will be a year of considerable expense and the Horse will need to keep a close watch over outgoings. This is not a time for taking risks or indulging in too many expensive indulgences. To avoid problems and having to make too many economies, care and a certain restraint are needed.

RELATIONS WITH OTHERS

The Horse places great store on his social life and 1998 will be no disappointment. Parties, functions, events – the Horse will be much in demand and will also have the opportunity to build up some new friendships. For the unattached Horse, romance is well aspected. Domestically, too, these will be rewarding times and the Horse will value the support, encouragement and advice he is given by those close to him. His relations with others mean much to him and in 1998 his personal life will be rich and rewarding.

THE GOAT

The Goat has a warm, friendly and understanding manner and gets on well with most. He is generally easy-going, has a fond appreciation of the finer things in life and possesses a rich imagination. He is often artistic and enjoys the creative arts and outdoor activities.

However, despite his engaging manner, there lurks beneath his skin a sometimes tense and pessimistic nature. The Goat can be a worrier and without the support and encouragement of others can feel insecure and be hesitant in his actions.

To make the most of himself and his abilities the Goat should aim to become more assertive and decisive as well as more at ease with himself. He has much in his favour, but he really does need to promote himself more and aim to be bolder in his actions. He would also be helped if he were to sort out his priorities and set about his activities in an organized and disciplined manner. There are some Goats who tend to be haphazard in the way they go about things and this can hamper their progress.

Although the Goat will always value the support and backing of others, it would also be in his interests to become more independent in his actions and not be so reticent about striking out on his own. He does, after all, possess many talents, as well as a sincere and likeable personality, and by always giving of his best, he can make his life rich, rewarding and enjoyable.

Advice for the Goat's Year Ahead

GENERAL PROSPECTS

What the Goat undertakes and achieves over the year will have important implications for the future. This is a year which will contain significant change and while the Goat may feel unsettled by some of the events that take place, many of them will prove important and necessary prerequisites for the improved times he will enjoy over the next few years. By making the most of his talents and skills, the Goat will do much to enhance both his position and prospects.

CAREER PROSPECTS

The Goat needs to stay alert to all that is happening. Many changes will take place over the year, some of which will hold interesting possibilities for the Goat. However, in order to progress, he will need to show some flexibility in his outlook and be prepared to make the most of the conditions that prevail. The determined and enterprising Goat can achieve much over the year and prepare for the advances and successes he will make in 1999.

FINANCE

The Goat will need to watch his level of spending over the year and make sure he budgets accordingly when making large purchases or entering into any new transaction or commitment. Money and savings spent during the Tiger year could take some time to replenish. Goats, be warned!

RELATIONS WITH OTHERS
The Goat will find himself much in demand with both family and friends and many pleasurable occasions are indicated. With the high level of activity over the year, the Goat's family, social life and hobbies will all be of considerable value to him.

THE MONKEY

Lively, enterprising and innovative, the Monkey certainly knows how to impress. He has wide interests, a good sense of fun and relates well to others. He also possesses a shrewd mind and often has a happy knack of turning events and situations to his advantage.

However, despite his versatility and considerable gifts, the Monkey does have his weaknesses. He often lacks persistence, can get distracted easily and also places tremendous reliance upon his own judgement. While his belief in himself is a commendable asset, it would certainly be in his interests to be more mindful of the advice and views of others. Also, while he likes to keep tabs on all that is going on around him, he can be evasive and secretive with regard to his own feelings and activities, and again a more forthcoming attitude would be to his advantage.

The Monkey also possesses a most enterprising nature, although in his desire to succeed he can sometimes be tempted to cut corners or be crafty. He should recognize that such actions can rebound on him!

However, the Monkey is resourceful and his sheer strength of character will lead him to an interesting and varied life. If he can channel his considerable energies wisely and overcome his sometimes restless tendencies, his life can be crowned with success and achievement. Added to which, with his amiable personality, he will enjoy the friendship of many.

Advice for the Monkey's Year Ahead

GENERAL PROSPECTS

Not the easiest of years for the Monkey, but his resourcefulness and ability to adapt to fast-changing situations will be very much to his advantage. In 1998 he will need to stay alert to all that is going on and make sure he acts in conjunction with others rather than remains too independent. This is a year which calls for considerable care, but to compensate for some of its more challenging aspects, what the Monkey achieves will do much to prepare the way for the more significant advances he will make in succeeding years.

CAREER PROSPECTS

A challenging year ahead with the prospects of new and sometimes daunting responsibilities. However, the Monkey thrives on challenge, and his enterprise and resourcefulness will see him through. He will emerge from the year wiser, more experienced and in an excellent position to progress further. In carrying out his activities, though, the Monkey should identify his priorities, avoid overcommitting himself and, as far as possible, ensure he has the support and backing of others. The long-term significance of what the Monkey accomplishes in the Tiger year can be considerable indeed.

FINANCE

In 1998 the Monkey would do well to keep a tight control over his purse strings. The temptation to spend could sometimes prove irresistible, though – if so, the Monkey would do well to plan his major purchases rather than succumb to too many whims or indulgences. A year also to avoid undue risks or speculations.

RELATIONS WITH OTHERS

Although the Monkey can look forward to many pleasurable occasions with his family and friends, care is still needed. As far as possible, he should actively involve them in his activities as well as seek their views on any matters that might be concerning him. Generally, his relations with others will go well, but if any difficulties do emerge the Monkey should try to sort the matter out quickly rather than allow it to continue unchecked in the background. There are too many other important and enjoyable things for him to do than get embroiled in squabbles. Monkeys, take note, tread carefully and enjoy – as most will – the many pleasant occasions the year will bring.

THE ROOSTER

With his considerable bearing and incisive and resolute manner, the Rooster makes an impressive figure. He has a sharp mind, keeps well-informed on many matters and expresses himself clearly and convincingly. He is meticulous and efficient in his undertakings and commands much respect. He also has a genuine and caring interest in others.

The Rooster has much in his favour but there are some aspects of his character that can tell against him. He can be candid in his views and sometimes over-zealous in his actions, and without forethought he can say or do things he later regrets. His high standards also make him fussy – even pedantic – and he can get diverted onto relatively minor matters when, in truth, he could be occupying his time more profitably. This is something all Roosters would do well to watch. Also, while the Rooster is a great planner, he can sometimes be unrealistic in his expectations. In making plans – indeed, with most of his activities – the Rooster would do well to consult with others rather than keep his thoughts to himself. By doing so, he will greatly benefit from their input.

The Rooster has considerable talents as well as a commendable drive and commitment, but to make the most of himself he does need to channel his energies wisely and watch his candid and sometimes volatile nature. With care, he can make a success of his life, and with his wide interests and outgoing personality will enjoy the friendship and respect of many.

Advice for the Rooster's Year Ahead

GENERAL PROSPECTS

An interesting and positive year ahead. Although the Rooster may have to forsake some of his current plans and ideas, the events of the year will bring some interesting possibilities and openings for him. To benefit from these, the Rooster will need to show some willingness to adapt and make the most of the situations in which he finds himself. In many cases, these will help to renew his impetus to do well and to make the most of his many fine abilities.

CAREER PROSPECTS

Changes are in store which could entail the Rooster taking on new and additional duties or moving to a completely different type of position. Some of the year will be challenging, occasionally unsettling, but the Rooster will do well and, in his efficient and meticulous manner, rise up to all that is asked of him. This will not necessarily be an easy year, but he can accomplish much and will be able to improve on his position.

FINANCE

A positive year for financial matters. However, while the Rooster will feel more secure with the general upturn in his fortunes, he should not let this lull him into complacency or tempt him into extravagance. In 1998 he would do well to keep a watchful eye over his spending and plan and choose his purchases carefully.

RELATIONS WITH OTHERS

Both domestically and socially the Rooster will find himself much in demand and can look forward to many pleasurable occasions with both family and friends. For those Roosters seeking friends or romance the year is favourably aspected, with the summer being an auspicious time.

APPENDIX
THE DOG

Loyal, dependable and with a good understanding of human nature, the Dog is well placed to win the respect and admiration of many. He is a no nonsense sort of person and hates any sort of hypocrisy and falsehood. With the Dog you know where you stand and, given his direct manner, where he stands on any issue. He also has a strong humanitarian nature and often champions good and just causes.

The Dog has many fine attributes, although there are certain traits that can prevent him from either enjoying or making the most of his life. He is a great worrier and can get anxious over all manner of things. Although it may not always be easy, the Dog should try to rid himself of the 'worry habit'. When tense or concerned, he should be more prepared to speak to others rather than shoulder his worries all by himself. In some cases, they could even be of his own making! Also, the Dog has a tendency to look on the pessimistic side of things and he would certainly be helped if he were to look more optimistically on his under-takings. He does, after all, possess many skills and should justifiably have faith in his abilities. Another weakness is his tendency to be stubborn over certain issues. If he is not careful, this stubbornness could at times undermine his position.

If the Dog can reduce the worrying and pessimistic side of his nature, then he will not only enjoy life more but also find he is achieving more as a result. He possesses a truly admirable character and his loyalty, reliability and sincerity are appreciated by all he meets. In his life he will do much good and befriend many — and he owes it to himself to enjoy life too. Sometimes it might help him to recall the words of another Dog, Winston Churchill: 'When I look back on all these worries I remember the story of the old man who said on his deathbed that he had had a lot of trouble in his life, most of which never happened.'

Advice for the Dog's Year Ahead

GENERAL PROSPECTS

After the tribulations of the last few years, now is the time for the Dog to draw a line over the past and look forward to the more favourable times of the Tiger year. In 1998 he should set about his activities with optimism and renewed vigour. He can now accomplish much and make the progress that has for some time proved so difficult. A positive and constructive year and the Dog should aim to give it his best.

CAREER PROSPECTS

When the Dog is committed to an objective he can attain much. In 1998 his resolve and sense of purpose will be recognized and rewarded and will do much to help his progress. Throughout the year he should pursue any opportunities he sees as well as promote his skills and ideas. The Dog can make excellent headway over the year and should make every effort to improve on his current situation.

FINANCE

A generally good year for financial matters, although the Dog should aim to put any spare money he has to a specific purpose or save it rather than be tempted to spend it too readily. With travel well aspected, he could do well to set some money aside for holidays and breaks.

RELATIONS WITH OTHERS

An active and enjoyable year ahead. The Dog's family and friends will bring him pleasure as well as give him much useful support, encouragement and advice. There will also be parties and social occasions for him to look forward to, with the prospects of making some new and valuable friendships. Romance, too, is well aspected. Overall, 1998 will be a gratifying year for the Dog and if he has been wanting to improve his social life, he really should take positive steps to bring this about now. The aspects will support him well.

THE PIG

Genial, sincere and trusting, the Pig gets on well with most. He has a kind and caring nature, a dislike of discord and often possesses a good sense of humour. In addition, he has a fondness for socializing and enjoying the good life!

The Pig also possesses a shrewd mind, is particularly adept in dealing with business and financial matters, and has a robust and resilient nature. Although not all his plans in life may work out as he would like, he is tenacious and will often rise up and succeed after experiencing setbacks and difficulties. In his often active and varied life he can accomplish much, although there are certain aspects of his character that can tell against him. If he can modify or keep these areas in check then his life will certainly be easier and possibly even more successful.

In his activities the Pig can sometimes overcommit himself and while he does not want to disappoint, he would certainly be helped if he were to set about his activities in an organized and systematic manner and give himself priorities at busy times. He should also not allow others to take advantage of his good nature and it would be in his interests if he were sometimes more discerning. There will have been times when he has been gullible and naïve; fortunately, though, the Pig quickly learns from his mistakes. He also possesses a stubborn streak and if new situations do not fit in with his line of thinking, he can be inflexible. Such an attitude may not always be to his advantage.

The Pig is a great pleasure-seeker and while he should deservedly enjoy the fruits of his labours, he can sometimes be indulgent and extravagant. This is again something he would do well to watch.

However, though the Pig may possess some faults, those who come into contact with him are invariably impressed by his integrity, amiable manner and intelligence. If he uses his talents wisely, his life can be crowned with considerable achievement and the good-hearted Pig will also be loved and respected by many.

Advice for the Pig's Year Ahead

GENERAL PROSPECTS

This will be a demanding but important year for the Pig. By rising to the challenges given him and making the most of the changes that occur, he will learn much, gain valuable experience and prepare the way for the more favourable times that await him later in the year and in 1999. The effects of the Tiger year are often far-reaching.

CAREER PROSPECTS

The Pig would do best to concentrate his energies on areas in which he has most experience and aim to build on that experience. In the Tiger year he will greatly impress others with his drive and commitment and do much to enhance his prospects. He should also pay close attention to the changes that occur over the year, for out of these could arise future opportunities. A busy but constructive year.

FINANCE

An expensive year is indicated and the Pig should not spend without regard to his current financial situation. This is a year for careful financial management.

RELATIONS WITH OTHERS

Despite the active nature of the year, the Pig will delight in both his family and social life. There will be many occasions he will greatly enjoy and he will also have the opportunity to make some new friends and acquaintances. At busy times, though, he should not hesitate to ask for assistance rather than try to cope with too much single-handed. Overall, as far as personal matters are concerned, this will be a generally positive, albeit busy, year.